International African Library 17
General editors: J. D. Y. Peel and David Parkin

THE POLITICS OF CULTURAL DIFFERENCE IN NORTHERN CAMEROON

International African Library

General Editors
David Parkin *and* J. D. Y. Peel

The *International African Library* is a major monograph series from the International African Institute and complements its quarterly periodical *Africa*, the premier journal in the field of African studies. Theoretically informed ethnographies, studies of social relations 'on the ground' which are sensitive to local cultural forms, have long been central to the Institute's publications programme. The *IAL* maintains this strength but extends it into new areas of contemporary concern, both practical and intellectual. It includes works focused on problems of development, especially on the linkages between the local and national levels of society; studies along the interface between the social and environmental sciences; and historical studies, especially those of a social, cultural or interdisciplinary character.

Titles in the series:

THE POLITICS OF CULTURAL DIFFERENCE IN NORTHERN CAMEROON

PHILIP BURNHAM

EDINBURGH UNIVERSITY PRESS
for the International African Institute, London

For Jennifer
hegɔ bɔnsɛnɛ

© Philip Burnham, 1996

Edinburgh University Press Ltd
22 George Square, Edinburgh

Typeset in Linotronic Plantin
by Speedspools, Edinburgh, and
printed and bound in Great Britain by
Redwood Books, Trowbridge, Wilts

A CIP record for this book is available
from the British Library

ISBN 0 7486 0812 5

CONTENTS

LIST OF ILLUSTRATIONS

ACKNOWLEDGEMENTS

The initial fieldwork on which this book is based, from 1968 to 1970, was supported by the Wenner-Gren Foundation and by the University of California at Los Angeles. Research grants from the University of London and the Economic and Social Research Council have helped to finance subsequent visits. Periods of writing time were funded by the Maison des Sciences de l'Homme, the Ecole des Hautes Etudes en Sciences Sociales, the Ecole Pratique des Hautes Etudes, and by University College London. To all these organisations, I express my gratitude. I would also like to thank Basil Blackwell (Publisher) Ltd for permission to reprint passages from my chapter in *Asian and African Systems of Slavery* (ed. James Watson, 1980).

This book is about, and for, the residents of the Department of the Mbere; I thank the large number of them who have helped me in my attempts to understand their society. I trust that although some will find what I have written contentious, they will accept that I have done so in the spirit of constructive enquiry. I would also like to thank the Cameroon Government's Ministry of Higher Education and Research, the various sub-prefects and prefects of the Meiganga *Arrondissement* and the Department of the Mbere, as well as the numerous canton chiefs, village headmen and *ardo'en*, who have facilitated my research over the years. Despite the many negative remarks that one reads nowadays about post-colonial African political regimes, let it be recorded that I have experienced nothing but helpful responses from these authorities throughout my stays in Cameroon.

Over the years, I have benefited greatly from the intellectual stimulation and advice of the staff and students of the Anthropology Department at University College London. In particular, I must mention my West Africanist colleagues Murray Last, Paul Richards, Mike Rowlands, Barrie Sharpe and the late M. G. Smith. At the risk of offending the numerous other people who have contributed materially and intellectually to this project, I also want to thank Elisabeth Copet-Rougier, Henri Bocquené, the late Ndoudi Oumarou, Phil and Cece Noss, Thomas Christensen, Adzia Denis, Abbo

Secretaire, Eldridge Mohammadou, Peter Geschiere and the other anonymous reader of this manuscript. Of course, none of these helpful individuals bears any responsibility for the faults of which this work, no doubt, has its full share.

Finally, I want to thank my children, Emily and Matthew, who have patiently lived with this project, both in London and in Cameroon, for all their years to date.

FRONTISPIECE: The late *Ardo* Seini, a Jafun leader from the Yarimbang area.

1

INTRODUCTION

On 15 July 1991, there was an outbreak of violence in the town of Meiganga in north-central Cameroon. At the time, the country was in the throes of a widespread campaign of popular protest, commonly referred to as '*villes mortes*', against the policies of President Paul Biya and his regime – in particular his opposition to constitutional reform and multi-party elections. In towns and cities across Cameroon, the *villes mortes* general strike shut shops, offices and other public facilities. But in Meiganga, this boycott was not universally supported and on the July morning in question, Gbaya women who regularly sold foodstuffs in the central market place brought their produce for sale in the normal way.

This was seen as a provocation by certain Muslim youths of the town who, in common with the politically dominant Fulbe and other Muslims throughout northern Cameroon, were strong supporters of the anti-Biya *villes mortes* campaign. These young men attempted to enforce the boycott by attacking the Gbaya market women, beating them and spilling their foodstuffs. Some Gbaya men who were nearby tried to protect the women but they too, including a prominent elderly pastor of the Lutheran church, were badly beaten. The violence escalated and several Gbaya men were killed, but the response to these attacks was not long in coming. When other Gbaya men in Meiganga heard the news, they armed themselves with their hunting weapons and descended on the Fulbe residential quarters of town, killing as many as possible of those whom they deemed to be collectively responsible. Peace was finally restored by the intervention of the army and gendarmes. The number of persons slain in the reprisal phase is disputed by various sources. The report in the government newspaper at the time (*Cameroon Tribune*, 22 July 1991), seeking to play down the affair, cited only nine deaths and about fifty wounded.[1] Some months later (8 April 1992), the same newspaper admitted that there had been some fifty deaths and about 100 wounded. Eyewitness estimates, on the other hand, speak of as many as 100 slain.

Unfortunately, although this deadly episode was confined to one day in July 1991 and national, multi-party parliamentary elections were held in March 1992, there was more violence to follow. It began at Meidougou, a crossroads town some 17 kilometres from Meiganga, when a long-smouldering dispute between Gbaya factions concerning the town headmanship was ignited by a disagreement over the date the new moon had been sighted to signal the end of the Ramadan fast. The incumbent Muslim Gbaya headman, and his Gbaya and Fulbe supporters, accomplished the public prayers marking the end of the fast on 4 April 1992, whereas the dissident Gbaya Muslim faction performed them on the following day. A dispute erupted later in the day between the opposing parties and, during the night, the assistant imam of the town mosque, a Fulbe, was murdered. When news of this murder reached Meiganga it inflamed the Fulbe youth there, who considered it to be a continuation of the inter-communal violence of the previous year. Seeking revenge, they headed toward Meidougou, gathering forces as they went and killing several Gbaya on the way. The gendarmes who attempted to halt their progress only succeeded in turning them back toward Meiganga, and when they arrived there, they continued their rampage, attacking the compound of the Gbaya canton chief, destroying several vehicles and committing further murders. But again, once mobilised, the Gbaya of Meiganga proved to be more effective fighters and their riposte was even more deadly than the 1991 carnage. Some of the Fulbe were lured into the bush and ambushed there. Bodies floated in the River Yoyo outside town. Many deaths occurred at the new transport park, where more than twenty buses and lorries owned by Muslim merchants were burnt by the Gbaya. The number killed in this second episode will never be known since many bodies were buried in the bush to avoid detection, but eyewitnesses agree that it was more murderous than the first. The violence lasted several days before it was brought to an end by the army.

In comparison with the large-scale massacres and wars that have plagued many independent African countries in recent years – Rwanda, Somalia, Liberia and so forth – the number of deaths cited above, even granted that the larger estimates are probably nearer the truth, might seem unremarkable. But for me, having worked in Meiganga and its district[2] on and off since 1968, this descent into inter-ethnic violence came as a bolt out of the blue. As I reflected on it, I realised that my sense of shock did not come simply from the sadness that I felt for friends and acquaintances involved but also stemmed from the fact that I had never expected events to come to such a pass.

But if the inter-ethnic violence of 1991 and 1992 did come as a surprise, it was not because I had failed to pay sufficient attention to the markedly plural ethnic composition of the society of the Mbere Department, or because I held an idyllic view of local inter-ethnic relations. On the contrary, this was an issue on which I had been conducting research ever since my first period of fieldwork in Cameroon from 1968–1970. During the very week that I learned of the first Meiganga clash, I had been working on a seminar paper about inter-ethnic relations in northern Cameroon. In it I devoted several pages to discussing the grievances felt by various of the ethnically defined segments of the society of the Mbere Department concerning their perceptions of political, economic and other forms of social disadvantage, in relation to neighbouring groups and the national government.

On a broader scale too, many commentators on the African scene had been arguing that the growing, continent-wide pressures in favour of multi-party elections, more strongly supported by the western donor countries following the demise of the Cold War, entailed a significant risk of offering a newly legitimated context for the expression of ethnic politics. But this was a generalised consideration; it was the specific focus and immediacy of those tragic events of 1991 and 1992 that stirred me to complete this book – to draw together the material I have been collecting on inter-ethnic relations in northern Cameroon over the past twenty-five years in an attempt to explore the reasons for such a tragedy.

But 'reasons' may be identified at several different analytical levels and from various points of view. There is the level of the event versus the level of structure; there are the contrasting perspectives and motivations of the actors concerned; there are the justifications and explanations after the fact; and there are local, culturally specific social practices versus more global social forces. At the very least, it seemed to me important to avoid falling prey to the fallacy of an overly deterministic analysis that would see these events as the inevitable outcome of social structural causality. On the other hand, my understanding of the Meiganga violence suggests that it can justifiably be taken as representative of much more widely distributed social processes within the regional society of northern Cameroon, and possibly further afield in Africa. This book is therefore more concerned with the level of structure rather than event, and focuses on an analysis of the social processes and cultural logics which have defined, redefined, and continue to give content to inter-ethnic relations in northern Cameroon from the late pre-colonial period through to the present.

In some current anthropological circles, even to mention the words 'ethnic group' is to stand accused of siding with a colonialist anthropology that employed a highly reified and ideological notion of the 'tribe' to serve its particular ends. According to Amselle (1990: 22, my translation), for example: 'the invention of ethnic groups is the joint work of colonial administrators, professional anthropologists, and those who combine these two qualifications.' Often linked with such theoretical positions is the view that to focus on ethnic conflicts in the recently independent states of Africa is an anti-progressive position, one that is inappropriate for social scientists working in these countries. Congruent with this latter argument, although the product of more pragmatic political considerations, is the Cameroon government's public position on the question of ethnicity. With discrimination on the basis of ethnic criteria formally outlawed in the Cameroon constitution, Cameroon government officials seldom fail to use any public occasion to condemn tribalism as the chief threat to national unity.

In response to arguments like Amselle's, I would briefly answer (for now) that, although his contention may indeed be valid in certain cases, it is certainly not a tenable historical generalisation for Africa (to say nothing of other parts of the world), as the North African historian Ibn Khaldun (1967), although writing in the fourteenth century, would have told him. As we shall see in the next chapter, concepts of ethnic difference played prominent roles in framing *pre*-colonial social relations in what is now northern Cameroon, although this does not necessarily mean that the conceptual boundaries and ethnic referents of the nineteenth century are the same as those of today. As Gledhill (1994: 69) aptly remarked: 'The distinctive cultural structures inherited from the past leave traces in the present, but the colonial process also produced strong discontinuities in development and a restructuring of established institutions, practices and beliefs . . .' Surely, the challenge here is to construct a fully historicised account of ethnic identities, not one that conveniently pins their existence on the whipping boy of colonialism.

As for the more pragmatic arguments against ethnic allegiances from those saddled with the task of governing modern African states, with which I have more sympathy, I can only reply that to call a goat a sheep is no more an aid to understanding animal classification than is calling ethnicity by another name an aid to understanding political process. Such linguistic subtleties will not make the problem disappear.

Given that the notion of ethnicity provokes such strong reactions and is central to the theme of this book, it is important for me to explain at the very outset what I mean and what I do not mean by this concept. Although ethnicity is not synonymous with cultural difference, culture is the source material out of which ethnic difference is fashioned. If we understand culture, in its most basic sense, as consisting of what an individual learns through socialisation into a particular society, I take it that it is a basic feature of developing human behavioural competence to learn to respond to other actors' behaviours in terms of an assumption of shared interactional (cultural) meanings. To the extent that an individual perceives the meaning that he or she attributes to an interaction as not being shared with a fellow actor, that individual may account for this experience in a variety of ways, relating possibly to problems of misinterpretation or trust, differences of personality or social roles, or various other reasons. But to the extent that an individual perceives that the differences in motivation of another actor's behaviour are due to that actor's socialisation into another culture, the stage has been set for subsequent behavioural interaction to be phrased in terms of ethnic difference.

Much or little can then be built on these basic, and probably universal, interactional foundations.[3] Cultural differences may be viewed simply as minor encumbrances in achieving successful interactions or may be evaluated positively as an opportunity to enrich one's range of cultural experience. As an American who has lived for more than twenty years in London, I note that many of my cultural differences are not ethnically marked at all by the natives. Others – like the different vocabulary used at a hardware store (sorry, an ironmonger's!) – are only minor irritations to the smooth flow of interaction. And some – which elicit veiled comments about 'pushy Americans' – demarcate a more solid ethnic boundary. Such categorical distinctions may be given political weighting: either at the dyadic interactional level as a feature of micropolitics or at the inter-group level as a feature of macropolitics (cf. Jenkins 1994). Given the mutual behavioural orientations of actors in such settings, definitions of ethnicity are also subject to feedback processes, to objectification and reification. Thus, if I know that you define me in a certain way, I may behave in relation to this categorisation, either opposing or confirming it, which in turn may affect your subsequent definition of me, and so forth. In fact, as many authors have remarked, the recognition of ethnic difference necessarily implies a 'we/they' dichotomy, which means that an ethnic group cannot exist on its own – in a social vacuum. However, ethnic difference may often be 'naturalised', that is, treated as a 'god-given' fact of nature rather than as a socially constructed and historically mutable cultural phenomenon. Such naturalising ideologies are found especially often in association with patterns of phenotypic ('racial') difference, although of course are by no means restricted to such situations.

Although ethnic identity construction may be analysed primarily as a reflex of dyadic inter-personal interactions, such interactions are typically situated within broader frameworks of collective discourse, including appeals to shared historical 'knowledge', cultural 'traditions', legal, political or other 'rights', and so on. These collective discourses, in turn, serve to articulate ethnic categorisations with larger scale processes of political competition, domination and resistance which, in the present day, are most often played out with reference to the more globalising discourses of the modern state system. In this historical context, concepts of ethnic identity and difference therefore become part and parcel of nationalism – the political principle or philosophy which 'holds that the political and the national unit should be congruent' (Gellner 1983: 1; see also Smith 1986 and Jenkins 1994: 209).[4]

It is, of course, the potential political content of inter-cultural relations, both the micropolitical nuances of everyday inter-personal interactions as well as the collective weight of inter-group, 'we/they' oppositions, which forms the main subject of attention in research on ethnicity. Furthermore, it is this focus on the potential for political conflict which attracts much of the unfavourable comment and the many efforts to 'deconstruct' the concept of ethnicity, seeing it as an inevitably nihilistic or pessimistic perspective on human affairs. In the hands of some social scientists, the ethnicity concept may well be guilty of these charges. The common, although increasingly outmoded, conceptualisation of ethnicity as being the expression of primordial ties or attachments (Shils 1957; Geertz 1963), combined with an unhistoricised view of tradition, has indeed been found wanting in attempts to account for social change. I want to make it quite clear that my analytical approach to ethnicity has nothing in common with this primordialist position. Although I do argue that ethnically defined behaviour is a function of basic, essentially universal, human interactional competences, the cultural differences and interpretations of difference on which ethnic demarcations are based are clearly subject to historical change, transformation and dissolution. However, rather than acting as if ethnic differences either do not exist or are simply the ideological results of a colonial or anthropological plot, it is surely important to give careful attention to the sociopolitical processes which underlie the historical development of a society such as Cameroon: processes which are embedded in the locally specific and always changing cultural realities which the concept of ethnicity seeks to capture.

Neither is it the case that, simply by labelling a conflict as 'ethnically based', one has said very much about the content of that political struggle. Not only are different ethnic boundaries frequently constructed on quite different cultural and historical bases, such that their degrees of coherence, permeability and durability can vary greatly, but inter-ethnic relations are also fundamentally affected by variation in the logics of the cultural beliefs and practices of the different ethnic sections concerned, and by their varying patterns of articulation with more global structural practices. I emphasise this last point since, following Barth's (1969) influential and almost exclusive emphasis on mechanisms of ethnic boundary maintenance, some ethnographers have tended to give inadequate attention both to the analysis of the cultural knowledge and practices of the constituent units of ethnically plural societies, as well as to their historical transformations.

As we shall see in later chapters, inter-ethnic relations in the Mbere Department are fundamentally affected both by the contrasting modes of ethnic boundary maintenance (or permeability), as well as by the different cultural logics and practices of the three major ethnic segments discussed in this work – the highly incorporative Fulbe (town Fulani) category, the exclusivist Mbororo (pastoral Fulani) category, and the socially encapsulated Gbaya category. Moreover, as I shall argue throughout this book, each of these differing conceptions of ethnic grouping themselves have the potential for greater or lesser degrees of ethnic exclusivity (or inclusivity), which has been variably expressed at different periods in their histories.

The analytical problem, then, that this book seeks to confront is the need to establish a correct 'dosage' of global versus local explanatory factors for the present political conjuncture in the Mbere Department, and northern Cameroon more generally, including careful attention to the degree of reciprocal self-definition, boundedness or mutual inter-penetration of local, culturally specific logics. At the same time, these explanatory factors need to be set within the flow of history – a history that gives space for human agency and cultural specificity, while acknowledging the structuring force of state power and macroeconomic relations in the pre-colonial, colonial and post-colonial periods.

As I have already indicated, the topic of this book has been on my mind for a long time. Originally, however, I did not set out to work in northern Cameroon or on inter-ethnic relations at all. During my postgraduate studies at the University of California at Los Angeles, I had decided to work on an ecological theme among one of the forest-dwelling, Bantu-speaking societies of southwestern Cameroon – the Mbo people inhabiting the area around Nkongsamba. However, inter-ethnic violence intervened to affect my research focus, even prior to my arrival in Cameroon when, in 1967, there was a major outbreak of fighting between Bamileke squatters and the autochthonous Bakossi people at Tombel, adjacent to the territory of the Mbo. Quite naturally, the Cameroon government was hesitant to grant me research permission to work in that area and, on the advice of Claude Tardits, then head of the Anthropology Department at the Federal University in Yaounde, my wife and I found ourselves carrying out research far to the northeast instead, among the Gbaya people of the Meiganga *Arrondissement*.

At the outset of my fieldwork, my knowledge of the published literature on northern Cameroon societies was quite limited, since within several weeks of my initial reorientation toward the Gbaya, we had established residence in a small Gbaya village. Having already experienced this false start in beginning my field research for the PhD, and with much of my research funding already frittered away by the long delay in obtaining government research permission, I felt I had to focus rapidly on a research topic that promised to yield a viable PhD thesis with minimum risk. For this purpose, an ethnographic study of the Gbaya people of Meiganga *Arrondissement* seemed made to order and this indeed is what transpired. However, as I explained in my 1980 monograph on the Gbaya, *Opportunity and Constraint in a Savanna Society*, I was forced to confront, from the very beginning of my fieldwork in the Meiganga area, the prominently plural ethnic character of this social setting, in which the Gbaya constituted only a bare majority of the total population. Seen from the Gbaya perspective, inter-ethnic contacts were constant features of their daily activities, fundamentally colouring their social and historical perceptions and affecting their economic livelihoods, their political relations, their religious beliefs and many other aspects of their lives.

At a theoretical and methodological level, I had had some preparation for confronting such a field experience, having participated during my postgraduate studies at UCLA in a major seminar organised by two of my supervisors, Leo Kuper and M. G. Smith, on the topic of 'Pluralism in Africa', eventually published in 1969 in a book of that title. And so, although most of my first year in the field was concentrated on my Gbaya research, I soon submitted a grant application to the Wenner-Gren Foundation seeking supplementary funding to carry out research specifically on the topic of ethnicity in Meiganga. When I learned in mid-1969 that this application had been successful, I was able to extend my stay in Cameroon to some twenty-one months in all, about nine months of which were devoted more or less entirely to the ethnicity issue.

In mulling over this larger project that I had embarked upon, my initial thought was that, up to that time (and still largely today), studies of inter-ethnic relations in Africa and elsewhere had been carried out from a one-sided perspective. That is to say, an anthropologist, having gained a first-hand knowledge of one group on the basis of intensive ethnographic fieldwork, would then write of inter-ethnic relations from that group's point of view, having only a cursory or second-hand knowledge of the other segments of the multi-ethnic society. The reason for this state of affairs was plain to see, since the amount of field research involved in a project that aimed at equally intensive coverage of all significant segments of a multi-ethnic social unit, including the probable need to learn a second or third field language, would be quite daunting. In the Meiganga case, this would entail, at minimum, a knowledge of the Gbaya and Fulbe languages (Fulfulde), with Mbum and Hausa also being of use, and extended periods of residence in at least five different ethnically defined units. While I was not so naïve as to think that I could eventually accomplish all the elements of such a comprehensive research plan, I must admit that, even after my first twenty-one-month stay in Cameroon, I was not entirely clear just how much more fieldwork on this theme would be desirable or necessary or possible. Since that time, during the seven subsequent visits I have made to Cameroon up to 1994, my ideas about this research have continued to evolve in an ongoing process of dialogue, both with the increasing volume of field data, as well as with the ever-growing theoretical and comparative ethnographic literature related to this theme. At times, the project has seemed a never-ending one, as a perfectionist impulse to collect yet more data tended to override my desire to see the book on the shelf. But, as I have said, the events of July 1991 intervened to give me a timely reminder that the project needed to be finished.

Ultimately, then, in the research on which this book is based, I have employed just two indigenous local languages – Gbaya and Fulfulde, but I have managed to accomplish extended periods of participant observation among all the major ethnic groups that comprise Mbere Department society.

The more field research I carried out, the more I came to realise that the character of this multi-ethnic society was more than simply the sum of its culturally distinct and locally observable parts. This is the result of the fact that the processes of mutual accommodation between co-residential, but culturally discrete groups, tend to generate emergent and, to some extent, shared cultural properties between these groups, as Fredrik Barth (1969) has argued. But equally, these emergent cultural properties also evolve under the influences of larger-scale social forces operating on regional, national or international levels, which serve to articulate, at least partially, the local with the global.

THE GEOGRAPHIC AND SOCIAL SETTING

The Mbere Department is an area of some 17,000 square kilometres of well-watered Guinea savanna and wooded stream valleys, located on the south-eastern edge of the Adamawa Plateau at altitudes ranging from 900 to 1,500 metres above sea-level. Comprising the most easterly part of the Adamaoua Province of Cameroon,[5] it is bounded on the east by the Central African Republic, while to the south are the lowland forests of southeastern Cameroon. To the north, below the Adamawa Plateau escarpment, stretch the hotter and drier plains of the Benue valley.

The social geography of the Mbere Department is largely determined by colonially inspired policies of population resettlement and by its under-developed road network, which radiates from Meiganga, the largest town of the district, which recorded a population of 31,852 in the 1987 census. The principal north-south highway of Cameroon, rapidly transformed in the rainy season into a muddy morass, runs through Meiganga on its way to Ngaoundere, the provincial capital, some 150 kilometres to the north. Running due west of Meidougou, a crossroads town about 17 kilometres south of Meiganga, is the 200 kilometres of well-paved road (eventually scheduled to form part of the east-west Trans-African highway) leading to the railway town of Ngaoundal and on to Tibati. Travelling northeast from Meiganga is the lightly travelled 150 kilometres of the Fada-Djohong-Yarimbang road, which runs toward the northwestern Central African Republic and Chad beyond, with spur roads branching to the frontier market town of Ngaouwi.

Along all these roads, dotted at intervals of several kilometres, are the many small villages and a few larger market towns inhabited primarily by Gbaya farmers, interspersed in some areas by more multi-ethnic villages in which Fulbe agro-pastoralists and traders predominate. The Mbororo, on the other hand, do not generally live alongside the roads. During the seven-month rainy season they live in relatively permanent encampments scattered throughout the savannas while for the rest of the year they lead a more mobile life, moving to and from the dry season grazing areas to the south.

The Mbere Department is still relatively thinly peopled with a population

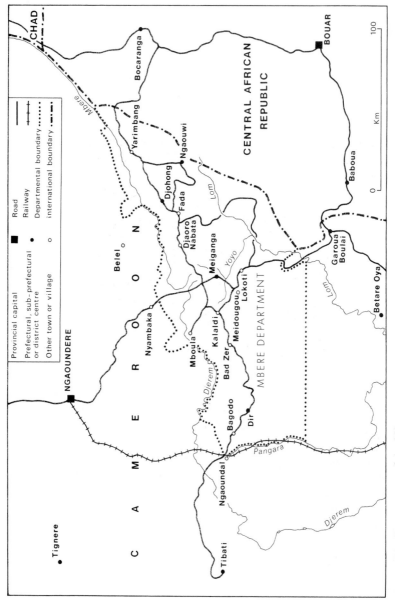

Map 1: The Department of the Mbere.

density of about five per square kilometre, although the population has grown steadily since the 1960s when I first began my research. According to the official census of 1966, the population of the then Meiganga *Arrondissement* numbered about 64,000. This figure had risen to 89,912 in the 1976 census (République Unie du Cameroun 1976), while the most recent census of 1987 enumerated the population of the Mbere Department at 126,921 (République du Cameroun 1987). Due to the effects of the inter-ethnic violence of 1991 and 1992, the population of the Department has probably not increased substantially in the last few years, since there has been a significant out-migration by local traders which is likely to have more or less cancelled out the growth by natural increase.

Of the three censuses mentioned, only the 1966 census contained information on 'ethnicity', which classified the population of the Meiganga *Arrondissement* as shown in Table 1.1 below. The ethnic labels used in this census,

TABLE 1.1: Population of Meiganga *Arrondissement* in 1966 by ethnicity.

Gbaya	33,850
Mbororo	19,218
Fulbe	6,617
Hausa	1,987
Mbum	376
Bamileke	286
Congo	245
Bornuan	235
Ewondo	208
Laka	192
Arabs	128
Europeans	51
Functionaries	626
Total	64,022

with the exception of the 'functionary' category (evidently the Cameroon government wished to convey the impression that its administrative employees were immune to ethnic allegiances!), correspond very closely to the generally accepted ethnic terminology used in daily discourse in Fulfulde, Gbaya and French, the major languages spoken in the region. Some brief remarks about each ethnic category are appropriate here, by way of preliminary introductions to our cast of characters.

The Gbaya are by far the largest ethnic unit of the Mbere Department although today they still probably comprise only a bare majority of the total (i.e., on the order of 65–70,000 people). They are the most north-westerly of the Gbaya-phone peoples – a population of perhaps one million scattered across the western Central African Republic and adjacent parts of eastern Cameroon.

Practising a mixed economy centred on the cultivation of manioc and maize, combined with some livestock raising, hunting and gathering (see Burnham 1980a), the Gbaya of the Mbere Department participate in trading activities only to a limited degree. They are today considered by the Cameroon government to be autochthonous to the region and, on these grounds, have the right to fill the six canton chieftaincies, which constitute a level of political organisation intermediate between village headmen and the sub-prefectural administration of the *arrondissement*. However, as we shall discuss more fully in the next chapter, most of the Gbaya clans are, in fact, relative newcomers to the region of the Mbere Department; they drifted into this area from the east during the nineteenth century, gradually outnumbering and assimilating the longer-resident Mbum, who today exist as a distinct ethnic unit in only a few villages in the area. A generally healthy and growing population in recent decades, the substantial rate of Gbaya natural increase since the 1960s has probably been equalled, or even exceeded, by the significant rates of in-migration of several other ethnic groups resident in the Mbere Department.

Since the early decades of the twentieth century, the excellent pastures of the Mbere Department have attracted many pastoral Fulani, usually referred to as '*Mbororo*' (plural *Mbororo'en*), and their large herds of cattle are the chief source of the Department's wealth. Their more mobile existence living scattered in family-sized encampments throughout the bush, combined with many other distinctive cultural features, differentiates them markedly from the settled Fulani, commonly referred to as '*Fulɓe*' (singular, *Pullo*), who also inhabit the region. The settled Fulani practise a diverse range of liveli-hoods, focusing particularly on settled agro-pastoralism and trade. Although both pastoral and settled Fulani, as native speakers of Fulfulde, classify themselves together as '*Fulɓe*' in contrast to 'pagan', formerly-servile, non-Fulani groups (termed '*Haaɓe*' in Fulfulde), in most contexts they draw a clear distinction between themselves by using the terms 'Mbororo' versus 'Fulbe' (or other more pejorative slang labels), and I will use this same convention throughout this book.[6] On the other hand, when I wish to refer to the shared traditions of common cultural and racial origin which are said to unite Mbororo and Fulbe at a more historically distant and inclusive level of social segmentation, I will refer to them together as 'Fulani' (a term of Hausa origin which has become conventional in English). In addition to being the native language of the Fulani, Fulfulde serves as the lingua franca of the Mbere Department, as it does for much of the rest of northern Cameroon. Since the 1966 census, Mbororo population in the Mbere Depart-ment has probably increased only modestly, due to significant out-migration to more southerly regions of Cameroon and to the Central African Republic. The Fulbe category, on the other hand, has expanded considerably primarily as a result of in-migration to the Department.

The Hausa, the Bamileke, the Bornuans (that is, Kanuri and other groups from Bornu), and the Arabs (including North Africans, Sudanese, Choa Arabs from northern Cameroon and Chad, and Yemenis) are all mainly involved in commercial and trading activities and reside predominantly in Meiganga or in a few of the larger villages. As will be discussed more fully in the next chapter, Hausa and Kanuri traders have been visiting and residing in the Mbere region since as early as the 1830s or 1840s and today play dominant roles in the cattle and kola nut trades and in butchering. The Bamileke, natives of the western province of Cameroon (who are often referred to locally as *'Garafi'* from the pidgin English for 'Grassfielders'), run dry-goods shops, bars, bakeries and other commercial enterprises which they established in the region from the late 1950s onwards as European merchants progressively withdrew from this sector.

All these commercially oriented ethnic groups increased their numbers substantially from the 1960s through the 1980s, as the trading economy of Meiganga and other towns benefited from the economic growth consequent on the expansion of salaried government employment associated with the promotion of the Mbere Department to prefectural status. During this period, the centre of Meiganga town, despite still being the site of the Gbaya canton chief's compound and the various government administrative offices, came to be populated primarily by Fulbe, Hausa and the other commercially-oriented ethnic groups. The Gbaya, on the other hand, having sold off their compounds downtown, now mostly reside around the Protestant and Catholic mission stations away from the centre, or in the surrounding semi-rural settlements that are progressively being incorporated into the encroaching town. However, the growth of Meiganga, which remains a town whose economy is reliant upon the salaries of the government and mission employees and on its role as a regional trading centre, has markedly slowed or even gone into decline in the last few years. This has been due in part to the national economic crisis, especially since 1987 when the Cameroon government instituted the first of several radical cuts in the salaries and perquisites of its employees as part of an IMF-mandated structural adjustment programme. Meiganga's economic decline has also been exacerbated by the episodes of ethnic violence, which have cast a pall over the local trading economy and caused numerous traders to depart for calmer locations.

The term 'Congo' in the census is commonly used in the region to refer to non-Gbaya labour migrants from the neighbouring Central African Republic. All of these people use Sango as a vehicular language among themselves but use Fulfulde or French in inter-ethnic relations in Cameroon. The majority of the 'Congo' are drawn from the Kpana people (a group of the Mbum language family) north of the town of Bocaranga. Included in this category as well are members of other Central African and Chadian Mbum-speaking peoples often referred to as *mbum babal* in Fulfulde, as well as the Kare, Manja and Banda. The flow of migration from the CAR has grown in the post-independence period as a result of the relative poverty of that country, and the numbers of 'Congo' in the Mbere Department today are surely proportionately greater than in the 1966 census. Substantial 'Congo' residential quarters are to be found in the environs of Meiganga and in several other towns, and these now house significant numbers of second-generation migrants as well as more recent arrivals.

The small population of Laka in the Mbere Department also owe their presence to in-migration, although in much less happy conditions. The Laka of what is today southwestern Chad were the target of many of the slave raids conducted in the latter part of the nineteenth century by Fulbe and Gbaya war parties, and most of the Laka remaining in the Mbere Department today continue to live in a semi-dependent relationship with the households of Gbaya canton chiefs or Fulbe notables.

The Ewondo category in the 1966 census served as a collective label for migrants from southern Cameroon who speak Ewondo, or one of the Bantu languages related to Ewondo (for example, Bulu or Fang). In 1966, the level of western-style schooling of this group was higher than that of other populations in the Mbere Department, and they were usually employed as schoolteachers or in other white-collar occupations. A substantial number of Ewondo, as well as Bamileke, Duala and other Cameroonians from the better-educated south and west, also formed part of the 'Functionary' category in the census. As just mentioned, the number of white-collar jobs significantly expanded from 1983 with the administrative upgrading of the Meiganga *Arrondissement* to prefectural status as the Department of the Mbere and, since this coincided with the change in national leadership from Ahmadou Ahidjo, a Fulbe northerner, to Paul Biya, a Christian southerner, many of these new posts were filled by Ewondo and other educated southerners and westerners.

Finally, the European category in 1966 was composed primarily of missionaries, both American and Norwegian Protestants and French Catholics, plus a handful of elderly French colonials who still attempted to maintain their local business interests. Today, the number of Europeans has declined, although the Protestant and Catholic missions remain active.

This, then, is our cast of characters and their general locations in the Mbere Department landscape. To a significant degree, as I have described, much of the daily lives of the peoples of the Mbere Department takes place in spatially segregated, mono-ethnic settings. On the other hand, certain situations are characteristically multi-ethnic in social composition – especially in the larger towns and marketplaces. The ethnography that follows therefore tends to adjust its focus back and forth between multi-ethnic and mono-ethnic perspectives. However, as I have already suggested, this division is, to a considerable extent, an artefact of presentation, since social behaviours in even mono-ethnic settings are often predicated on meanings and motivations emergent from the pronounced multi-ethnic character of the region.

As the preceding paragraphs will have made clear, the discussions in this book are firmly rooted, first and foremost, in the data I have collected on the multi-ethnic society of the Mbere Department. But to a significant degree, this study also has wider relevance. Of course, any ethnographically based study is bound to a certain empirical focus which will determine its limitations to a greater or lesser extent. But, in my view, many of the social processes documented for the society of the Mbere Department are common to a much larger area of northern Cameroon, and the West African savanna zone more generally, and reflect both long-term as well as more recent tendencies toward a regional society-in-formation. Such questions of local versus more global perspective will emerge here and there throughout the following chapters.

2

THE HISTORICAL CONSTITUTION OF A MULTI-ETHNIC SOCIETY

In large measure, the social composition of the present-day Mbere Department is the outcome of nineteenth- and early twentieth-century historical developments. The historical origins of current patterns of inter-ethnic relations in the Department are still therefore viewed by its inhabitants as relatively recent and not referrable to some quasi-mythical past. In many contexts of ethnic interaction, historical accounts relating to the nineteenth century retain a sense of immediate relevance for social relations in the present day.

Of the ethnic groups now resident in the Department, only the Mbum appear to have been present there in any numbers at the start of the nineteenth century. The data available for the period of the early nineteenth century prior to the Fulbe conquest of the Adamawa region are very few and consist of little more than sketchy, sometimes fanciful, oral traditions and toponyms (see Mohammadou 1986 for summaries of some of this material; also Von Briesen 1914). Nonetheless, the existence of several independent Mbum chieftaincies and villages within, or on the margins, of what is now the Mbere Department can be reliably documented (Faraut 1981; Burnham, Copet-Rougier and Noss 1986: 102). For the early nineteenth century as well, there is some oral history evidence that the first of the Gbaya had begun to penetrate the area, although many of the Gbaya clans that presently inhabit the region were resident at that early date in the territory of what is now the Central African Republic (Burnham, Copet-Rougier and Noss 1986: 102–4).

THE FULBE CONQUEST OF ADAMAWA

The event that set in motion the social forces that were fundamentally to transform the society of the Mbere region was the declaration of Muslim holy war (*jihad*) by the Fulani leader Shehu Usumanu bi Fodiye (Usman dan Fodio) in faraway Gobir in 1804. At that date, our sources indicate that there were no Fulani permanently resident in any part of the Adamawa Plateau, let alone on its eastern margins in the Mbere region. But various

Fulani clans, who had lived for some time in the Benue river valley along the borderland of the modern states of Nigeria and Cameroon, rallied to the call of the Shehu and undertook to extend his holy war into what is now northern Cameroon. It was one of these clans, the Wolarbe (*Wolaarɓe*), who play the major role in our story.

Various Wolarbe clan fractions directed their *jihad* against the pagan tribes of the Benue valley and southwards on the Adamawa Plateau and, during the first half of the nineteenth century, managed to establish a series of conquest states including Tchebowa, Demsa, Garoua, Gourin, Tchamba, Boundang-Touroua, Ngaoundere, Tibati, Kontcha, Tignere and Banyo (Strümpell 1912; Mohammadou 1978; 1981; 1983). One prong of the Wolarbe *jihad*, led by Ardo Njobdi of Boundang (*ardo* – chief, literally 'leader'; plural *ardo'en*), focused its principal attacks against the several Mbum groups living around Ngaoundere. Although the conquest of the Mbum and their neighbours the Duru was not completed by Ardo Njobdi himself – he withdrew to Boundang in 1839 (Mohammadou 1978; 1981; Froelich 1954: 14) – Njobdi's successors were able to consolidate their hold on Ngaoundere over the next decade and transform it into one of the most important Fulbe states on the Adamawa Plateau.

The Fulbe of Ngaoundere became more sedentary during this period, setting up a more elaborate system of territorial administration and establishing a sizeable walled capital which counted more than 10,000 inhabitants in the late nineteenth century (Ponel 1896: 207). Throughout the nineteenth century, the rulers of Ngaoundere continued to stand in a loose relation of vassalage to the Emir of Adamawa (Fombina) at Yola, and through him to the Sultan of Sokoto, owing to Yola an annual tribute of 1,000 slaves, 1,000 cattle and ten large elephant tusks (Abdoullaye and Mohammadou 1972; Mohammadou 1978; see also Lacroix 1952: 34). However, Ngaoundere was sufficiently strong and distant from Yola so that, for long periods of its history, this tribute was only paid when it suited Ngaoundere to do so.

By the 1850s, Ngaoundere's desire for territorial expansion *per se* began to dim. The Fulbe state had already laid claim to extensive tracts of lightly populated land near to home, and its emphasis progressively shifted from full-scale territorial conquest to a less direct exploitation of its peripheries via slave raiding, relations of vassalage, and trade. Hemmed in on most sides by other Fulbe powers, Ngaoundere's main attacks were aimed toward the south and east, in particular against the Gbaya, Laka, Kaka (Mkako) and Yangere peoples, who lived 200 kilometres or more from Ngaoundere town in what is now the Central African Republic, Chad and eastern Cameroon (Mohammadou 1978). The effects of these contacts on the society of the Mbere region will be examined in some detail, after a discussion of the incorporative processes of the Ngaoundere state.

The Adamawa *jihad* was undertaken by relatively small groups of Fulbe who were outnumbered by the autochthonous pagan groups of the region. Ngaoundere was no exception in this regard, and the rapid integration of conquered Mbum and other peoples into the Fulbe state, which transformed large numbers of former enemies into effective elements of the state political and economic apparatus, was the key to Ngaoundere's remarkable political success. We have only limited historical information concerning the lifestyle of the Wolarbe Fulani who waged this war of conquest (see Mohammadou 1978) but we do know that: 1) they were not an Mbororo clan – Mbororo clans existed as culturally and politically distinct entities at this period but they played no significant role in the *jihad*; 2) the Wolarbe had not been practising an urban lifestyle prior to the *jihad*, although they were familiar with the urban political forms of such neighbouring states as Bornu and the Hausa emirates (see Bassoro and Mohammadou 1980; Mohammadou 1983); 3) these Fulani clans possessed a mixed economy dominated by cattle herding but which also included some cultivation that was undertaken principally by slaves settled in slave agricultural villages; 4) the cattle husbandry practised by these Fulani groups involved a significant annual transhumance from a relatively settled wet season base, the focus of which was probably the agricultural villages of the slaves of the Fulani; 5) at least a rudimentary system of political offices, with titles for both freemen and slaves, was in operation prior to the *jihad* and had probably been adopted by the Wolarbe during an earlier period of residence on the marches of Bornu; and 6) few of the Wolarbe were especially known for their Islamic learning and the branch of the Wolarbe who established the Ngaoundere state utilised Bornuan personnel as religious specialists (Mohammadou 1978: 273–4; Njeuma 1978; Burnham and Last 1994).

If we draw a comparison between the social organisation of pre-*jihad* Wolarbe and better-documented cases of semi-pastoral Fulbe groups composed of both free and slave elements living in a similar environment, it seems probable that the initial group of Wolarbe that conquered Ngaoundere did not exceed 5,000 in number, including women, children and slaves. But in the course of several decades of fighting against the indigenous peoples of the Ngaoundere region, the Fulbe were able to conquer and reduce to slave or tributary status large groups of local populations who substantially outnumbered their Fulbe conquerors. These military successes were assisted by alliances between Ngaoundere and other Fulbe states as well as by the progressive incorporation of pagan elements into the Ngaoundere army (Mohammadou 1978).

Making use of Smith's (1969: 108–9, 133–4) terminology, we can describe the state structure of Ngaoundere as being characterised by clearcut patterns of differential incorporation, with systematic, codified principles of legal advantage and disability routinely applied to Fulbe and other categories of freemen versus the various socially differentiated categories of tributary or servile status. Defeated pagan village populations located near Ngaoundere town were often allowed to remain on their traditional lands (Mohammadou 1978: 280). Their chiefs (*arnaaɓe*, singular *arnaaɗo*) were awarded titles, and the whole village unit was allocated to the *tokkal* (political following) of a titled Fulbe or slave official in the Ngaoundere court, who became responsible for collecting annual taxes and raising levies of soldiers for Fulbe war expeditions (Froelich 1954: 26–7). In return, the 'pagan' group's loyalty to Ngaoundere was rewarded principally by opportunities to secure booty in war, and this incentive was probably the primary factor which allowed the Fulbe to secure the allegiance of conquered groups so rapidly.

The *tokke* (plural of *tokkal*) which formed the basis of the Ngaoundere administrative system, had their origins in the leadership patterns of mobile pastoral society and were not territorially discrete domains ruled by resident overlords. Rather, *tokke* were sets of followers (the verbal root of *tokkal* is *tokka* – which means 'to follow'), both Fulbe and members of vassal peoples, who were distributed in a scattering of different rural villages or residential quarters in town and who were allocated to individual office holders living at Ngaoundere at the behest of the Fulbe ruler (*laamiiɗo*). Such a spatially dispersed administrative organisation lessened chances of secession by parts of the Ngaoundere state and yet was an effective means of mobilising and organising an army and levying taxes.

In addition to local subject pagan peoples, the size of the servile population at Ngaoundere was further enlarged by slaves captured at distances of several hundred kilometres from Ngaoundere town itself. These captives were brought back for resettlement at Ngaoundere either as domestic slaves or as farm slaves in slave villages (*dumɗe*, singular *rumnde*). This long-distance raiding, which was a regular occurrence from the 1850s up through the first decade of the twentieth century, was a large-scale phenomenon, and European observers at the end of the nineteenth century estimated that as many as 8–10,000 slaves might be taken on these raids annually (Coquery-Vidrovitch 1972: 76, 204–5; Loefler 1907: 225; Ponel 1896: 205–7; Archives AN3 and AN4). Those captives who were not settled at Ngaoundere were sold to Hausa or other traders, and Adamawa soon gained the reputation as a slave traders' Eldorado (Passarge 1895: 480). By the second half of the nineteenth century, Adamawa had become one of the principal sources of slaves in the Sokoto Caliphate (Lacroix 1952: 34; see also Bassoro and Mohammadou 1980: 84).

Summing up the demographic situation at Ngaoundere in the nineteenth century, we can say that it is likely that at no time following the establishment of the Fulbe state did the proportion of slaves and vassals to freemen ever fall below a one-to-one ratio and that for most of the period, the ratio was probably more like two-to-one. Twentieth-century census figures, although they can be applied retrospectively only with the greatest of caution, tend to support this interpretation. Thus, in 1950, there were approximately 23,000 Fulbe living in the Ngaoundere state as compared with 35,000 non-Fulbe who were still identifiable as ex-slaves, vassals or servants of the Fulbe (Froelich 1954: 25). It goes without saying that by the late colonial period, when all legal disabilities and constraints on movement of persons of servile status had been removed for some decades, the proportion of servile to free persons can be expected to have dropped. But nonetheless, as late as 1950, we still encounter more than a three-to-two ratio.

Whatever the exact number and proportion of slaves in the pre-colonial period, they were not all of uniform social or legal status. The Fulfulde language makes a distinction between *dimo* (plural, *rimbe*) and *maccudo* (plural, *maccube*), meaning respectively 'freeman' and 'slave', a discrimination paralleling the basic one made in Koranic law (Ruxton 1916). Membership in the legally free category was attainable through birth to two free parents, through birth to a slave concubine having relations with a freeman, or through manumission. A slave concubine herself, having borne a free child, would also become free on the death of her child's father. Free offspring of slave concubines were not jurally disadvantaged and were considered to be members of the Fulbe ethnic group. Manumitted slaves were known as *rimdinaabe* (singular, *dimdinaado*), a term formed on the same verbal root as *dimo* but with the addition of causative and passive infixes, which literally means 'one who has been freed'. Although a freedman suffered no subsequent legal disabilities, his low birth could be socially disadvantageous, particularly when it came to contracting marriage.

The term *maccudo*, when used in its broader sense, referred to all subject pagans (also known as *haabe*, singular *kaado*) regardless of their exact legal or social situation. Jurally speaking, within this broader category of *maccube*, there was a clear distinction made, for taxation and other purposes, between on the one hand conquered tribute-paying groups and protected pagan groups who were permitted to live on their traditional lands under the control of their own chiefs, and on the other captive individuals (known as *jeyaabe*, from the verbal root *jeya* – to possess or own) who were brought back to Ngaoundere for sale as slaves. Vassal groups including various Mbum and Duru populations living near Ngaoundere were required to pay annually the Koranic *jizya* tribute to the state, consisting minimally of a large basket of millet of about 20 kilograms per household (Mohammadou 1978: 280; Froelich 1954: 48; Ruxton 1916). Slaves, on the other hand, were not taxed, since their masters fed and clothed them and provided their other basic needs. Despite the distinctions which existed between the slave and vassal categories in Koranic law, it would however be an error to draw an overly sharp line between the two groups. In practice, the Fulbe clearly viewed the vassal populations as functionally similar to slaves and did not hesitate to demand extra produce or labour from them as required. (See similar remarks for Kano by Lovejoy 1981: 223.) Many concubines were also procured from vassal groups, and the status of these women often differed little from that of concubines of slave status. In the last analysis, the most important point with regard to vassal groups at Ngaoundere was that the Fulbe still regarded these people as potential reservoirs of slaves and if these groups and their leaders did not continue to submit to Fulbe demands, they would be raided and reduced to total slavery (Passarge 1895: 297).

Even among the slave population at Ngaoundere itself, there were marked variations in status. Slaves could be owned by private owners or by the state. In the case of private ownership, slaves normally performed farming or herding work or could serve as domestic slaves in the master's household. The state owned substantial numbers of farm slaves as well, but there was also a category of court slaves (a few of whom were eunuchs) linked to the office of ruler, the *laamiido* (Passarge 1895: 490–1). Many of the latter performed domestic tasks in the ruler's compound while others served in government or military offices. For example, the offices of *sarki lifida*, the leader of the heavy cavalry, and *sarki bindiga*, the leader of the corps of musketeers, were both slave titles (Passarge 1895: 267; Froelich 1954: 79). Farm slaves settled in a slave village (*rumnde*) had the hardest lives, while the court slaves could in certain cases wield important powers and live a life of relative ease, supported by state resources and disposing of their own slaves (Passarge 1895: 489–90).

One problematic issue with regard to the Fulbe system of slavery at Ngaoundere is the question of the increasing rights enjoyed by at least some of the slaves who had been born in captivity (*dimaajo*, plural *rimaibe*). Some form of progressive modification of slave status would seem to be implied by a situation where slaves might hold important public offices and where, at least in legal theory, masters were under the obligation to convert their slaves to Islam and the enslavement of Muslims was illegal. Although the full details of this practice are not clear, it appears that in the case of household and court slaves who had been raised as Muslims in their masters' households, their owners were morally, although not perhaps legally, barred from selling them. On the other hand, farm slaves in Ngaoundere, as elsewhere in the Sokoto Caliphate (Lovejoy 1981: 221,225–6; see also Bassoro and Mohammadou 1980: 82–5), were subject to a more severe regime, and they and their children were sold at their masters' will.

At first glance, the presence of numerous slave farming settlements around Ngaoundere might lead one to the conclusion that the principal economic dynamic of the society was based on the extraction of an agricultural surplus from the servile population by the Fulbe state and private slave-owners for sale on the market. Careful consideration of the case, however, leads to the rejection of this conventional 'slave mode of production' interpretation (*contra*

Büttner 1967). Ngaoundere's reputation during the nineteenth century was built on the importance of its trade, and yet agricultural commodities as well as the output of Ngaoundere's rudimentary craft production played virtually no role in this commerce (Lacroix 1952: 32–3, see also Flegel 1883; 1885). The transport of bulky foodstuffs for long distances by human or donkey porterage was uneconomical, and the lightly populated Fulbe states of southern Adamawa had few difficulties in feeding their populations in any case. The agricultural produce of the slave settlements was used to support the ruler's court and the related administrative and warfare apparatus, and the growth in the number of slave settlements around Ngaoundere during the nineteenth century was principally linked with a political and demographic strategy of increasing the manpower available to the state.

On the other hand, Ngaoundere maintained an important pastoral component in its economy throughout the nineteenth century and slave herdsmen were often used in this activity (Passarge 1895: 261). Cattle did serve as an important form of tribute and general means of exchange between the states of Adamawa as well as between Ngaoundere and its pagan peripheries where cattle were exchanged for slaves. But the labour requirements of cattle production at Ngaoundere were not large and consequently cannot constitute an adequate explanation for the voracious appetite for slaves of the Ngaoundere state from its foundation.

The slave raiding activities of Ngaoundere had their own in-built and self-perpetuating rationale. The majority of the slaves taken in raids were sold to long-distance slave traders, and it was more as means of exchange than as means of production that slaves constituted the principal source of Ngaoundere's wealth (Bassoro and Mohammadou 1980: 84). Captives who were resettled in slave villages at Ngaoundere primarily served to strengthen the slave-raiding machinery, by producing food to feed more warriors and/or by serving as warriors themselves. The continued existence of the Ngaoundere state in its nineteenth century form clearly depended on its slave raiding and trading, activities which implied a continuing integral relationship within a regional system between Ngaoundere and its pagan peripheries.

Most Fulbe slave raiding expeditions took place during the dry season and normally lasted for several months, although in some cases they stretched over several years (Passarge 1895: 275; Charreau 1905: 78–9; Strümpell 1912: 84). A sizeable proportion of Ngaoundere society would participate in these major raids, and one French traveller reported that when he visited the town in 1893, 3,000 out of the total population of 11,000 were absent for this purpose (Ponel 1896: 207). Once the war party, complete with women and domestic slaves to look after the warriors' needs, had travelled to within striking range of the enemy, a fortified military camp (*saŋyeere*) was established to serve as a safe base (Ponel 1896: 205). The *saŋyeere* also served as a slave market after the captives had been taken. The ruler of

Ngaoundere profited heavily from these raids, since he claimed a minimum of 50 per cent of the slaves taken. When the ruler's titled slaves commanded such a slaving expedition, he still had rights to the whole booty, although he would of course reward his officers well. The bulk of the slaves taken were sold by the successful warriors to Hausa and other traders who visited the *saŋyeere* for this purpose, and these captives were then exported for resale in the slave markets of the Sokoto Caliphate and Bornu.

It was within the context of this regional system that the multi-ethnic society of the Mbere region developed during the latter half of the nineteenth century. The early attacks of the Wolarbe Fulbe overran the autochthonous Mbum and scattered Gbaya settlements of this area, probably in the early 1840s. Local territorial control was established using Ngaoundere's Mbum Mana[1] vassals as administrators at the town of Mboula, a staging point on the Djerem river about 100 kilometres from Ngaoundere on its southeastern trade route. Somewhat later, probably around 1850, an even more important centre of Fulbe influence developed at the town of Kounde, which was located a few kilometres beyond the present-day eastern frontier of Cameroon at the headwaters of the Mambere river in the Central African Republic (and some 200 kilometres as the crow flies from Ngaoundere).

At its origin, Kounde was a small patriclan-based grouping of the Gbaya Lai people. The Lai, under their war leader Nguimo, were defeated by a Fulbe force under the leadership of Kaigama Zarami, a titled vassal of Mbum Mana origin. In recognition of this victory, Zarami was made chief of Kounde and, during the latter half of the nineteenth century, this town became both an important base for slave raiding against the Gbaya, Laka and other peoples of the region and a focus of Fulbe tributary relations and trade. At its peak in the 1890s, under Kaigama Zarami's son and successor Iya Kounde, the Kounde political formation's raiding sphere was very large, extending in particular to the north and east to southern Chad and the Ouham river valley (Burnham, Copet-Rougier and Noss 1986).

The town of Kounde itself was surrounded by a wall of some four kilometres in circumference (Charreau 1905: 11–14), and the *jaoro* (chief) of Kounde and the other Mbum residents, who numbered only a few hundred, lived along with about fifty Laka domestic slaves and the principal Muslim traders within its defensive perimeter. During this period, some 2–2,500 Muslim traders were based at Kounde – this population fluctuating with the arrival and departure of long-distance trading caravans from various towns in the Sokoto Caliphate. Beyond the town wall, some 4–5,000 Gbaya lived directly under the control of Kounde, scattered over the neighbouring hillsides. Further afield, Kounde's political control, maintained on behalf of Ngaoundere, extended to a radius of some sixty kilometres, although some of the tributary relations on which it was based were not strongly institutionalised. Also located in the area were several *dumde* (slave settlements) and their

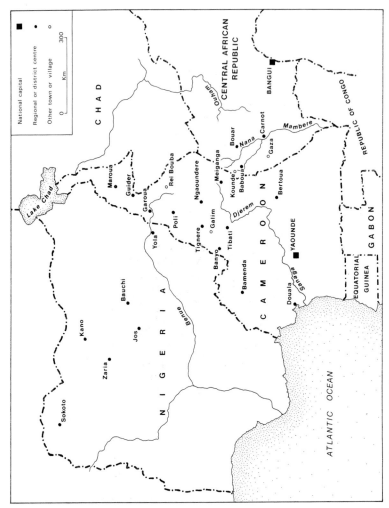

MAP 2: The Republic of Cameroon.

agricultural plantations, which belonged to the titled officials and important traders of the town.

This sketch of the social composition of Kounde, which along with several other tributary towns such as Mboula, Baboua, Bertoua[2] and Gaza is quite well documented for the late nineteenth century, tells us much about the extension of Fulbe political and cultural influences, both direct and indirect, into peripheral areas such as the Mbere region. As has been discussed at length in earlier work (Burnham 1980a; Copet-Rougier 1987; Burnham: in press), Gbaya political organisation prior to the impact of Fulbe-initiated influences, was markedly fluid. Gbaya patriclan territory groupings were unstable alliances of dispersed, extended-family hamlets which would co-operate in the face of external threats but which asserted their independence at other times. The leaders of such clan groupings exercised their roles primarily during wars, both offensive and defensive, but had few political resources to draw upon to shore up their leadership in other situations.

In this fluid political setting, it is apparent that the arrival of the Fulbe, although posing a grave risk of death or enslavement, also offered important opportunities for Gbaya leaders to enhance their political power within their own followings and even further afield. Gbaya clans that were subject to Fulbe overlordship funnelled annual tribute payments to the Fulbe through the hands of their clan leaders. As the explorer de Brazza explained (Archives AN1, my translation),[3] Gbaya clans that had submitted to the Fulbe without opposition were permitted to remain on their lands and

> their chiefs go to Ngaoundere, receiving there the investiture in the name of (*laamiido*[4]) Abbo . . . Populations that put up resistance are raided and the sons of chiefs and other important young men are taken to Ngaoundere and brought up in contact with the Fulbe and Hausa. Then, after several years, they are sent back to their homeland where they rule the country in the name of Abbo.

We have only limited records of the tribute levied by the Fulbe on Gbaya clans but the amounts involved do not appear to have been too heavy. For example, Charreau (1905: 28) reported that the village of Bingue near Baboua paid an annual tribute to the *laamiido* of Ngaoundere consisting of slaves, salt, mats and ivory but received a return gift of cattle which, in Gbaya eyes, was often of equal value. From the Fulbe point of view, of course, tribute received from the Gbaya was still an important source of wealth even when the value of counter-gifts was set off against it, since commodities like slaves and ivory fetched very high prices when traded westward through the Sokoto Caliphate (Flegel 1885).

For Gbaya war leaders, such tribute relations with the Fulbe were the source both of valuable trade items, which could be distributed to followers, and of military equipment such as weapons, padded armour and horses, which were of use in conducting slave raids further afield. Increasingly during the late nineteenth century, powerful Gbaya leaders, working in concert with the Fulbe of Ngaoundere much in the way that Kaigama Zarami and his successor Iya Kounde did at Kounde, were able to consolidate their political control not only over their immediate clan followings but also over neighbouring Gbaya clans and other nearby peoples. This constituted a strong nucleating force on the populations living within their ambit. Although the strongest Gbaya leaders do not themselves seem to have established slave settlements along the lines of the Fulbe *rumnde*, they did manage to hold subordinated groups under close control, insisting that they relocate their villages nearer to the leader's own settlement.[5] At the same time, these nucleating forces also had an opposite reaction among Gbaya and other groups seeking to escape the control of these expanding centres of political power, which led to movements, dispersals and intermingling of populations in areas at the limits of power of Ngaoundere and her vassals (Burnham: in press).

Another social factor that was actively at work within the developing multi-ethnic society of the Mbere region and adjacent areas was the Muslim 'Hausa' trader population, which has already been mentioned on several occasions. This category included both itinerant, long-distance traders as well as traders residing in centres like Mboula and Kounde on a longer-term basis. These men were not natives of Ngaoundere and although they are often referred to in the literature as 'Hausa' and used the Hausa language in their commercial activities, they were not necessarily of Hausa origin either. Their ethnic origins were diverse and included Kanuri, Jukun, Nupe, Wangarawa, Mandara and Choa Arab as well as Hausa.[6] On the whole, these traders manifested weak political allegiances and constituted a floating population which circulated widely throughout the savanna zone of West Africa. They would trade wherever it seemed most profitable, and the great concentration of these men in Ngaoundere's southeastern frontier regions is good evidence for the high profitability of the trading opportunities available in this area at that time. Even with little trading capital, a long-distance trader who was willing to assume the risks of operating in this dangerous region in the nineteenth century stood the chance of amassing substantial wealth after only a few visits. The economic details of this 'Hausa' trade are fascinating and have been discussed at some length elsewhere (Burnham 1980b; Flegel 1885; Duffill 1985), but our interest here is not so much economic as political, religious and cultural.

Although it appears that small numbers of very daring Muslim traders may have operated in the Mbere region during the 1840s, from about 1850 onwards, as the Fulbe consolidated their control over their southeastern marches, much larger numbers of these traders began to be attracted to this area (Barth 1857, II: 613–21; Burnham 1981). At first these men moved in large, well organised and armed trading caravans of several hundred members, but as security conditions improved, they began to be accompanied by their wives and domestic slaves and some settled for extended periods in the growing trading centres such as Mboula and Kounde.

It was in conjunction with their strategy of indirect exploitation of their southern frontier zones that the rulers of Ngaoundere supported the establishment and maintenance of permanent colonies of Muslim traders among the Gbaya (Mizon 1895: 358–9; Flegel 1885; Passarge 1895: 275; Archives AN1 and AN2). These Hausa and other Muslims living as traders in the Mbere region and beyond were governed by their own local officials, former caravan leaders entitled *madugai* (Hausa, singular *madugu*), appointed by Ngaoundere. These Muslims paid taxes through their local leaders to the Fulbe state (Charreau 1905: 21, 28; Mizon 1895: 358–9). The activities of these colonies of traders under their leaders served to funnel the lucrative trade of this region through Ngaoundere and bolstered the effectiveness of the uncertain tribute relations with the Gbaya and other pagan peoples. *Madugai* also collected caravan taxes on all long-distance traders passing through the area, welcomed strangers and emissaries, and acted as the leaders of the local Muslim community. These communities of Muslim traders constituted important sources of Islamic influence (Tessmann 1937: 175–6), since some of their members had made the pilgrimage to Mecca, were literate in Arabic, and gave instruction in the Koran. This influence mainly made itself felt on the leaders and other elders of local non-Muslim peoples like the Gbaya who, as Tessmann (1937: 174–5) and others (Mizon 1895: 358–9; Archive AN1) noted, saw in Islam a new road to power. On the other hand, the mass of these pagan peoples remained unconverted and little influenced by Islam.

Summing up our understanding thus far of the structure and ethnic composition of the Ngaoundere state, the central administrative organ of the state was the *laamiido* and his court, which mirrored the composition of the wider society in being composed of both free and slave officials. The category of freeman in Ngaoundere society was in turn segmented into the descendants of the original Fulbe conquerors (including offspring of both Fulbe and non-Fulbe wives and concubines), the members of the non-Fulbe 'Kambari' Muslim categories (most of whom were traders), and the category of freedmen and Muslim converts from the subjugated non-Fulbe populations of Adamawa. The two most striking characteristics of the Ngaoundere state were its great incorporative capacity of conquered populations and its reputation as a trading 'Eldorado' – features which were closely linked to the state's slave raiding and trading apparatus. At the same time, Ngaoundere's political and economic influence extended far beyond the territory that it could effectively administer and stimulated tendencies toward political centralisation among formerly uncentralised peoples like the Gbaya on its peripheries (Copet-Rougier 1987).

THE MAJOR GBAYA MOVEMENTS INTO THE MBERE REGION

At the time of the first European penetration of the Mbere region, during the decade of the 1890s, the Lom river marked the approximate western frontier of a major concentration of Gbaya who spoke what today is often referred to as the '*Gbaya Yaayuwee*' dialect. These Gbaya groups were living within the sphere of influence of Kounde, Ngaoundere's Mbum-led vassal town. As explained above, to the west of these Gbaya in the Mbere region, Mbum populations also predominated at the villages of Mboula, Manden (near the site of present-day Meiganga town), Mbusa (near the present-day town of Garoua Boulai), Nyambaka and along the Mbere river valley (Faraut 1981). Further to the north, other Gbaya groups had reached the lower Mbere and Lim river valleys south of the modern town of Baibokoum in Chad, where they confronted elements of the Laka and Mbum peoples with whom they maintained generally hostile relations (Burnham, Copet-Rougier and Noss 1986).

The Gbaya Yaayuwee of the Lom valley, in company with other culturally similar clans of the Yaayuwee and Gbaya Kara dialect groups inhabiting the valleys of the Mambere, the Nana, and the Yibi rivers, lived at this time within the sphere of influence of the political formation at Kounde described above. With the arrival of the French from the south under the command of de Brazza, Kounde and its allied Gbaya tributary populations came under direct European military pressure to cease its slave-raiding activities on behalf of Ngaoundere (Archives AN2; AN4; M1; M2 and I1; also Burnham: in press). These events culminated in a major battle (the second of two) in 1896 near the village of Sakani where a force under the leadership of Fulbe title holders and their Mbum, Duru and other slave officers, and containing cohorts of slave and tributary troops recruited from Gbaya, Yangere and other pagan peoples, was defeated by a force of French officers, Senegalese *tirailleurs* and Gbaya and other native auxiliaries. Having killed or scattered the forces at the disposal of Iya, the Mbum chief at Kounde, Alphonse Goujon, the commander of the French force, proceeded systematically to dismantle the town's slave-trading apparatus by ordering the removal of the Muslim trading community at Kounde to the new French administrative post at Carnot some 200 kilometres further south.

For the Gbaya clans resident in the Lom valley, who were implicated in Iya Kounde's slave-raiding activities, this upheaval made it advantageous to move westwards, out of the sphere of French colonial administrative control and also beyond the influence of the political formation at Kounde. Archival and oral history sources provide especially good documentation for the movements at this time of the *Bugwi* and other allied clans of the Gbaya Yaayuwee, under the leadership of Dogo Lokoti, who crossed the Lom and established villages on its western banks in the years immediately after

1896. Other Gbaya Yaayuwee clans pushed further west as the power of the Fulbe declined in the face of German colonial expansion at the turn of the century in Cameroon, peopling the lands between the Pangara and Djerem rivers at the western margins of the Mbere region (Burnham 1981).

A second major movement of Gbaya clans into the Mbere region, which probably occurred in the last decade or two of the nineteenth century, followed a more northerly route. Departing also from the upper Mambere basin, these groups followed the Nana river basin to the headwaters of the Lim and passed over into the Mbere river valley. Eventually these groups peopled the whole of the Mbere valley and are today recognised as linguistically and historically distinct from the Gbaya Yaayuwee dialect group, although closely related.

For the Mbum at Mboula and elsewhere in the Mbere region who were closely linked as vassals to the Ngaoundere state, the rapid decline of Fulbe power with the advent of colonial rule also led to a major diminution of their own political power. A vestige of one of these Mbum Mana political formations is still visible today at the now insignificant village of Mboula but, for the other more scattered Mbum populations of the Mbere region, the arrival of large numbers of Gbaya led to their gradual assimilation through intermarriage within that rapidly expanding people. Mbum cultural influences on the Gbaya Yaayuwee are nonetheless still noticeable today – especially in the large amount of borrowed Mbum vocabulary present in the Gbaya dialect spoken in the Mbere Department.

Despite the early French penetration of the eastern marches of Ngaoundere's territory, it was Germany which claimed Adamawa, including the Mbere region, as part of its colony of Kamerun. In establishing control over this region, German forces assaulted Ngaoundere in 1901, killing Lamido Abbo in the attack (Stoecker 1968: 68 *et seq.*). A successor was soon appointed and, throughout the period of German control up to the First World War and for more than a decade afterwards under the French, the Ngaoundere state apparatus was used by the colonial power to administer the peoples of the Mbere region via a system of indirect rule. This mode of colonial administration, based on the recognition of political distinctions between the Fulbe, the Mbororo, the Gbaya and the various other peoples inhabiting Adamawa, perpetuated the basic patterns of differential incorporation that had characterised the pre-colonial Fulbe state structure, while imbuing them with new content which will be discussed below.

THE MBORORO ARRIVAL IN THE MBERE REGION

It was during this period of early colonial rule that the final major element of the multi-ethnic society of the Mbere region was put into place, with the arrival of the nomadic pastoral Fulani (Mbororo). In contrast to the Fulbe, all the Mbororo clans now resident in the Adamaoua Province of Cameroon migrated to this area during the last decades of the nineteenth century or later and therefore played no role in the Adamawa *jihad*. Early Mbororo penetration of the Adamawa Plateau seems to have been restricted to its western reaches, especially within the territories of the Fulbe states of Banyo and Tignere, and the Mbere region did not receive significant Mbororo population until the beginning of the twentieth century.

As Dognin (1981) has documented, the early Mbororo migrants to Adamawa experienced considerable difficulties in the unsettled political conditions that prevailed, and their herds often fell prey to depredations either from the Fulbe states or from local pagan peoples. But as increasingly peaceful conditions came to prevail following the colonial conquest of Cameroon, more and more Mbororo groups migrated from neighbouring parts of northern Nigeria to the Adamawa Plateau, drawn by the excellent reputation of its environment for cattle husbandry. Both the German colonial administration (like the French after them), as well as the Fulbe rulers of Ngaoundere and the other Adamawa states, were pleased to see this influx of the cattle-rich Mbororo, whose presence represented great wealth for the local economy.

The last two decades of the nineteenth century and the first decade of the twentieth were the main periods of arrival and dispersal within Cameroon of the principal Mbororo clans that are known collectively as the '*Jafun*' (plural *Jafun'en*) and which are the predominant Mbororo grouping in the Mbere Department today. First penetrating the northwest of the Adamawa Plateau region from the Benue valley and from areas further west in Nigeria, these pioneer Jafun groups spread rapidly eastwards across the lightly populated Adamawa landscape and southwards into the Bamenda Grassfields. This was a time of considerable political competition and uncertainty for these Jafun groups as the *ardo'en* (leaders) of various clan fractions jostled for dominance.

Also at issue was the question of the relationship between the Mbororo and the political structures of the people already established in the Adamawa region, not least, of course, the colonial authorities. In certain areas, for example at Galim near Tignere, the Jafun encountered armed resistance from local pagan chiefs who attacked their herds and sought to prevent them from settling. The rulers of the Fulbe states of Banyo, Tignere, Tibati and Ngaoundere, for their part, sought to establish the traditional mode of relationship between Muslim Fulbe state and nomadic pastoral Mbororo – claiming the right to legitimate by investiture local Mbororo leaders and extracting a grazing tax (*chofol*) and, often, other less legitimate prestations, from the Mbororo living within their territories. In short, in a variety of ways, the Mbororo groups living within the ambit of the Fulbe city states of Adamawa were subject to a system of fiscal and administrative differential incorporation imposed by the Fulbe, despite the common cultural heritage of the two Fulani peoples. This system, which was essentially the same as that in effect in the other states of the Sokoto Caliphate, clearly was of pre-colonial origin, although it was progressively adjusted and changed by the colonial powers.

The German colonial administration made an early attempt to accommodate the growing Jafun population with their large herds in western Adamawa (Dognin 1981). To begin with, in 1906, they mounted a military expedition against the local pagan people at Galim, attacking them with machine guns and artillery and exiling their chief. In 1910, the Germans created an Mbororo canton (*bezirk* Lompta, also spelled Lomta) centred on the mineral springs at Galim, and appointed Ardo Hoba as a superior chief not subject to the neighbouring Fulbe state of Banyo.

This administrative experiment came to grief as a result of the German defeat in the First World War but was revived by the French, first in 1921 under the leadership of Ardo Tonga and, again in 1922 in a more grandiose manner under 'Lamido' Babba Haram. In the latter case, the French commandant of Ngaoundere envisioned the creation of a political grouping of all Mbororo in Adamawa, Wodaabe as well as Jafun. But, as Dognin (1981: 146) notes, this plan provoked the immediate dispersal of many of the Mbororo groups concerned. Although some of the Jafun clan fractions did settle for a brief period at Lompta, it ultimately proved no more successful than the previous administrative arrangements since the Jafun superior chief displayed the same tendencies to extract cattle tribute from the pastoral groups under his control as had the Fulbe rulers previously.

Various Jafun *ardo'en* soon emerged as competitors to Babba Haram and seceded from the Lompta political formation, dispersing widely throughout Adamawa and Bamenda. It was at this period during the 1920s that the territory that was to become the Mbere Department was first penetrated in significant number by Mbororo groups. At first used as a dry season grazing zone, the Mbere region became a place of refuge for Mbororo escaping the exactions of Fulbe chiefs and the Lompta experiment. This period of 'flight' (Fulfulde *perol* – the same word used to speak of Mohammed's hegira from Mecca) is today closely bound up in oral accounts and poetry (Lacroix 1965) with the name of Ardo Idje, a charismatic *ardo* of the Faranko'en clan. Idje assumed the leadership of the Faranko'en migratory group following a violent confrontation with retainers of Lamido Issa Maigari of Ngaoundere in which the former *ardo*, Bi Abba, was killed. Idje made peace with Ngaoundere and settled for a time on the north side of the Mbere River valley around Belel. However, after several years during which his reputation as a leader grew and he attracted more Mbororo clan fractions around him, he asserted his independence from the Fulbe and in 1920 moved with his followers to the eastern Ubangi-Shari (Dognin 1981: 148; see also Dupire 1970: 243–4).

It is instructive to note, *inter alia*, that although Ardo Idje's renown was very much linked with his successful resistance against the exactions of sedentary chiefs, he himself, having arrived in the western Ubangi-Shari, was named *chef supérieur* of the Mbororo there by the French administration and soon began to engage in the same types of exactions as those from which he and his followers had fled. This turnabout in Ardo Idje's behaviour points to some interesting contrasts in the modes of political leadership and legitimacy that distinguish the role of Mbororo *ardo* from that of the colonially created office of *chef supérieur* (or *laamiido*, for that matter), a theme I shall return to shortly. It also illustrates, as Dupire (1970: 520–1) has suggested, that a *chef supérieur* mode of organisation has a marked potential for development of stratification and autocratic political power, whether the chief be Mbororo or Fulbe, from which 'the nomads have attempted to escape, during the course of their history, by flight.'

The Jafun clans that first settled in the Mbere uplands in the 1920s had all resided previously in the Lompta canton, and their mode of settlement and seasonal displacement reflected the effects of this experience and their earlier sojourns around Yola and Bauchi. Although the independent, seasonally mobile family encampment with its herd remained (and still remains) the normative settlement pattern of Mbororo groups in the Mbere region, senior, politically influential Jafun men and their families tended to adopt a more sedentary lifestyle and settled permanently in an agricultural village of their slaves (*labbaare* – compare with the Fulbe notion of *rumnde*). Many Jafun men owned slaves, who were acquired as children via Hausa traders from neighbouring non-Fulani peoples (see Dupire 1970: 446–7). Small-scale slave trading of this sort, often involving the purchase of children from peoples like the Gbaya, continued in the Adamawa region well into the 1930s (see Bassoro and Mohammadou 1980: 84; VerEecke 1994). Male slaves served as herdboys during their youth and early adulthood. On reaching middle age, slaves would be permitted to settle and cultivate on their master's behalf, usually on the well-manured sites of former cattle camps. Female slaves served as domestic servants in their master's encampment and, upon reaching puberty, were often taken as concubines by their masters. In the Mbere Department today, villages such as Fada, Ngaouwi, Garga and Diehl owe their origins to the sedentarisation of Jafun leaders from the Dabanko'en and Seganko'en clans in this way.

EARLY COLONIAL RULE AND THE CREATION OF THE MEIGANGA *ARRONDISSEMENT*

As already mentioned above, the various populations of the Mbere region continued to be administered, under the Germans and during the first decade of French colonial rule, via a system of indirect rule which employed the Ngaoundere state system as political intermediary. This meant that, with no European colonial officers permanently resident in the Mbere region, the Fulbe of Ngaoundere retained an almost free hand in their relations with the Gbaya and the Mbororo. Slave-raiding activities in the Mbere region and further afield therefore continued largely unabated up through the First World War. The Fulbe also made onerous exactions from subordinate populations like the Gbaya, including corvée labour, sometimes under the guise of traditional tribute payments and sometimes in their role as collection agents for German and then French taxes. In some respects, Fulbe power over the peoples of the Mbere region was even enhanced during the early colonial period, since they could call down German or French punitive expeditions against populations whom they judged to be too intransigent (Burnham 1980a: 47). Indeed, throughout this early period of colonial rule, the Gbaya were subject to German and French military (rather than civil) government, and the officers in charge seem to have considered their goal to be pacification as much as administration.

In addition to this system of indirect rule, both the Germans and the French pursued policies of village 'regroupment' which were particularly directed against the Gbaya with their highly dispersed settlement pattern (although the creation of the Mbororo canton at Lompta also reflected similar concerns). Gbaya were required to relocate their residences in larger nucleated villages along the main trails so as to facilitate the collection of taxes, the recruitment of porters, and other activities of colonial surveillance and administration, and the houses and crops of recalcitrants were burned. Leaving aside the oppression of the Fulbe as well as the military action of the First World War, the level of administrative violence was especially severe on the part of the Germans. However, the French also used severe policing methods and, for much of the early colonial period, the Gbaya took refuge in flight to the bush. Indeed, both the Gbaya and the Mbororo made ample use of settlement mobility as a mode of resistance against colonial rule.[7]

An event of the early French colonial period, which was to have great significance subsequently for social relations in the Mbere region, was the establishment of a Protestant mission by American Lutheran missionaries at Mboula in 1924. The French colonial administration was very hesitant to allow missionaries to work in what was viewed as a dangerous region, and formal permission was not initially accorded. But this did not deter the Reverend Gundersen and his small band of co-workers of the Sudan Mission, who began work anyway (Christiansen 1956). In fact, the conflictual, multi-ethnic politics of this region constituted one of their main reasons for choosing to work in the area. In the missionaries' view, the Gbaya were a 'heathen' people who obviously resented the domination of the Fulbe of Ngaoundere and would therefore convert willingly to Christianity as an evident source of salvation both in this life and the next. Although this analysis was to prove correct in the long run, at the outset Christian conversion took place only very slowly since, particularly for Gbaya leaders, Islam and the associated Fulbe politico-economic system still enjoyed great prestige (Burnham 1982).

In July 1928, large sections of western Ubangi-Shari and eastern Cameroon, including the Mbere region, were thrown into even greater turmoil with the outbreak of the Karnu (*Koŋgo Wara*) Rebellion. This revolt was precipitated by the preachings of a Gbaya prophet named Karnu living in the village of Nahing, located between Baboua and Bouar in the Ubangi-Shari (now the Central African Republic). Karnu claimed to possess supernatural powers which, if used as he directed, would cause the French and the Fulbe to depart and leave the Gbaya in peace. Fighting began when Karnu's followers attacked a group of Mbororo and further attacks followed against Hausa traders and a French agricultural agent. On the strength of these early successes, Karnu's fame spread and Gbaya groups from far afield sent emissaries to learn of his methods. By the autumn of 1928, violence had spread throughout much of the western Ubangi-Shari and adjacent parts of eastern Cameroon, including the Mbere region, and the French sent several companies of troops to restore order. On 11 December 1928, Karnu was killed in an engagement at his village, following which the rebellion in the Baboua-Bouar area rapidly subsided. Violent outbreaks continued elsewhere, however, including clashes in the Mbere and Pangara valleys in Cameroon, and even as late as 1933, dissidents were still being hunted down and punished.

The participation of Gbaya groups in the revolt was patchy (Burnham and Christensen 1983: 6–7). In the Mbere area, the Gbaya chief Dogo Lokoti and the Mbum chief at Mboula sided with the French while the Gbaya leaders Alim in the Mbere valley and Gbangen in the Pangara valley rallied the local dissident clans. This pattern of allegiances correlated closely with the political alliances of these leaders. Certain groups had cultivated links with the Ngaoundere state and its German and French colonial successors and, on the basis of these ties, had managed to establish themselves as officially recognised chiefs. These men and their close followings refused to support the revolt. In contrast, for subordinate groups, the Karnu movement was seen as an opportunity to be rid of both French and Fulbe overlordship.

The Karnu Rebellion convinced the French colonial administration, once and for all, that their system of indirect rule of the Mbere region via the Ngaoundere state was untenable; the Gbaya had to be freed from Fulbe exploitation. The establishment of a separate *arrondissement*, with its district administration centred on the town of Meiganga, had several other advantages from the French point of view, despite being more costly. Although earlier experiments with an independent Mbororo canton at Lompta had failed, the development of the Meiganga *Arrondissement* as an Mbororo district offered a new opportunity to achieve similar aims. The French administration felt that it was important to maintain a separation, both spatially and politically, between the Fulbe and the Mbororo. In addition to wishing to counteract the Fulbe tendency to exploit any Mbororo groups under their control, there was also the fact that the French veterinary service wanted to prevent the mixing of Fulbe and Mbororo cattle. The mobile Mbororo herds were viewed as a potentially dangerous source of infectious disease, and the veterinarians also wanted to avoid interbreeding of Mbororo stock with the Fulbe *wudale* (singular, *gudaali*) strain, a more commercially useful beef cattle breed. Virtually from the date of its foundation in 1929, therefore, the Meiganga *Arrondissement* was administered by the French as a specifically Mbororo cattle-herding district from which Fulbe herds were excluded. (Conversely, Mbororo groups with their herds were forbidden to enter the neighbouring Ngaoundere *Arrondissement*.) This policy is usually referred to by the Fulfulde term *hadaande*

COLONIAL POLITICAL ECONOMY IN THE MEIGANGA *ARRONDISSEMENT*: 1929-60

Once the administrative authority of the Fulbe *laamiido* of Ngaoundere over the peoples of the Mbere region had been ended, canton chiefs drawn from the Gbaya people were henceforth regarded by the French as the *chefs de terre* within the Meiganga *Arrondissement*, on the grounds that the arrival of the Gbaya in this district had pre-dated that of the Mbororo. The formal exclusion of settled Fulbe agro-pastoralists and their herds, and the separation of the *arrondissement* from Fulbe administrative control, were facts of great significance for the subsequent development of inter-ethnic relations in the area. The Mbororo were able to set up generally favourable relations with the Gbaya villagers near whom they camped, bartering dairy products for agricultural produce and employing Gbaya men to build houses and perform other labour services as required.

The role of the Gbaya canton chief itself was essentially an artificial creation to suit French colonial requirements in domains such as tax collection, labour mobilisation, and the adjudication of minor court cases. Initially, the villages of the Meiganga *Arrondissement* were organised into five cantons (Mboula, Lokoti, Pangara [Dir], Djerem [Bagodo], and Mbere [also called Doumba or Djohong]). Later, in the 1950s, as the importance of the Mbum chief of Mboula declined, Mboula was abolished as a canton chieftaincy and replaced by Kalaldi. Meiganga, which was only a small village of some 250 people at the time of the establishment of the *arrondissement*, was also later elevated to separate canton chieftaincy status, after an initial attempt to persuade the chief at Lokoti to relocate to Meiganga had failed. Gbaya canton chiefs, while enjoying superior powers within the *arrondissement* in comparison to Mbororo *ardo'en*, did not wield the same degree of political power as had the chiefs of the Fulbe states. Although disputes about cattle damage to Gbaya crops occurred continually, Mbororo were generally able to resolve these to their satisfaction by the judicious distribution of gifts, particularly to the Gbaya canton chiefs.

However, as the Mbororo became increasingly numerous in the Meiganga *Arrondissement* and the French sought to encourage and stabilise this economically important influx of cattle herders, the local colonial administrators evolved a system of taxation and administration which was specifically designed to permit the Mbororo to be governed directly by the French, without resort to Gbaya canton chiefs as intermediaries. This system, based on the use of a separate head-tax roll for mobile populations such as the Mbororo, was known as the *rôle supplémentaire*. On the one hand, settled agricultural populations like the Gbaya were henceforth to be annually censused and head taxed, village by village, on the '*rôle primitif*', using their village and canton chiefs as tax collectors. On the other hand, mobile and transient populations such as Mbororo herders and itinerant, non-Gbaya traders were to pay their taxes directly to the sub-prefecture where they were recorded on a separate census roll – the *rôle supplémentaire*. Although the official rationale for this dual structure of census and taxation was that effective administration of mobile populations required such special arrangements, the French colonial administration made no bones about the desirability of effectively segregating the local structures of taxation and administrative control along ethnic lines in this way.[8] In particular, it obviated the necessity for Mbororo *ardo'en* to forward the taxes of their followings to the sub-prefecture through the hands of the Gbaya canton chiefs, a procedure which the Mbororo found demeaning and which also enhanced the potential for the canton chiefs to extort cattle from them.

Following the establishment of the French administrative presence within the Meiganga *Arrondissement*, their efforts were increasingly directed toward developing the economic potential of this area. An important barrier to this development during the 1930s was the poor local transport situation. There were no well-surfaced roads at this time, and this prevented the export of bulky foodcrops such as manioc, the major Gbaya crop. Some small alluvial gold mines were opened up by European entrepreneurs in the 1930s but the deposits were soon worked out. Nonetheless, this activity did provide the Gbaya with some experience of wage labour and with the marketing of crops to provision the miners.

The motor-road network of the Meiganga *Arrondissement* was constructed primarily during the decade of the 1940s, using local labour levies (recruited under the provisions of the colonial *indigénat* code [Archive M5; LeVine 1964: 101 *et seq*.) as well as Italian prisoners of war. As these routes were constructed, the colonial administration pursued active measures to relocate the Gbaya population along the roads according to its conception of an economically and administratively rational population distribution. For example, the many Gbaya villages inhabiting the fertile Mbere rift valley were forced to move to the new road which ran along the heights of the southern Mbere valley escarpment. In this new location, they were more easily accessible to the French administration and were also supposed to be in a better position to engage in agricultural trade to provision the numerous Mbororo encampments in this upland zone. However, this relocation proved to have severe drawbacks, in particular the fact that the soils of this upland plateau were not suited to Gbaya agricultural methods.

However, the road network, which was largely completed by the early 1950s, did make possible a major expansion in the regional market economy. Several European and Syrian/Lebanese commercial firms established themselves in Meiganga, as did increasing numbers of Hausa and Bamileke lorry operators and traders. A system of periodic markets was established in the larger villages and towns, which further enhanced the attractiveness of the region to Fulbe and Hausa petty traders, and a *beurrerie* was founded in 1948, with a network of purchasing points for Mbororo milk and butter (Christiansen 1956: 249). On the other hand, French attempts to get the Gbaya to cultivate cash crops such as coffee, tobacco and cotton were passively resisted and came to nothing (Burnham 1980a: 61).

To an ever-increasing extent from 1930 onwards, Mbororo cattle were viewed as the chief economic resource of the *arrondissement*, and local colonial policy was formulated with this mainly in mind. The primary focus here was the production of beef cattle for export to the towns of southern Cameroon, with Hausa cattle traders and butchers playing the principal role in this commerce. In fact, a 1955 report of the colonial agricultural service baldly stated that their first goal was to promote cattle husbandry, with assistance to farmers like the Gbaya, the majority population, being only a secondary consideration (Archive M3). Another index of the differential treatment of the Gbaya and the Mbororo by the French in the Meiganga *Arrondissement* is that while the Gbaya were subject to colonial labour prestations, the Mbororo were informally exempted.

This state of affairs was especially galling to the Gbaya in view of the fact that Gbaya labour levies were sometimes required to construct cattle vaccination parks and other facilities of use mainly to the Mbororo (Archives M4). Moreover, the archives reveal that French colonial administrators often gave support to the self-image of the Fulani as masters of non-Fulani peoples like the Gbaya. Thus, for example, the Fulbe and their *serviteurs* were allowed to refuse to labour on road construction (Archive M5), and Mbororo herders living near Ngaouwi complained to the commandant at Meiganga that Gbaya were not willing to work in sufficient numbers on Mbororo farms (Archive M7).

The immediate post-Second World War period also witnessed the establishment of a second Christian mission with the arrival of French Catholic priests and nuns (*Oblats de Marie Immaculée* and *Filles de Jésus de Kermaria*). Although by this date, the American Lutheran missionaries were well entrenched among the Gbaya people and Protestant Gbaya were nearly as numerous as Muslims and animists combined, the Catholic missionaries made some strides in French language teaching and vocational education, fields which the Americans, as well as the French colonial administration, had neglected. Nonetheless, few inhabitants of the Meiganga *Arrondissement* received even primary schooling during the colonial period.[9]

In relation to the main theme of this book, the period of French rule is especially noteworthy for the ways in which pre-colonial ethnic distinctions were utilised as the basis for colonial administration. Although ethnically based differential incorporation had been a feature of the Fulbe pre-colonial state system, the French used this principle in an even more thoroughgoing manner for purposes of taxation, labour recruitment, village resettlement and chieftaincy, judicial procedures, agricultural development, and many other activities. As administrative modes of surveillance became more effective in the later decades of colonial rule, there were few domains of public life where ethnicity was not significant in determining a person's relationship with the colonial state – a fact which doubtless reinforced, while subtly redefining, the content of ethnic differences in the Mbere region.

NATIONAL INDEPENDENCE AND POST-COLONIAL DEVELOPMENTS

Independence was granted to French Cameroon on 1 January 1960, and the effects of this change gradually made themselves felt in political backwaters in the north such as the Meiganga *Arrondissement*. While President Ahmadou Ahidjo, a Fulbe from Garoua, consolidated his hold over what was rapidly transformed into a one-party state, northern Cameroon served as his power base, with conservative Muslim regional and local governments in charge in most areas. A good example of this political strategy was Ahidjo's tight control over the territorial administration in the north, exercised on his behalf by his longtime friend and fellow Fulbe Ousmane Mey, 'the immovable governor' (to borrow a phrase from Bayart [1986: 10, my translation]) of the whole of northern Cameroon.

In common with other former French colonies, the independent Cameroon government is effectively divided into two parallel and separate bureaucracies. On the one hand, there is the territorial administrative system reaching from the president down through province, department, *arrondissement* and district levels, and equipped with its own police force – the gendarmerie. On the other, there is the ministry-based administrative system, reaching from the president, through the cabinet members and their ministries, and down to the local offices of the ministries, known as delegations, which are usually sited in the prefectural towns. During Ahidjo's quarter-century of rule, the power of the territorial administration in northern Cameroon greatly outweighed that of the ministerial system, since the ministerial delegation offices were very thinly distributed on the ground in the few prefectural centres and the territorial administration disposed of many more political resources. In towns below the prefectural level (such as Meiganga before 1983) and in the vast rural areas of northern Cameroon, the territorial administration was the sole manifestation of central government power, and certain prefects and sub-prefects ruled their domains in a patrimonial style reminiscent of traditional Fulbe chiefs.

As regards recruitment to this all-powerful territorial administration in Adamawa, Ousmane Mey operated virtually a mono-ethnic policy in favour of appointees drawn from the Fulbe or 'Fulbeising' category. For example, during virtually all of Ahidjo's period as head of state, the Meiganga *Arrondissement* was governed by Fulbe or Fulbeised Muslim sub-prefects. One may also note in passing that a selective recruitment policy was applied to the personnel of the elite *Garde Républicaine*, a corps of gendarmes which had served as Ahidjo's personal bodyguard and which played a central role in the 1984 coup attempt against Paul Biya, Ahidjo's southern Christian presidential successor. Recruits to this unit were drawn predominantly from Fulbe or Fulbeising ethnic groups for the officer positions and from northern 'pagan' groups for the non-commissioned ranks.[10]

The dominance of Fulbe political culture in the territorial administration of northern Cameroon led to numerous abuses of power and cases of corruption, some of which I was able to observe in a discrete manner during my early periods of fieldwork between 1968 and 1980 but which have now become topics of public discussion since the departure from office of Ahidjo in 1982. More important for our present topic, however, is the fact that the Fulbe territorial administrators found it generally advantageous to perpetuate many of the ethnically based structures of differential incorporation and Fulbe forms of political culture that have their historical roots, as we have seen, in pre-colonial and colonial patterns of inter-ethnic relations.

Ahidjo's resignation on grounds of ill-health in 1982 in favour of his successor Paul Biya set in motion a series of major political changes which were to have wide-ranging impact throughout the country, especially in the north (Monga 1986). Soon after his resignation, Ahidjo's health worries apparently diminished, and he returned to active political life in his role as president of the sole national political party, the UNC (*Union Nationale Camerounaise*). There ensued a power struggle between Ahidjo and Biya, during which Biya weeded out ministers seen as loyal to Ahidjo and moved to break up Ahidjo's northern power base.

One of the early administrative changes made by the Biya government as a direct response to the perceived political threat emanating from northern Cameroon was to divide the monolithic northern province into three provincial units, with their capitals at Ngaoundere, Garoua and Maroua. As Bayart (1986: 10) has noted, in making this change, Biya was attempting to capitalise upon the long-standing rivalry between the traditional Fulbe elites of these three major cities of the north and to exploit the frustrations of Maroua and Ngaoundere at Ahidjo's systematic preferment of his home town, Garoua. Concomitant with Ngaoundere's promotion as capital of the Province of Adamaoua, the town of Meiganga was elevated to the status of the prefectural headquarters of the Department of the Mbere, and a major expansion of the local administration was carried out. For the first time since the early 1960s, the Mbere Department was headed by a southern Christian prefect, and a large proportion of the expanded prefectural and ministerial delegation services, not to mention those of the police services (*Sûreté* and *Gendarmerie*), were staffed by southern Cameroonians.

In the face of these moves by Biya, Ahidjo retreated to his villa in the south of France. In August 1983, Biya announced that a plot had been uncovered. Ahidjo was implicated, tried in absentia, condemned to death and then pardoned. In April 1984, a bloody and unsuccessful attempted coup, in which the northerner-dominated *Garde Républicaine* played a leading role, did take place but was soon crushed by loyal army units (see Monga 1986). Many northerners implicated in the plot (including Gbaya and others hailing from the Mbere region) were executed or imprisoned for lengthy terms, often on the basis of 'administrative detention' or unfair trials (Amnesty International 1984; 1985; 1986; 1987; 1989 and Monga 1986: 160–4). From that time on, the Biya government progressively strengthened its grip on the reins of power, only to be challenged in the 1990s by political movements calling for democratic, multi-party elections.

Another important element in Biya's political programme was the abolition of the UNC and the creation in 1985 of a new party, the RDPC (*Rassemblement Démocratique du Peuple Camerounais*), under a banner proclaiming '*renouveau*', liberalisation and democratisation (despite the fact that there was still only one legal party in Cameroon). Nonetheless, as Bayart (1986: 20) and DeLancey (1989: 167 *et passim*) note, the mid-1980s was a period marked by relatively greater freedom in public life than heretofore – a fact which is apt to be forgotten in the 1990s thanks to Biya's growing unpopularity.

Within the Mbere Department, it was particularly the Gbaya people who had entertained hopes at the time of Ahidjo's retirement that Biya's appointment might usher in for them a period of greater political influence and employment opportunities, thanks to a likely decline in Fulbe power in the north. These hopes were further bolstered by the rhetoric of prominent early Biya appointees to the Mbere departmental administration, which was widely judged by Gbaya to be 'pro-farmer' (and therefore anti-pastoralist and anti-Fulani). Indeed, in my own interviews with local officials during this period, almost all of whom hailed from southern Cameroon, I was struck by the way in which they seldom missed an opportunity to condemn the traditionalism and ethnic favouritism of the Ahidjo period, as well as the alleged backwardness and recalcitrance of Fulbe and Mbororo to economic and political progress.

However, Gbaya optimism in this regard has largely proved to be unfounded. As mentioned above, Gbaya discontent with the Biya regime began to mount following the 1984 coup attempt and the imprisonment of members of the *Garde Républicaine*. The Gbaya have become further disillusioned as they arrived at the view that, even within their 'own' Mbere Department regional government, southern dominance had simply been substituted for Fulbe dominance in access to senior administrative posts.[11]

On the economic and infrastructural fronts within the Mbere Department, the post-independence period has witnessed many significant changes. Primary education expanded markedly from the late 1950s onward, with continued active involvement of the Lutheran and Catholic missions as well as the state. A government secondary school was opened in Meiganga in 1980. The town of Meiganga was connected to public electricity and an efficient telephone service, while many villages and towns in the department were provided with a clean water supply. The level of government employment also expanded, particularly in the early 1980s, thanks to the elevation of Meiganga to prefectural status (with its many new delegation offices representing ministries such as social services, planning, finance, equipment, tourism and the Ministry of the Interior) and the establishment of Djohong as a sub-prefecture.[12] However, Meiganga remains a town with no industrial base which is heavily dependent on the salaries of government and mission employees as well as on its role as a regional trading entrepôt. For this reason, as mentioned in the introduction, Meiganga has been hard hit since 1987 by the national economic crisis and accompanying structural adjustment measures.

The completion of the Yaounde-Ngaoundere Transcamerounais rail link in the early 1970s led to the rapid growth from point zero of the rail depot town of Ngaoundal, on the western margin of the *arrondissement*. This was soon followed by the paving of the Meidougou-Ngaoundal-Tibati road, which opened the way for Ngaoundal to compete with Meiganga as a commercial centre. During the same period, the village of Ngaouwi, on the frontier with the Central African Republic, also grew rapidly in commercial significance as a centre for cross-border trade and smuggling.

Cameroon's national economic decline from the mid-1980s (linked with a major drop in state oil revenues), followed by the public service austerity programme and swingeing cuts in government salaries instituted in 1987, further contributed to the unpopularity of the Biya government. This has been followed, during the 1990s, by political turmoil associated with the economic weakness of the state and the abortive attempts to introduce multi-party democracy. Sadly, as explained above, these changes produced the sparks which ignited the violent inter-ethnic conflicts in the Mbere Department in 1991 and 1992. These recent political developments will be discussed in Chapter 7 but first, in the following chapters, we will look in more detail at the social practices and ideologies defining the three principal ethnic categories of this region.

CONCLUSION

This chapter has rapidly reviewed the historical emergence, over the last 150 years, of the multi-ethnic society of the Mbere Department. During most of this period, the most important conditioning factors affecting the quality of inter-ethnic relations in the region have been the structures of differential incorporation of the pre-colonial Fulbe state of Ngaoundere, and its German and French colonial successors. While the incorporative capacity of the nineteenth century Ngaoundere state was quite remarkable, it was based on warfare, slavery, vassalage and concubinage, underpinned by the hierarchy of social categories defined by Muslim law. Despite the ideology of the *jihad*, the conversion to Islam of conquered 'pagan' peoples was not strongly emphasised in practice. And although certain individuals from conquered groups such as the Mbum and Gbaya did gain considerable power and wealth through their association with the Fulbe state, acquiring in the process much of Fulbe Muslim material and conceptual culture, they did not become assimilated within the Fulbe ethnic category. Instead, they retained their natal ethnic identities and were administered by their own chiefs or vassal officers. In other words, the Fulbe state system was socially inclusivist in orientation but the defining logic of the Fulbe ethnic category remained exclusivist. As a result, during the pre-colonial period, the Fulbe ethnic category expanded much more slowly than the Fulbe state – relying primarily on demographic recruitment by birth, either to free Fulbe women or to slave or vassal concubines.

German and French colonial rule in northern Cameroon also functioned on the basis of ethnically defined systems of differential incorporation. However, certain of the changes that were instituted in the colonial period were to have major impacts on the structures of ethnic boundary maintenance, and associated cultural logics, defining the different ethnic components of Mbere Department society. This point is especially well illustrated by the effects of the abolition and (gradual) decline of slavery on the Fulbe ethnic category, which is one of the principal themes of the next chapter.

THE FULBE ETHNIC CATEGORY AND ITS INCORPORATIVE POTENTIAL

As we have seen in Chapter 2, the multi-ethnic composition of the Mbere Department owes much to the events set in motion at the beginning of the nineteenth century by the Adamawa *jihad*. The present-day constitution of the Fulbe ethnic category in particular results from the operation of social processes in the pre-colonial Fulbe states of northern Cameroon such as Ngaoundere, Tibati and Rei Bouba that were created in the course of that holy war. The system of social stratification of these Fulbe states was based on the large-scale differential incorporation of population derived from neighbouring non-Islamic, 'pagan' (*haaɓe*) peoples, who were relegated to the tributary or servile status categories prescribed by Islamic law (Ruxton 1916; see also Mohammadou 1978: 280 and Bassoro and Mohammadou 1980). As for the social status of 'freeman' (*dimo*, plural *rimɓe*) in these states, it is important for us to consider the social composition and internal stratification processes at work in this category in more detail at this point, in view of their implications for subsequent developments within the Fulbe ethnic category more generally.

Although Azarya in his 1978 work entitled *Aristocrats Facing Change: the Fulbe in Guinea, Nigeria and Cameroon* has taken the opposite view,[1] it is my contention that the Fulbe groups that undertook the Adamawa *jihad* were not differentiated along aristocratic versus commoner descent lines and that, subsequent to the establishment of the Fulbe conquest states of Adamawa, despite the centralisation of power in the hands of the *laamiido* and his titled officials, the dominant social cleavage remained that between Fulbe freemen and *haaɓe* slaves or vassals, as opposed to that between so-called aristocrats versus commoners. As we have seen in the preceding chapter, Fulbe clans like the Wolarbe who took a prominent role in the Adamawa *jihad* were leading a mobile agro-pastoral existence at the beginning of the nineteenth century, and there is no evidence for any significant degree of descent-based differentiation of social status within the freeman category at that time. Indeed, it is instructive to note that the leaders of those Fulbe clans were referred to by the term '*ardo*', a title which was indicative of a much more limited degree of centralisation of powers and institutionalisation of political succession than their later designation as '*laamiido*' implied. Moreover, aside from Moddibo Adama, most of the other leaders of the Adamawa *jihad* such as Ardo Njobdi were not renowned for their Islamic learning prior to the advent of the holy war (Burnham and Last 1994; Burnham: in press).

Of course, the military successes of Ardo Njobdi and his Fulbe followers greatly increased their reputations, their wealth (especially in slaves and slave estates) and their power. With the establishment of the Ngaoundere state, the state treasury began to receive substantial flows of wealth from the various taxes and tributes that could be levied by a Muslim state (Froelich 1954; Lacroix 1952; Ruxton 1916: 31 *et passim* and Dognin 1981), as well as from sales of slaves and other booty taken in subsequent campaigns. But as is clear from our nineteenth century sources, this access to increased wealth was not restricted to the ruler and his state treasury but was open to titled officials, both freemen and slaves, and to private individuals active in both warfare and trade.

This relative fluidity of economic status was also enhanced by the operation of the system of titled offices in the Ngaoundere state, which was effectively more praebendal than patrimonial (Weber 1947). The number of specialised political titles attached to the court of the *laamiido* of Ngaoundere that were reserved for Fulbe freemen was relatively small, although in keeping with the *tokkal* concept of leadership derived from their experience of a mobile pastoral existence, Fulbe freemen could establish themselves as leaders (*jaoro'en*, singular *jaoro*) of settled agro-pastoral communities and thereby play a role in the life of the court and the state government. On the other hand, titled slave officials were numerous and important in many of the Adamawa states including Ngaoundere (and not just in Tibati and Rei Bouba), and the court officials of slave status were utilised by the *laamiido* to counteract oppositional tendencies among Fulbe competitors for power.

It is relevant to note in this regard that the primary rule of succession to the office of *laamiido* (and probably to several others of the non-religious positions open to Fulbe freemen) which operated in these Fulbe states was that a candidate had to be the son (by either a legitimate wife or a slave concubine) of a previous holder of the office. In the context of the large-scale polygamy which was prevalent in Fulbe circles, this rule ensured that there would normally be numerous eligible candidates (which enhanced the effectively praebendal as opposed to patrimonial character of the political system), while at the same time having the effect of excluding unsuccessful fraternal lines from future competition.

The available data (Froelich 1954; Mohammadou 1978; Lacroix 1952) indicate that there were two levels of corporate political organisation which are relevant for an understanding of the operation of a pre-colonial Adamawan state. First, there was the ruler and his court of titled officials, many of whom were not freemen nor were they ethnically Fulbe. Secondly, there were the ethnically defined categories of freemen including, of course, the Fulbe but also the Hausa and the Bornuans (known collectively as Kambari) whose interests were separately represented within the court by individuals holding the titles of *Sarki Hausawa* and *Mai Bornu*. As suggested above, the first level is best analysed with reference to theories of state formation and functioning, while the second must be understood in relation to the social structural mechanisms and cultural logics which maintained the distinctiveness of Fulbe ethnic status within the freeman category.

During the pre-colonial period, as we have seen, Fulbe ethnic status was firmly anchored within the legally defined system of differential incorporation operating in Ngaoundere and other Fulbe states. The administrative procedures through which this differential incorporation was maintained were chiefly those of the *tokkal* political following, explained in the previous chapter. This structure defined citizenship and excluded the Mbororo, for example, who were required to pay the *chofol* pasturage tax when resident in Ngaoundere's territory, whereas Fulbe and other free citizens of the state were exempt from this levy (Froelich 1954). In addition to their status as free citizens of the Ngaoundere state, members of the Fulbe category were differentiated from other categories of Muslim freemen on the basis of two other factors – race and cultural norms.

By the term 'race', I am referring to the set of phenotypical features which are considered, both by Fulani peoples as well as by their non-Fulani neighbours, to be characteristic of the Fulani – Fulbe and Mbororo taken together (see, for example, Dupire 1981: 170). These phenotypical features include a lithe build, a light coppery skin colour (termed 'red', *bodeejum*, by the Fulani), an aquiline nose and fine lips. On the other hand, it must be emphasised that this is only a cultural ideal or stereotype; many Fulani in the past, as is the case today, would not have exhibited this set of characteristics, given the substantial intermixing of Fulani and negroid peoples throughout their recorded history.[2]

As for Fulbe cultural identity during the pre-colonial period, we do not possess much detailed data on this point, although it is clear from contemporary manuscript data (Last 1989: 558) that an ideology of Fulbe cultural distinctiveness and superiority played a significant role in recruiting followers to Shehu Usumanu's holy war.[3] This cultural ideology, known as *pulaaku* in Fulfulde, will be discussed at greater length in this and later chapters.

COLONIAL AND POST-COLONIAL MODIFICATIONS OF FULBE ETHNIC IDENTITY

Following the colonial conquest of the Fulbe states of northern Cameroon, the gradual decline of slavery and the demise of the *tokkal* structure, progressively larger proportions of the populations of these states became freed from the pre-colonial power structures discussed above and the connection was loosened between Fulbe ethnicity and Fulbe state political structures. As more peaceful conditions became the norm, there was a substantial increase in the spatial mobility of the northern Cameroonian population in general and, in particular, the development of a substantial 'floating' population of recently freed slaves (VerEecke 1994). These social changes, in turn, set the stage for a more rapid assimilation of non-Fulbe into the Fulbe ethnic category.

Although the Fulani racial ideal continued to be highly valued in opposition to negroid features (which evidenced slave or *haabe* ancestry), phenotypic features were not reliable indicators within northern Cameroonian society of an individual's political or economic status. For example, many of the rulers of the Fulbe states of Adamawa in the colonial and post-colonial periods have had negroid features because they were the offspring of non-Fulbe concubines. This continuing inter-breeding served to further increase the already substantial heterogeneity of this population and also ensured that phenotypic traits could not act to deny membership in the Fulbe ethnic category to individuals whose phenotypic features did not correspond to the Fulani racial stereotype. This situation is described by Emily Schultz, who carried out research on ethnicity and Fulbeisation in the Fulbe-dominated town of Guider in northern Cameroon during the 1970s, as follows (1979: 20–1):

> In northern Cameroon the racial factor, although important in the past for Fulbe ethnic identity, is no longer significant in urban areas like Guider, following one hundred years of inter-marriage between the light-skinned, Caucasian-featured [*sic*] Fulbe nomads and the darker-skinned, indigenous non-Fulbe peoples.

The colonial changes toward a more open boundary of the Fulbe category within northern Cameroonian society can be compared with the situation in northern Nigeria during the pre-colonial period where, as Lovejoy has argued (1981: 211; see also Al-Hajj and Last 1965), recruitment efforts by the *jihad* reformers, linked with debates over conceptions of 'free' versus 'slave' status, also led to changes in the definitional bases of the Fulani and Hausa ethnic categories. In the pre-colonial northern Nigerian context, where the predominantly Fulani reformers were protesting against, among other things, the un-Islamic practice of Hausa rulers and slave owners of enslaving Muslims, the term 'Fulani' took on the expanded meaning of 'free' and Muslim, versus '*haabe*' and 'slave'. On the other hand (Lovejoy 1981: 211):

> As the caliphate was consolidated after 1804, the term *Hausa* broadened to signify the Muslim peasantry and merchant class, as opposed to the Fulani aristocracy. Hausa society in turn became more heterogeneous, and people were usually identified in terms of origins. This pluralistic conception of ethnicity, in which Hausa was now the umbrella for a complex mixture of diverse people, was probably more important than the simplistic dichotomy based on religion.

In Ngaoundere as in most of the other Fulbe states of Adamawa, the situation differed somewhat from that in Hausaland, primarily as a result of the fact that the *jihad* had been conducted entirely against non-Muslims, as opposed to purportedly backsliding Muslims, and in a region that had been beyond the ambit of any pre-existent Hausa cultural influence. When the many ethnic groups of this region submitted to or were enslaved by the Fulbe conquerors, the label '*haabe*' that was applied to them could therefore have no uniform cultural referent beyond that of 'subject pagan'. It was Fulbe culture and Islam, embedded within the incorporative Fulbe state structure, that was the new way of life on offer, although full access to this lifestyle did not open up widely until after the colonial conquest.

Of course, a more wide-ranging adoption of Fulbe ethnic identity did not happen overnight, since the Germans and the French continued to use Ngaoundere and the other Fulbe states as intermediaries in their systems of indirect rule. Particularly in the more remote Fulbe states such as Rei Bouba, but also in Chamba and Banyo among others, the Fulbe chiefs and their courts managed to retain a relatively high degree of day-to-day autonomy from the colonial government (and even, to a significant degree, from the independent Cameroonian government under the Ahidjo regime), and influences of the pre-colonial Fulbe system of social status, including legally sanctioned differential incorporation and servitude, remained visible well into the post-colonial period.[4]

Change in an individual's ethnic identity from one of the non-Fulbe and non-Muslim ethnic groups to Fulbe ethnic status, a process which has often been referred to in the literature as 'Fulbeisation' (Dupire 1962: 39; Callies 1968: 130; Burnham 1972; Azarya 1978; and Schultz 1979 and 1984), has offered individuals a number of potential advantages during the colonial and post-colonial periods in Cameroon. For ex-slaves who had lost touch with their natal ethnic groups, Fulbe identity was virtually the only ethnic option on offer but, even for many members of non-Fulbe ethnic groups in northern Cameroon who had not been enslaved, migration to town and adoption of Fulbe ethnicity were and are still seen as socially and economically advantageous under certain conditions (Podlewski 1966: 13–15; 1971: 104,

118 *et passim*; Schultz 1979: 191 *et passim*). During the majority of the post-independence period, with the political affairs of Cameroon being dominated up to 1982 by the Fulbe president Ahmadou Ahidjo and his close northern associates, it has also been highly advantageous to be identified as a member of the Fulbe ethnic category when seeking government employment or other state-controlled opportunities.

The process of Fulbeisation involves change in three main social domains, which can be thought of as ethnic boundary mechanisms in Fredrik Barth's sense (1969). These boundary criteria are: adherence to Islam, use of Fulfulde as principal language, and overt behavioural consensus with Fulbe cultural norms and ideals. As has been noted in various studies of northern Cameroon societies (Podlewski 1966; Burnham 1972; Schultz 1979: 213; 228), this process of ethnic passing into the Fulbe category is often accomplished during an individual's lifetime, although depending on the interactional strategies adopted by that individual and given the existence of social ranking criteria within the category, this ethnic change may sometimes be more one of degree than of kind in the first generation. For this reason, I often speak of 'Fulbeising' individuals to refer to persons who adhere to the above-mentioned boundary criteria defining the Fulbe category, but whose previous ethnic affiliations are still detectable in their social behaviour. We will describe some of the nuances of the Fulbeisation process as we consider each of these three major facets of ethnic redefinition in turn.

ISLAM AND FULBE ETHNIC STATUS IN NORTHERN CAMEROON

Adherence to Islam is a pro forma prerequisite for entrance into Fulbe society, for despite inevitable variations in degree of piety, all Fulbe in northern Cameroon are at least nominally Muslim. Indeed, the Fulbe continue to derive much prestige from their leadership of the *jihad*, a glorious history which is still enshrined in an oral literature of praise songs and epic poems (Lacroix 1965; Haafkens 1983), as well as in modern printed texts. From this perspective, throughout much of northern Cameroon, Islam may be seen as a particularly Fulbe cultural property. Lacroix aptly explained the situation in the following terms (1966: 402, my translation):

> for the Fulbe, especially those of Nigeria and Cameroon who are descend-ants and heirs of the great tradition of Uthman dan Fodio, being Muslim and being Fulbe are easily confused. Islam justifies and explains in their eyes the social and political system which they have created and which they benefit from; it reinforces, at the same time, their sense of being 'different' from the peoples surrounding them. In this regard, one may speak of a sort of appropriation of Islam by the Fulbe for their own benefit – a fact which helps to explain their lack of inclination to proselytise.

In the final line of this quotation, Lacroix is referring to the often remarked failure of the rulers of the pre-colonial Fulbe states of Adamawa to actively pursue the proselytisation of Islam among the conquered pagan groups after the *jihad*. In part, Lacroix attributed this failure to the greater economic rewards that Fulbe rulers could gain by exploitation of non-Muslim subjects as opposed to those who had converted. But I would also argue, with Lacroix, that during the pre-colonial period, the Fulbe displayed a relatively conservative attitude toward conversion of their subject peoples due to the fact that Islam had become one of their principal mechanisms of ethnic boundary maintenance.

The relative exclusion of non-Fulbe groups in Adamawa from Islamic conversion could not be effectively maintained in the more fluid social conditions after the colonial conquest and the abolition of slavery. But Islamic morality and Fulbe custom had become so closely associated during the pre-colonial history of northern Cameroon that when a non-Fulbe has converted to Islam in more recent times, they are seen as opting for Fulbe culture at the same time. Schultz (1979: 272) explains this process as it operates in the town of Guider north of the Benue river:

> since Fulbe racial characteristics have lost their importance as defining features of the urban Fulbe in Guider, Islam is free to operate in a universalistic manner, recruiting into the Fulbe way of life many dark-skinned individuals of non-Fulbe origins. Yet because being Muslim and being Fulbe are synonymous in Guider, given the prevailing view of ethnicity, non-Fulbe who Islamise and commit themselves to urban Fulbe culture are seen to have changed ethnic groups and to have become Fulbe.

In other words, as the character of the social boundary demarcating the Fulbe ethnic category progressively shifted from exclusionary to assimilative during the colonial period and afterwards, the universalistic ideology of Islam found freer expression.

Today, non-Muslims living in the north are frequently chided or entreated by their Muslim acquaintances about their non-believer status, and I was not exempted from such exhortations. Indeed, as Schultz (1979: 187–90) notes, Fulbe scorn and insults directed at 'pagans' have become significant factors promoting Islamisation and Fulbeisation of non-Fulani peoples in northern Cameroon. For example, the following story, which was told to me on several occasions both in Fulbe and in Mbororo circles, explains the torments awaiting the unbeliever in hell and, at the same time, makes use of a folk (and probably false) etymology for the Fulfulde word *keefeero* (unbeliever, cf. Arabic *kafir*) to make a racial slur against the *haabe*. According to this story, unbelievers are sent to burn in hell and their burnt skin is then scraped off. They are then burnt and scraped again, repeatedly, to increase their suffering. The Fulfulde verbal root for 'scrape', *hefa*, becomes *kefa* in its plural forms according to rules of consonantal shift, and my informants claimed that this is the root for the noun *keefeero*. This etymology is also said to explain the black skin of pagans (as opposed to the 'red' skin of the Fulani). This story conveniently ignores the fact that, if this etymology were correct, the word would be *kefeero*, not *keefeero*, and Taylor's Fulani-English dictionary listing of the verbal root of *keefeero* as *heefna/keefna*, meaning 'to recant', is probably the more accurate.

While the greater ease of Islamic conversion has facilitated the more rapid assimilation of population within the Fulbe category in recent decades, it has also contributed, as Lacroix noted (1966: 404), to the prevalence of a shallow and heterodox adherence to Islam among many of the partly assimilated and Fulbeised populations of Adamawa today. In demonstrating one's allegiance to Islam as a minimal step toward Fulbeisation, it is only necessary to perform the five daily prayers and, since these may be said inaudibly and/or in private, there is no convenient means for others to check an individual's full mastery of the Koranic verses.[5] In any case, the basic prayers appear to be widely known, even among non-Fulbe 'pagan' or Christian populations in the north. For example, in one predominantly Christian Gbaya village where I lived, I observed a group of children reciting Muslim prayers in the form of a game, much like 'Peter Piper' tongue-twisters in English. On the other hand, as Schultz (1979: 227–8) noted in Guider and as is also the case in Ngaoundere, Meiganga and elsewhere in Adamawa, non-Fulbe or Fulbeising converts to Islam are sometimes reluctant to perform their prayers in public, since they risk the ridicule of the Fulbe for not accomplishing them correctly.

In the face of such risks of ostracism, an individual wishing to convert to Islam as part of the process of Fulbeisation may well try to cement his membership of his new community by seeking out a patron to initiate him into the faith.[6] He may approach a Muslim friend, an employer or a Koranic schoolteacher or other locally recognised *mallum* to give him basic religious instruction and on completion he may undergo a formal 'baptism' (*'yiiwugo islama*) ceremony. Such a formal and publicly recognised conversion is likely to improve the convert's status within his community of adoption but, according to my observations, it does not necessarily absolve him from Fulbe jibes or suspicions of what Schultz (1979: 191; see also Lacroix 1965: 22 *et passim*) has aptly termed 'utilitarian Islamisation'.

Beyond the basic marks of membership or conversion to Islam, symbolised by performance of daily prayers, relative devotion to the faith offers a scale of social ranking within the Fulbe ethnic category, with many institutions such as Koranic schools, religious orders, and the pilgrimage, and numerous symbols including writing tablets, charms, prayer beads and various items of clothing forming the basis for visible differentiation of status in the religious sphere. Several of these dimensions of Islamic belief and practice in northern Cameroon society will be discussed in later sections.

SOCIOLINGUISTIC ASPECTS OF FULFULDE SPEECH IN NORTHERN CAMEROON

Most inhabitants of northern Cameroon, regardless of ethnic status, speak at least 'market' Fulfulde as a vehicular language. Thus language does not pose an effective barrier to participation in Fulbe life, although accomplishment in the language has great sociolinguistic significance as a ranking mechanism within the Fulbe ethnic category. Fulfulde is a language based on some twenty-five noun classes (the number varying with dialect), which play a fundamental role in the formation of plurals and in adjectival agreement with nouns, among other things (Arnott 1970; Noye 1974). There is also a system of initial consonantal alternation, which renders the formation of plurals, as well as the conjugation of verbs, even more complex. Thus, for example, in the following examples of plural noun formation (Table 3.1), we see that the initial consonants change (*p-* to *f-*, *d-* to *r-*, *k-* to *h-*, etc.) as well as do the noun class endings (*-o* or *-ɗo* to *-ɓe*, the singular and plural noun class endings for humans), with only the middle portion (root) of the words remaining constant.

TABLE 3.1: Some singular and plural forms in Fulfulde.

Singular	Plural
pullo	*fulɓe* = Fulani/-s
dimo	*rimɓe* = freeman/-men
kaaɗo	*haaɓe* = subject pagan/-s

Among non-native Fulfulde speakers who use Fulfulde as a vehicular language, many such complexities deriving from the noun class system tend to be ignored and simplification of the sort common in pidgin or creole languages is usual (Romaine 1988). For example, either the singular of a noun may be used as an invariant form and the plural formed by adding an adjective like 'many', or the plural form may be used as invariant and the singular formed by adding the numeral 'one'. Thus, in pidgin Fulfulde, the plural of 'chicken' (*gertogal*) might be formed as '*gertogal duuɗi*' (literally, 'chicken many') rather than as '*gertoɗe*' (chickens), the correct Fulfulde form. These and many other simplifications and adjustments common in multi-ethnic settings in northern Cameroon have been analysed by several different linguists (Lacroix 1959; 1962; 1967; Noss n.d.; Noye 1971; and Nelson 1972) and reveal a graded series of levels of competence which are closely related to the social contexts in which these forms of language are spoken. Noss (n.d.), for example, speaks of a continuum of language forms ranging from the pidgin Fulfulde spoken as a vehicular language by non-native speakers (often referred to as '*bilkiire*' or '*fulfulde luumo*' – 'marketplace' Fulfulde) to *fulfulde laamnde* ('clear' or 'proper' Fulfulde) of native speakers.

Native Fulfulde speakers themselves remark and make value judgements upon such variations in linguistic competence. Thus, at Ngaoundere for example, Fulbe informants recognise several types of Fulfulde spoken by inhabitants of the town and tend to correlate these linguistic forms with ethnic and racial differences. In contrast with *fulfulde laamnde* which is integral to the Fulani conception of a 'proper' way of life (*pulaaku*), Ngaoundere Fulbe identify *kambariire* as a less correct form of Fulfulde, which is said to be spoken by persons of mixed parentage resulting from marriages between Fulbe and Mbum or other pagan groups of the Adamawa region.[7] Less correct even than *kambariire* is *bilkiire*, a term which is often used in a pejorative sense to refer to the jabbering of a simpleton. Looking further afield, some of my informants at Ngaoundere made comparisons between the Fulfulde dialects spoken in the major Cameroonian towns of Maroua, Garoua, and Ngaoundere in terms of their 'pureness' according to the perceived degrees of intermixture of 'races' in these locales. On this reckoning, Maroua Fulbe speak the 'clearest' Fulfulde because at Maroua, Fulbe are said only to marry other Fulbe. The dialects of Fulfulde spoken at Garoua and Ngaoundere, on the other hand, are much less pure, it is said, since there has been much racial intermixture in these towns since the *jihad*. Such folk interpretations of Fulfulde dialectical variation are of interest because they coincide, as we shall see, with Fulani ideological notions concerning the purported genetic inheritance of cultural traits.

In a more scientific vein, Noye (1971) has remarked upon the greater 'conservatism' of the Maroua dialect of Fulfulde, compared to those of Garoua, Ngaoundere and elsewhere on the Adamawa plateau. Likewise, Lacroix (1959) compares the *fulfulde laamnde* of Maroua with what he calls the 'standard' Fulfulde spoken in urban centres south of Maroua such as Garoua and Ngaoundere, which is characterised by some grammatical simplification. It is evident that not only have the complexities of the noun class and verbal conjugation systems been more fully retained in Maroua, but that the Fulfulde spoken in the more southerly Adamawan towns also displays more influences derived from French.

Such an effect has been increasingly noticeable in Ngaoundere since the completion in the early 1970s of the railroad linking it with Yaounde, which has caused a massive influx of population from south and west Cameroon whose competence in French is generally much greater than that of northerners. Noss (n.d.) argues that French borrowings are especially apparent in passages dealing with 'modern' topics (for example, '*mi windi directement haa sous prefet*' – 'I wrote directly to [the] sub-prefect'), but I have found them to also be widespread in more routine contexts (e.g., '*mi yidi rentira*' – 'I want to go home' [cf. French *rentrer* – to go home]). Noss suggests that, in the face of the expansion of French-language schooling in northern Cameroon and greater contacts with French-language speakers from southern Cameroon, the use of *bilkiire* as a pidgin may decline. On the other hand, the population speaking creolised forms of Fulfulde as a first language is likely to expand, as children, especially those in the rapidly growing multi-ethnic towns and cities, tend to adopt a more 'international' form of the language. As I will argue later, the outcome and social impacts of these linguistic changes are likely to depend in large measure on the competition between the southern Christian modernist versus northern Muslim conservative tendencies within the developing regional culture of northern Cameroon.

CULTURAL CONSENSUS IN FULBE INTERACTIONAL CONTEXTS

The third and final criterion of incorporation into Fulbe society consists of at least an overt consensus to Fulbe ideals of behaviour and ethnic superiority; this is a simple step, formally speaking, although often a more difficult one, it would seem, in the context of day-to-day inter-personal relations. It is easy, as suggested above in the section on religion, for Fulbeising individuals to begin to utilise various items of material culture as outwardly visible symbols of their choice of lifestyle. Thus, in urban settings like Ngaoundere or Meiganga for example, the wearing of one of the Fulbe styles of robe (*gaarewol* or *ngapaleewol*, sometimes referred to by the Hausa term *gandura*) rather than the western-style dress favoured by Christian southern Cameroonians, serves as a visible statement of ethnic and/or religious allegiance on many public occasions. On the other hand, it is probably more difficult for an individual engaged in Fulbeisation to deal with Fulbe views of their own cultural superiority which, as mentioned above, are closely intertwined with their concepts of racial superiority.[8] Fulbe in the Mbere Department, as elsewhere in Adamawa, continue to be extremely disdainful of other peoples, often using among themselves insulting terms such as *haaɓe* (subject pagans), *maccuɓe* (slaves), and *baleeɓe* (black men) to refer to members of non-Fulbe ethnic groups. To be a member of Fulbe society, one must be willing to join in such in-group talk, even when the insults are directed at one's previous ethnic group.

As we have seen, the Fulbe of Adamawa, in common with other Fulani peoples, express their sense of cultural distinctiveness and superiority via their concept of '*pulaaku*', and the logic embodied in this cultural construct is a fundamental conditioning factor in their relations with the other ethnic groups alongside whom they live.[9] This complex concept embodies notions of good breeding (in the sense both of racial ancestry and refined manners), restrained behaviour, intelligence, awareness of cultural heritage, and adherence to Fulani customs. In its broadest usage, *pulaaku* refers to all of 'proper' Fulani behaviour, and any attempt to discuss this notion briefly is therefore doomed to oversimplify the matter. For example, a popular radio programme broadcast in Cameroon for many years on the *Sawtu Linjiila* (Radio Voice of the Gospel) Christian mission station used to feature regular discussion groups by Fulani panellists ruminating on different aspects of *pulaaku*, and the transcripts of these discussions alone would fill several volumes. However, to understand the concept of *pulaaku* in a broad comparative sense does not require us to establish a comprehensive catalogue of 'correct' cultural behaviours, since *pulaaku* is clearly a relativistic term, even though individual Fulani are liable to treat it as an absolute. Fulani normally assert that the mode of behaviour of their *own* group is the most correct one and that those of neighbouring Fulani groups (let alone non-Fulani peoples!), however objectively similar they may appear to the outsider, are inferior (see Dupire 1981: 170). So despite the essentialist nature of this Fulani discourse on their culture, it is plain that the notion of *pulaaku* does not in fact refer to a primordial source of Fulani tradition but reveals instead, in its recognition of the many microscopic variations of Fulani custom, the processes of change and adjustment continually at work in Fulani societies.

Although the nuances and implications of the concept will be explored further in later sections of this book, the main point of significance about *pulaaku* which must be emphasised at this stage is that it provides a set of purportedly absolute and traditional standards of ranking of social behaviour, both within and between the various categories of Fulani society as well as vis-à-vis non-Fulani groups. Within the socially heterogeneous Fulbe ethnic category in northern Cameroon, discourse on *pulaaku* is the special property of high-status members of the group, who use it to defend their status honour against the encroachments of those who have recently joined the ethnic category through assimilation. It is in such contexts that arguments phrased in terms of race or descent assume prominence (see Schultz 1979: 261) and ethnic jokes and racially disparaging remarks become the order of the day.[10]

The change of interactional patterns involved in the process of Fulbeisation seems to be most easily accomplished when an individual is living apart from members of his former ethnic group, who might otherwise continue to interact with him in terms of his old culture. Referring to this tendency in the context of a discussion of Islamic conversion, Lacroix (1966: 404, my translation) commented:

> conversion (to Islam) appears to the more enterprising of the non-Fulbe as an effective means of social mobility which permits them, if not completely to melt into Fulbe society, at least to integrate themselves into elite Fulbe settings. Among some of the neighbouring or subject 'pagan' peoples of the Fulbe, conversion certainly cannot be accomplished without serious risks of social conflict between the convert and

his former associates, especially in situations characterised by strong cultural boundaries. This is particularly the case in northern Adamawa, and here Islamic converts remain few in number. By contrast, conversion offers nothing but advantages to members of populations with weakened structures and to persons isolated from their places of origin.

As examples of the two extremes that Lacroix doubtless had in mind, we can take first the case of the Dowayo people living around Poli. As Barley (1983: 1–3, 60–2) has documented, the Dowayo have maintained a strongly defined ethnic boundary which can be interpreted in many respects as explicitly oppositional to Fulbe political and religious pressures.[11] Indeed, the Dowayo have incorporated a prominent role for a Dowayo man masquerading as an 'old Fulani woman' in their most important ritual cycle to symbolise the archetypical outsider – one who must be 'killed' by the sponsor of the ceremony. At the other extreme, there is the highly assimilative Fulbe society of the city of Garoua, into which so many non-Fulbe have been incorporated during the last century and a half that, today, to speak of a *'pullo garwa'* is to imply a mixed or non-Fulbe ancestry (see below as well as Schultz 1979: 230, 247; and Bassoro and Mohammadou 1980).

Given the interactional factors already described, it is not surprising that the relatively more anonymous and socially fluid settings of the larger towns and cities of northern Cameroon are the principal loci of the Fulbeisation process. Schultz (1979: 28, 226; 1984) has strongly emphasised the importance of the urban factor in her discussion of Fulbeisation in the town of Guider, while at the same time confirming Lacroix's point that an individual's change of ethnic identity is likely to lead to a break with family and former friends if carried out in a community near the person's natal home. As we shall see later for the Mbere Department, Meiganga is not a sufficiently large and anonymous urban setting to be a highly favourable milieu for members of non-Fulani peoples like the Gbaya who may wish to Fulbeise and, for this purpose, Ngaoundere is the nearest location where ethnic passing occurs on a large scale.

As has been described thus far, the decline in Fulbe state power from the colonial period onwards and the more permissive boundary conditions controlling admission to the Fulbe category have encouraged the development of the heterogeneous social amalgam that today is the Fulbe society of northern Cameroon. According to the available demographic studies of northern Cameroon which provide ethnically differentiated data, almost all of which are based on work carried out in the 1960s (Podlewski 1966; 1971; Callies 1968; but see Boutrais *et al.* 1984 for more recent data), the Fulbe category is being constantly augmented by the assimilation of non-Fulbe population, a process which can be accomplished within one generation as we have seen. This rate of assimilation appears to vary from one area of northern Cameroon to another, depending on local political-economic conditions, and is generally more accentuated in urban areas and in the region from the Benue river plain northwards than in the rural areas of the Adamaoua Province. On the basis of a demographic sample drawn from areas of Cameroon north of the Benue river, Podlewski (1966: 15) estimated that the rate of first generation assimilation of non-Fulbe to the Fulbe category was no less than 12 per cent of the whole Fulbe category, whereas his samples drawn among populations living on the Adamawa Plateau suggest that the first generation assimilation rate, while still significant, was likely to be somewhat lower on average (Podlewski 1971). On the other hand, as we shall see later in this chapter, this influx of persons into the Fulbe category only barely counteracts the low fertility rate characteristic of this population.

Up to this point, we have been considering in a rather general way the major social processes defining the boundary of the Fulbe ethnic category in northern Cameroon and their transformations during the past century. We have also discussed in a preliminary way some of the criteria of ranking within the Fulbe ethnic category in the modern day, although consideration of important political and economic dimensions of these stratificational processes will be deferred until later in this book. Now we will narrow focus and look at the Fulbe ethnic category as it is represented in the Mbere Department.

THE FULBE CATEGORY IN THE MBERE DEPARTMENT TODAY

As we have seen in the previous chapter, the foundation of the Meiganga *Arrondissement* in 1929 as a separate administrative entity had as its principal goal the ending of the subjugation of the local Gbaya and Mbororo populations by the Fulbe state of Ngaoundere. From that date onwards, the territory of what has now become the Mbere Department was officially declared to be off-limits to Fulbe agro-pastoralists, either for settlement or even for pasturing their herds during the dry season – an exclusionary policy referred to as *hadaande* (prohibition) in Fulfulde. For the most part, this interdiction was carefully enforced by the French and subsequently by the newly independent Cameroon government, with only minor incursions of Fulbe agro-pastoral settlements on the margins of the district (at villages like Djaoro Nabata and Mbarang) up until the mid-1970s when the *hadaande* began to be relaxed (Boutrais 1994).

Following this change in policy, the district received an increasing influx of Fulbe agro-pastoral groups who migrated from the northwest of the Adamawa Plateau and from further north and west in Nigeria (Boutrais 1994). Many of these movements were stimulated by the spread of tsetse fly in these areas as well as by growing population pressures in Nigeria. Although these Fulbe agro-pastoralists came from diverse clan backgrounds, many of them hailed from the region of Nigeria south of Yola, which had been the zone of departure during the nineteenth century of the Wolarbe and Kiri Fulbe founders of Ngaoundere, Tibati and other states of southern Adamawa. In the Mbere Department today, these Fulbe are often collectively referred to by the other residents as '*Mai'ine*', an ethnic label which appears to be derived from 'Mayo Ine' – the name of a river and district near Yola. Especially in areas where these newer migrants have established ethnically segregated villages and hamlets adjacent to Gbaya villages, this recent growth of Fulbe settlement has generated significant opposition among longer established inhabitants, who take special exception to the xenophobic attitudes of these more ardent Muslims. As we shall see later, such opposition was one of the precipitating factors in the violent episodes in Meiganga in 1991 and 1992.

Aside from these recent arrivals who are mainly located in the northeastern sector of the department, the Fulbe population of the Mbere Department is largely comprised of relatively small numbers of market traders, craftsmen and Islamic specialists living in separate Fulbe residential quarters in Meiganga and in the larger multi-ethnic towns. There are also some western-educated Fulbe holding posts in the government administration. The Fulbe residential quarters are recognised by the administration for tax-censusing purposes, and each is represented by a quarter chief (*jaoro*) who collects taxes and acts as an intermediary between the local government and the inhabitants of the quarter. The largest settlements may have several ethnically defined quarters including possibly several Gbaya quarters, a Hausa quarter, a 'Congo' quarter, and one or more Fulbe quarters. In such contexts, there is a tendency for a Fulbe quarter to be a sort of residual category where, in addition to inhabitants of unquestioned Fulbe descent, one is also liable to encounter an ethnically heterogeneous array of residents hailing from all parts of northern Cameroon and even further afield. Such a situation is in keeping with the assimilationist nature of Fulbe ethnicity in northern Cameroon.

As explained above, the incorporative character of present-day Fulbe ethnicity in northern Cameroon is closely linked with the universalistic (as opposed to sectarian) trend in Islam and, in general, popular Islam in the Mbere Department is very much bathed in this tradition. Islam in the Mbere Department has very little in the way of a scholarly or clerical orientation, even less than in those parts of northern Cameroon where the remnants of Fulbe state structures persist and certainly much less so than in the well-known centres of Islamic learning in Hausaland or Bornu. Although all Fulbe residential quarters of any size in the Mbere Department have a least one Koranic school, there are no facilities locally for more advanced Islamic learning. Most of the Fulbe imams and judges (*alkali'en*, singular *alkali*) who hold posts in the mosques and courts attached to Gbaya canton chieftaincies or to the Cameroonian state judicial system in the Mbere Department originated from outside the region. But even the qualifications of some of these Islamic specialists may be viewed as suspect by other conservative Fulbe *mallum'en* because, as one once commented, 'Would a real *alkali* work for a Gbaya chief?'. Another Fulbe *mallum* remarked to me, when discussing the level of Islamic learning among *mallum'en* of the Mbere Department, that these men are all 'merely *fukaraaɓe* (pupils)' with only a limited knowledge of Islam.

Throughout the 1970s, membership of Islamic brotherhoods such as the Tijaniyya or Qadiriyya, which are common elsewhere in Cameroon and Nigeria, was not widespread in the Mbere Department. My informal efforts during this period to estimate brotherhood membership in several of the larger villages and towns of the region revealed no Qadiriyya members at all and only a few Tijaniyya per village. In keeping with the tradition of Mahdist belief that has long been prevalent in Adamawa and in northern Cameroon more widely (see Lacroix 1966: 405–6 and Haafkens 1983), I also located a few Fulbe who claimed affiliation to the 'Mahdiyya'. However, this self-ascription did not imply collective participation in a brotherhood-like organisation but only a religious orientation involving certain additional ritual practices (see Haafkens 1983: 127–8).

The expansion in numbers of Mai'ine Fulbe in the Mbere Department from the 1970s onward introduced new and in some cases more radical elements into the Muslim population of the region. Membership of the Tijaniyya brotherhood is widespread among the Mai'ine, especially the Ibrahimiyya branch of Al Hajj Ibrahim Niasse (cf. Mohammed 1993: 126 *et seq.*). Some of the latter group, popularly known as '*Tarbiyya*' in Adamawa, seek access to Allah through ecstatic ritual practices and tend to be much less tolerant of different religions and of other Muslims (see Bocquené 1986: Chap. 14; Froelich 1962: 236). As already mentioned, on several occasions, they have come into open conflict with their non-Fulbe neighbours in the Mbere Department in recent years.

The Mai'ine Fulbe aside, popular Islam among the Fulbe of the Mbere Department is characterised by a distinctly this-worldly orientation which is consonant with the commercial activities of many of its adherents. Success in the here-and-now may be sought through recourse to the services of *mallum'en* who perform prayers (*do'a*), prepare Koranic amulets, and supervise 'drinking the Koran' (writing Koranic verses on a wooden tablet, then washing off the ink and drinking it) to seek Allah's blessings in a special undertaking or in case of illness. There is also widespread belief in, and considerable usage of, a range of distinctly heterodox or syncretic practices smacking of paganism (*yaafi*, cf. Hausa *tsaafi*) and/or sorcery (*siiri*) to achieve efficacity in everyday affairs. These include various forms of divination (*walaba*) including the search for lost or stolen property (*lekki yaashin*), magical protection from dangers, especially from iron weapons (*lekki bushin* or *lekki njamndi*), and potions ensuring success in matters of the heart (*lekki yusufu*). Those magical techniques which rely on the invocation of powers other than Allah and his word as revealed in the Koran, or which imply that human intervention alone can alter events, are clearly contrary to Islam. But as one Fulbe realist remarked to me, venal *mallum'en* resort to all manner of magical practices and then seek to legitimate these acts by appending the phrase '. . . if Allah wills it' to their incantations.

Many of these dubious practices are linked to beliefs in a spirit world inhabited by *ginaaji* (jinn) and Satan, which can be invoked through rituals to assist in the achievement of one's aims (see Bocquené 1986: 149). Illnesses may result from being possessed by *ginaaji*, which can be driven off or controlled either by orthodox Islamic incantations or by the techniques of a specialist in *girka* (the Fulbe equivalent of the *bori* spirit possession cult among the Hausa). Much talked about during my stays in various Fulbe villages was a particularly 'black' magical technique known as *lukudi* which was said to enable a person to obtain fabulous material wealth. According to my informants, this dangerous practice involved the night-long repetition of a secret phrase, acquired from a powerful *mallum*, in order to enlist the aid of the spirits or of Satan himself. On one occasion when a prominent Fulbe merchant died having suddenly been afflicted with dropsy, rumours were rife that he had employed *lukudi* to amass his wealth and had now been called to account.

Such stories reflect a view prevalent among certain pious Muslims in the Mbere Department that economic or political success is often morally tainted. They would point to the many rich merchants who had made the pilgrimage to Mecca and remark that one obtained no religious merit from accomplishing the pilgrimage if the funds for the trip derived from morally dubious sources. The title '*Al Hajji*' is widely used in northern Cameroon as a synonym for rich merchant, quite apart from its usual reference to a person who has made the pilgrimage. As for Mbororo Al Hajjis, one Fulbe *mallum* asserted that most of them had travelled to Mecca simply to obtain love potions!

Given the highly incorporative nature of the Fulbe ethnic category and the lack of a strong tradition of Islamic scholarship or other orthodox structures of knowledge transmission and control, it should not be surprising that there is a considerable range of heterodox beliefs and religious syncretism in the Mbere Department. Taking a topic such as sorcery for example, the many different non-Fulani peoples of northern Cameroon from whom the Fulbeised elements of the Fulbe ethnic category have been derived, display a great diversity of sorcery beliefs. Although uniformly classified by orthodox Islam as paganism, these sorcery techniques are still viewed as potentially efficacious and have been incorporated into a Fulbe cultural world where *mallum'en* employ both orthodox and heterodox methods to combat them. At times, the purported cultural provenance of such beliefs may be considered significant, as for example when certain ethnic groups are thought to be specialists in certain powerful techniques. But, more frequently, such knowledge has lost its ethnically specific label (if it ever had one) and been assimilated within the category of popular Islam.

To gain greater insight into the heterogeneous social composition of Fulbe residential quarters in the Mbere Department, we can turn now to the results of two 100 per cent surveys of life history and occupation I administered to heads of households residing in the Fulbe quarters of two multi-ethnic towns of the department in 1973. Each head of household was questioned concerning his place of birth, ethnic affiliation and/or descent grouping,[12] parents' ethnicity/descent, occupational history, previous locations of residence, reasons for migrating to the present place of residence, present number of wives, number of divorces, the ethnicity/descent of these wives, and their number of children. In addition, as far as possible, I also obtained the same data on each head of household in each quarter by interviewing several 'third parties' who were well placed to have such information – in particular two praise singers whose profession depended on knowing relevant facts about their potential clients. This 'second-hand information' proved very valuable, for although it was not necessarily to be considered more reliable than information collected directly, it gave me interesting perspectives on the process of public ethnic ascription in these contexts of ethnic assimilation.

In all, there were fifty-eight heads of household in the two Fulbe quarters. All were practising Muslims, which indeed is one of the few requirements for residence in such quarters. Thirty-two of the household heads (55 per cent) claimed Fulbe ethnicity and, of these, twenty-six provided me with details concerning their clan affiliations, place of birth, and parentage which were considered by my praise singers and other 'third party' informants to identify them unequivocally as 'true' Fulbe (*pullo pir*).[13] The other six self-ascribed Fulbe gave only very general information relating to their ethnic backgrounds such as '*pullo garwa*' or '*pullo mawra*', and my third-party informants considered it likely that these men derived from non-Fulbe backgrounds one or more generations in the past. (See the remarks above concerning the *pullo garwa* label.) A total of four heads of household in the two Fulbe quarters (7 per cent) refused to provide me with information about themselves during the surveys, and my third-party informants were unable to provide much amplification in these cases either. It goes without saying that reticence about ancestry on the part of these four individuals was consonant with the suspicions of my third-party informants that they derived from non-Fulbe parentage and had 'passed' into the Fulbe category.

The twenty-two other household heads surveyed can be grouped into three categories. Eleven household heads (19 per cent) identified themselves as members of various northern Cameroonian, non-Fulbe ethnic groups that were classified by the Fulbe as 'pagan' at the time of the *jihad* (three

Mundang, two Gbaya, two Guisiga, two Bata, one Guidar and one Musgum). Four others (7 per cent) were members of ethnic groups that were already Muslim in the pre-*jihad* period (two Kanuri, one Hausa, and one Choa Arab). And finally, seven household heads (12 per cent) were identified as '*maccube*' or former slaves.

This last category requires some additional explanation. Although slavery has been outlawed in Cameroon since colonial times, and in the present day to call a person a slave would normally be taken as a serious insult, several of the household heads had no hesitation when questioned in identifying their origins as '*maccube*'. (See Podlewski 1971: 118 on Laka slaves for a comparable case.) Others preferred to identify themselves to me as '*pullo*' but were commonly spoken of as '*maccube*' by other members of their quarter (although not in their presence, as far as I know). One head of household explained that he had been a household servant in the retinue of the *laamiido* of Ngaoundere in his younger days. Another man, who was currently working as a Koranic schoolmaster, identified himself as a 'freed slave' (*dimdinaado*) from Ngaoundere. Although the two men above had been born of slave parentage, most of the 'slaves' in my surveys had been born free as members of non-Fulbe ethnic groups and had been sold as children to Fulbe or Mbororo households. They had served as cattle herders (*gaynaako*, plural *waynaabe*) for their owners until middle age. The selling of children into slavery by poor families, as well as the kidnapping and sale of children by a few notorious slave traders, remained a relatively common practice in the Mbere area and elsewhere in northern Cameroon up until at least the mid-1930s (Bassoro and Mohammadou 1980 and VerEecke 1994). And in many Fulbe or sedentarised Mbororo villages in the 1970s, it was still relatively common to find elderly people who continued to work as servants for well-to-do Muslim families. There is, of course, no legal constraint which a slave 'owner' in the present day can use to force a 'slave' to remain in his service. However, since the relationship normally becomes transformed into one of part-time paid service, and many elderly *maccube* do not wish to give up the relative security that such a relationship offers, they freely choose to remain living alongside their masters.

As can be seen from the list of occupations in Table 3.2, the household heads in my surveys practised a great diversity of occupations, but in reviewing their life histories, several common career trajectories emerge. For a young man born into a poor family in northern Cameroon, the occupation of paid cattle herder is a frequently chosen option that permits him to see something of the world beyond his natal village while, at the same time, offering an opportunity to constitute a capital in the form of the cattle received in payment for this work (see Boutrais 1994: 191–2). The work involves living in rigorous conditions in cattle camps in the bush and is not very well paid (a *gaynaako* received a two-year-old heifer for every six months' work, plus

TABLE 3.2: Occupations of 58 household heads (some declaring more than one occupation).

Farming	33
Petty market trader	11
Mallum (and/or Koranic schoolmaster)	10
Cattle owner	6
Cattle herder	5
Cattle trader	4
Praise singer	4
Butcher	4
Tailor	3
Kola nut trader	3
Shop owner/trader	3
Barber	2
Quarter chief	2
Retainer of chief	2
Musician	2
Bulk cloth trader	2
Hat embroiderer	1
Leather worker	1
Mechanical repairs (esp. bicycles and radios)	1
Building construction	1

subsistence, in the Mbere Department during the 1970s), but many men in my surveys had undertaken such work in their early careers. The status of paid herder is a relatively low one. As mentioned above, it was a common practice among Fulbe and Mbororo cattle herders in the past to acquire young slaves to act as herd boys and, for an individual without recognisably Fulbe racial traits, to work as a paid herdsman is to lay oneself open to such servile imputations. As we shall see in the next chapter, this potential stigma acts as a disincentive to young Gbaya men who might otherwise consider working for Fulbe employers, since they are liable to be labelled '*baṛa mbisa*' (slave of the Muslims) by other Gbaya.[14]

Nonetheless, for a young man without a family background in trade or other non-farming occupation, working as a paid herdsman for at least a few years offers one of the few opportunities available in rural northern Cameroonian society to constitute a working capital. However, the mobile lifestyle of the paid cattle herder is seldom consonant with marriage, and few men continue in such employment beyond their early twenties.

To be a cattle owner, as opposed to being a paid cattle herder, is a high-status occupation within the Fulbe category. This is so much the case that, regardless of their actual occupation, almost all of the household heads in my surveys had stated their official occupation on the government's tax census records to be '*pasteur*' (pastoralist), in spite of the fact that pastoralists paid double the rate of head tax (*impôt forfaitaire*) compared with cultivators and were liable to cattle tax in addition. Indeed, making an official declaration for head tax purposes that one's occupation is that of 'pastoralist' appears to act primarily as a mode of Fulbe ethnic identification within the Mbere Department, and it is certainly an unreliable guide for census purposes as to an individual's principal occupation (or ethnic origin, for that matter). Most Fulbe men strive to own at least some cattle when money is available for investment (as do men of most ethnic groups in the Mbere Department), but in my surveys only 10 per cent of the household heads considered themselves sufficiently involved in cattle ownership to declare this as one of their occupations.

The major alternative non-farming employment for Fulbe or Fulbeising men in northern Cameroon is in some branch of trade or craft, perhaps working as a member of a trading consortium (for example, in the long-distance cattle, cloth or kola nut trade or in butchering) or in a service occupation centred on the marketplace such as tailor, barber or repairman. The Mbere Department has long had a name as a lucrative setting for trade – a reputation based during the pre-colonial and early colonial periods on its position as a frontier zone on the margins of the Ngaoundere state and, later, on the presence of the Mbororo with their large herds of cattle. The export of cattle to the south kept substantial sums of money flowing into the district, beginning as early as the 1940s. This trade peaked in the early 1970s as the local Mbororo herding population began to diminish, and has further declined since the mid-1980s when cattle prices began to fall in response to weakness in the Cameroon national economy.

As an indication of the continuing importance of cattle sales to the economy of the Mbere Department, during the period 1982–6 the *Service d'Elevage* registered an annual average of 50,000 head of live cattle exported from the department. The carcasses of another 7,000 head of slaughtered cattle were inspected by government veterinarians before sale by local retail butchers. These figures can therefore be taken as minimal estimates for the volumes of this trade. The 50,000 figure is probably fairly near the true value, given the relatively tight monitoring of cattle exports in the region, but the 7,000 figure is likely to be rather low, given the considerable number of cattle slaughtered clandestinely. During this same period, about fifty cattle dealers (*parkeejo* in Fulfulde) were licensed to trade in the Mbere Department. Most of these men head consortia of herdsmen and commission agents, who circulate through the rural areas collecting cattle for sale, bring them to central collection points, and 'convoy' them to the large urban centres in southern Cameroon by foot, by lorry or by rail (see also Boutrais 1994). A back-of-an-envelope calculation suggests that this cattle trade, whose source of supply was predominately Mbororo herds, represented something in the order of 3 billion CFA in annual income for the Mbere Department, or an annual average of about 25,000 CFA per resident of the region.[15]

Access to trading capital is naturally the main limiting factor affecting participation in the larger-scale and more lucrative trading activities. Young men from commercial family backgrounds often work for their father or other close relatives or fictive kinsmen. In this capacity, they gradually build up an independent trading capital from small profits earned on the side while assisting the senior member(s) of the trading enterprise, or they may eventually move to a senior position in the family firm. Less fortunate young men can try to raise capital by serving as paid herdsmen, as just mentioned, but in the present day, increasing numbers are attracted by what are perceived as more 'modern' occupations such as lorry or taxi driver or, perhaps, the occupation of '*dan komisio*' – a commission agent who solicits business for the passenger vans that ply the district. Possibly more lucrative, if decidedly more risky or even downright 'shady', are the opportunities for smuggling, diamond dealing, and other clandestine activities offered by the proximity of the Central African Republic frontier. Many of the household heads in my sample had spent periods of their earlier lives in the Central African Republic, and their life history data cast considerable light on the activities of Fulbe traders in that region. (See Bocquené 1986: 338–9, for an example of such stories.)

The village of Ngaouwi on the Cameroonian side of the Central African frontier, which grew from a small Mbororo cattle camp in the 1930s to a bustling trading entrepôt by the 1960s, and to an administrative centre with independent district status in the 1990s, is a notorious centre for such activities. Since the 1960s, during peak periods, as many as twenty large lorry-loads of consumer goods vanish each week over the frontier in the hands of traders/smugglers both large and small, and the large sums of money changing hands there attract a crowd of gamblers, drug dealers, confidence men and prostitutes in addition to more 'legitimate' traders. From the 1970s onward, the new railroad town of Ngaoundal, just beyond the western boundary of the Mbere Department, has had a similar boom-town reputation, although merchants from southern Cameroon are in active competition there with Fulbe and Hausa traders for economic and cultural dominance.

Although significant sums may be made in such 'wild west' frontier settings, many traders in the Fulbe category remain condemned, both because of their lack of capital and the heavy competition, to a life of petty trade. This trade is known colloquially by the pidgin term '*tabur*' (cf. table) which refers to the small, portable tables on which these men often display their meagre stocks of goods (*tarkase*, cf. Hausa *tarkace* – odds and ends). This petty trade keeps them active in the life of the marketplace, a symbolically important statement of their commitment to this domain within northern Cameroon society where Islamic and Fulbe values predominate. But these small-scale trading activities do not provide a sufficient livelihood and must normally be combined with subsistence farming. Farmland in the Mbere Department remains quite plentiful, and even Fulbe living in Meiganga town are able to farm if they so wish.

Many of the occupations engaged in by young Fulbe or Fulbeising men entail or permit mobile lifestyles, with frequent shifts of residence from the Fulbe quarter of one large village or town to another. Such mobility, as suggested above, often plays a part in many individuals' strategy or process (I use both words so as to leave open the question of intention) of Fulbeisation, since a change of residence can do much to obscure details of a person's social origins (cf. Schultz 1979: 229–31). Such younger men are not well represented in the surveys I am discussing here since they do not tend to establish stable households at this stage of their life-cycles. As many of the men in my surveys had approached middle age, on the other hand, they had adopted a less mobile lifestyle, marrying and settling down for extended periods. Only two of the fifty-eight household heads had been born in the Mbere Department (the two Gbaya),[16] but most had resided locally for considerable periods of time. Among the forty-nine men for whom I could establish length of residence at their present locale (excluding the two Gbaya men), the median period of residence was between fifteen and twenty years, and only one man out of these forty-nine had been resident at his present location for less than five years.

Aside from documenting a lack of recent mobility in this Fulbe population, these figures also indicate that at the time of my survey in 1973, there was a low rate of in-migration and household formation among commercially oriented Fulbe in this particular part of the Mbere region. This reflected a decline in trading opportunities which had begun in this area at the start of the 1970s. As will be described in later chapters, this period of economic decline was principally linked with worsening local conditions for cattle husbandry, which caused a substantial out-migration of wealthy Mbororo cattle herders to more favoured districts. Once again, the dependence of the local trading economy on the Mbororo and their cattle is highlighted, and the relatively high proportion of individuals practising what can be termed 'personal service' or entertainment occupations is explicable in these terms. I am referring here in the first instance to the praise singers and musicians who earn the bulk of their incomes through performances at Mbororo life-cycle ceremonies. We must also include here many of those practising the profession of *mallum* (plural, *mallum'en*) since, according to my interviews, the Mbororo provide the major part of their business of writing charms and preparing medicines. Three *mallum'en* in my samples also ran small Koranic schools.

With regard to the wives and children resident in the fifty-eight households in my surveys, I was able to collect only relatively limited data due to the Fulbe practice of wife seclusion, which was adhered to by the majority of the households. The men in my surveys were currently married, on average, to 1.6 women and had experienced 1.4 divorces per husband. The households in my surveys contained on average only 1.1 child per married woman. This last figure, of course, should not be confused with the total fertility of the married women in question, since it does not include deceased children or children who had been left behind with their fathers following divorce (information I was unable to obtain). Fifty-four per cent of the wives in my sample were of Fulbe ethnicity, and 54 per cent of the marriages in the sample were ethnically mixed.

In general, the Mbere Department has a reputation among the Fulbe men in my samples of suffering a shortage of Fulbe women who conform to the desired light-skinned Fulbe racial stereotype. One informant explained that, in these circumstances, it was likely that many Fulbe men would marry non-Fulbe women initially, but that if they were financially successful, they would later seek 'a light-skinned Fulbe wife' from one of the towns further north. This indeed had transpired in the case of several of the more wealthy men in my samples.

The data that I was able to obtain on marriage and fertility were generally consonant with the unstable marital situation and stationary or declining rates of population growth of the Fulbe which have been documented for much of the rest of northern Cameroon (and as early as 1910 – see Boyle [1910: 91]). These studies paint a quite consistent picture which reveals the systematic demographic effects of Fulbeisation and Islamisation – in particular a low rate of fertility linked with a high rate of divorce (Podlewski 1966: 19–22). During the 1960s in the area north of the Benue, the Fulbe category was in a situation of demographic decline which was only partially compensated for by the progressive assimilation of non-Fulbe population (Podlewski 1966: 23 *et passim*; see also David and Voas 1981 and Burnham 1974). Analysis of the national census results for 1976 (Boutrais *et al.* 1984: 155–7) also reveals a low, although somewhat ameliorated, rate of fertility among the Fulbe, the slight improvement since the 1960s being explained both by improved health-care provision as well as by the continuing assimilation of non-Fulbe population.

South of the Benue, and on the Adamawa Plateau in particular, the annual population growth rates during the 1960s in at least some of the Fulbe population samples were slightly positive at 1.0 to 1.5 per cent per annum (Podlewski 1971: 117). These more healthy Fulbe populations were agro-pastoral groups living in rural areas, among whom the rate of inter-ethnic marriage was quite low (that is, in an ecological situation that was not comparable to that in the Mbere Department, from which Fulbe agro-pastoralists were then excluded). On the other hand, in samples drawn from ethnically mixed marriages and from certain ethnic groups of Adamawa that have been subject to strong Fulbeisation and Islamisation pressures (such as the Laka, the Mbum and certain Duru populations), Podlewski (1971: 131; see also Callies 1968: 22, 76) recorded low or negative fertility and population growth rates comparable to those recorded among Fulbe north of the Benue (and probably comparable to the situation in my two sample populations).

This problem of low fertility in the Fulbe category was clearly recognised by the men in my sample. A Fulbe man, voicing the common Fulani view that 'pure' Fulbe are more intelligent than 'blacks' (*baleeɓe*), explained to me that one was faced with a clear choice – to marry a black woman and have a lot of dull children or to marry a light-skinned Fulbe woman and have only a few bright and beautiful children. He summed up his discussion with a proverb expressing this notion: '*Nda ko te'a keɓa ko dai nda*' (more or less literally, 'behold whom you marry, behold your offspring').

ASSIMILATION AND STRATIFICATION IN THE FULBE ETHNIC CATEGORY

This brief description of marital attitudes and practices in two heterogeneous and commercially oriented Fulbe/Fulbeising residential quarters in the Mbere Department has revealed that despite the strong incorporative processes that have affected such communities in recent decades, there remains a marked tendency toward stratification within this ethnic category based on criteria of wealth and concepts of racial descent. At the same time, it is apparent that the cultural logic inherent in the social processes which act to maintain the Fulbe ethnic category as the dominant (albeit assimilative) social grouping within northern Cameroon society embodies certain contradictions. We have seen that concepts of social dominance within the Fulbe category are often phrased in terms of *pulaaku*, an ideology which contains a prominent tinge of racial superiority. Although this focus on racial descent tends to be weaker in urban settings such as Guider or Rei Bouba where there has been a long history of massive incorporation of non-Fulbe populations by numerically small groups of Fulbe conquerors (Schultz 1979: 262; Shimada 1993; see also my earlier comments on *pullo gawra*), it is not absent even there (Schultz 1979: 248, 253–5, 261). And in Fulbe communities in Adamawa that are less heterogeneous in social composition and where claims to 'authentic' Fulbe genealogies are more frequently made, such as in Fulbe Mai'ine settlements, the characteristic Fulbe racial ideologies are even more accentuated.

On the other hand, the assimilative orientation of the Fulbe category, which is of crucial importance in insuring demographic expansion (or in some cases mere replacement) in the face of the low fertility rates characteristic of many Fulbe populations in northern Cameroon, is based to a significant degree upon the universalistic doctrine of Islam. From this perspective, as Lacroix (1965: 22) and Schultz (1979: 133, 262) have noted, an ideology giving too prominent an emphasis to a racial and/or descent basis for the Fulbe ethnic category would be politically dysfunctional, and it is therefore not surprising that such universalism may receive greater stress, especially in the more fluid social settings of larger towns and cities.

Trying to sum up a complex social situation, we might conceive of Fulbe ethnicity as mapping out a field of social debate and status competition in which *pulaaku*, concepts of race and descent, different understandings of Islam, and control over wealth receive variable emphasis depending on an actor's social position and on the social environment in which the interaction is taking place. Particularly for actors making strong claims to authentic Fulbe descent, the logic of *pulaaku* is often seen as encompassing and, in a sense, subordinating the social logic of Islam, thus giving the Islam of the Fulbe its particular cultural flavour. On the other hand, although success in the quest for wealth via involvement in trade or in cattle ownership can do much to enhance a person's status within the Fulbe category, this prosperity may be viewed as morally tainted by Muslims of a pietistic orientation.

Up to this point, I have not given much attention to political power as a stratificational factor within the Fulbe ethnic category in the Mbere Department. Certainly, given the absence of 'traditional' Fulbe chieftaincy structures locally, this omission is understandable. Moreover, in my view, it is possible to over-emphasise the significance of such 'traditional' political structures in underpinning the ascendancy of the Fulbe in northern Cameroon during the post-independence period (see Bayart 1986: 10 and compare Burnham 1991: 83). Of course, where such chieftaincy structures are still active, they do constitute a privileged locus of Fulbe values and a stimulus to Fulbeisation. In more isolated lamidates such as Rei Bouba or Chamba, the 'traditional' Fulbe political apparatus can still exercise repression on non-Fulbe peoples through demands for 'traditional' taxes or tribute in labour or in kind. But during the post-colonial period, the powers of the traditional Fulbe rulers have generally been in decline whereas, throughout Ahidjo's period in office, Fulbe political dominance within northern Cameroon was maintained or even strengthened.

As we have described in the preceding chapter for the Mbere Department, during the twenty-five years of Ahidjo's rule the key administrative posts at sub-prefectural and prefectural levels were staffed in large measure by personnel drawn from the Fulbe (or Fulbeising) ethnic category, and this pattern was repeated throughout the north. (See Azarya 1978: 168–71 for quantitative data supporting this contention.) In such conditions, the pursuit of links with the Fulbe-dominated local and regional government was a strategy that was actively followed by certain non-Fulbe political actors in the Mbere Department, both through the establishment of trans-ethnic political alliances as well as by the transformation of ethnic identities through Fulbeisation. Membership in the Fulbe ethnic category today may be based on minimal formal criteria and may say little more about an individual's behaviour other than indicating a basic politico-cultural orientation within regional and national Cameroonian society. Yet this ethnic categorisation is associated with a cultural discourse, embodied in the internally consistent and self-reinforcing set of cultural structures which Fulani term *pulaaku*, that offers itself as an encompassing logic of social interpretation, status evaluation and motivation available to the heterogeneous population of northern Cameroon society.

This is not to say, of course, that the establishment of Fulbe culture as the dominant regional culture in northern Cameroon is uncontested. One can note, for example, the development of a Christian modernist cultural orientation among many of the formerly pagan groups in northern Cameroon, an opposed politico-religious stance that has been promoted by the numerous Christian missions active throughout the north. This competition between different political cultures has become even more accentuated since the replacement of the Ahidjo administration by that of President Biya in 1982 and with the introduction of multi-party politics in the early 1990s – themes to which we will return in later chapters.

4

THE GBAYA ETHNIC CATEGORY: PERIPHERALISATION OR POLITICAL MOBILISATION?

Our analysis of the Fulbe ethnic category has revealed a particular combination of historical process and cultural logic which acts to generate and maintain the boundaries of this social unit. As we have seen, the highly assimilative present-day character of this complex and internally stratified category derives from the limited number and undemanding nature of its ethnic boundary criteria, chief among which is an actively proselytising Islam, combined with the historic political dominance of the Fulbe within the regional society of northern Cameroon.

Turning now to the Gbaya, we find ourselves dealing with an ethnic category which has been constituted and is maintained by quite a different set of social processes. As explained in earlier chapters, the Gbaya of the Mbere Department, who number some 65–70,000 today, are the most north-westerly extension of the million-or-so Gbaya-phone people who live thinly scattered throughout the western Central African Republic and adjacent Adamaoua and Eastern provinces of Cameroon. Although considered by the Cameroon government to be autochthonous to the Mbere Department and therefore to have the right to provide the legitimate *chefs de terre* of the region, the Gbaya are in fact only relatively recent arrivals in the area, having migrated from neighbouring parts of the Central African Republic during the nineteenth century.

WHENCE GBAYA ETHNIC IDENTITY?

With no written or oral sources for Gbaya history prior to the nineteenth century, we can say little about Gbaya ethnic identity before this period and cannot be sure whether or to what extent pan-Gbaya ethnic sentiments existed prior to their contact with the raiders and traders of the Muslim states. But, given the wide dispersal of Gbaya-phone groups over tens of thousands of square kilometres of lightly populated territory and the relatively low degree of ethnic consciousness that is evidenced in the available nineteenth century sources, it seems quite unlikely that the Gbaya-phone peoples, viewed as a totality, ever constituted a self-conscious ethnic group. Moreover, it should be noted that the notion of the 'Gbaya-phone peoples' is a typological construct of linguistic researchers (Monino 1988) which does not correspond precisely to any indigenous concept or to any culturally uniform or self-conscious whole even today. Thus, for example, *Boali* informants living some 100 kilometres northwest of Bangui in the Central African Republic whom I interviewed in 1969 did not consider themselves to be members of a Gbaya group, although their language has been classified by linguists as a Gbaya dialect.[1]

Although the 'Gbaya' ethnic label was in widespread use in the nineteenth century among both the Gbaya and their non-Gbaya neighbours (Barth 1857; Flegel 1883; Flegel 1885; Clozel 1896; Burnham 1981; and Rabut 1989),[2] the Gbaya themselves appear to have used the term most frequently in combination with sub-ethnic or clan names. Thus, for example, a series of names designating what can be called 'dialect tribes' (see Burnham, Copet-Rougier and Noss 1986) were in use in the late nineteenth century (for example, Gbaya Lai, Gbaya Dooka, Gbaya Mbodomo, Gbaya Kara and Gbaya Bianda), although we have no early record of the use of the term Gbaya Yaayuwee. These terms are used by Gbaya-phone groups today to refer to variations in Gbaya dialect and custom which are thought to be deep-rooted historically, and they can therefore be said to bespeak at least some degree of awareness of the widespread distribution, as well as the cultural variations and similarities, of Gbaya peoples.

In talking today with members of other Gbaya dialect tribes in eastern Cameroon or the western Central African Republic, the Gbaya Yaayuwee of the Mbere Department are often characterised as the most acculturated of Gbaya groups, on the basis of their long history of contact with the Fulbe and with Islam. Non-Yaayuwee Gbaya are liable to point, somewhat disparagingly, to the Yaayuwee preference for Fulbe-style, as opposed to western-style dress, and extended discussions with Gbaya informants on the theme of sub-ethnic distinctions will unearth many other perceived differences – from the Yaayuwee use of the bow and arrow as opposed to the spear as their usual hunting weapon to their house-building practices, including the enclosure of their residential compounds with mud walls or matting fences in the Fulbe manner.[3] On the other hand, questions directed to Gbaya which attempt to elicit a set of criteria defining a pan-Gbaya ethnic consciousness extending beyond the field of local political concerns do not yield fruit. Thus, there is no strongly enunciated discriminatory cultural logic among the Gbaya, comparable for example to the notion of *pulaaku* among Fulani peoples, which might give pronounced ethnic weighting to the acknowledged microcultural variations differentiating Gbaya dialect tribes. Equally, there are no Gbaya myths recounting their purported origin as a distinct society, in contrast to the situation among various Fulani peoples where such myths are widespread. And up until 1993, when a Gbaya ethnic association was founded in Cameroon for the first time, there were no publicly proclaimed common interests among the widely dispersed Gbaya-phone peoples that might have served as the basis for an incipient political movement – no pressures for the 'reunification of the Gbaya people' or the abolition of the artificial, colonially created frontiers between Cameroon and the Central African Republic which (might be said to) divide them. The significance of this very recent emergence of a Gbaya ethnic association will be discussed in Chapter 7.

According to our nineteenth century sources, Gbaya dialect tribes did not function as collectively unified political entities and the largest cohesive Gbaya political grouping in the immediate pre-colonial period was the unit which I have termed the 'clan territory'. As I have described at length in my monograph on the Gbaya (1980a: 19–28 *et passim*; see also Copet-Rougier 1987: 346 and Burnham: in press), Gbaya clan territory units were comprised of a set of dispersed hamlets which collaborated, primarily in external relations such as warfare, inter-group alliances and trade, under the direction of a leader whose position depended more on his personal qualities than on an institutionalised chieftaincy role. In fact, the membership of a Gbaya 'clan territory' was usually made up of elements drawn from several different clans, one of which would be recognised as dominant although the others would not lose their separate descent-based identities. Although members of these clan territories did recognise and defend the group's territorial boundaries against incursions by other groups, Gbaya clan territorial groupings were not presumptively perpetual corporate units, and their continued cohesion and very existence were contingent on the strength of the group's leader and the willingness of the various constituent hamlets to follow him. In general, in the pre-colonial period as now, Gbaya political formations were relatively fluid structures that were much affected by tendencies toward residential mobility at the hamlet level and redefinition of allegiances at the clan territory level.

The primary requisite for a group of Gbaya clansmen wishing to set themselves up as an independent clan territory unit was to be able to defend their interests in war. If they were not strong enough to do so, they ran a great risk of their territory being overrun and their people being killed or enslaved. Keeping in mind our aim to understand and account for the violent inter-ethnic clashes which have occurred in the past few years in the Mbere Department, it is important to recognise that Gbaya conceptions of personal damage and legal redress are deeply rooted in their historical experience of inter-clan and inter-ethnic violence in the pre-colonial period. Violence to persons was (and still is) viewed by the Gbaya as a collective concern of one's co-resident clansmen and, when members of several clans were co-resident in a single clan territory, this collective responsibility could extend to the whole membership of the multi-clan unit in relations with other clan territories. Death or injury of a fellow clan member required either compensation, usually in the form of a payment of a woman or child from the offending clan, or an equivalent retribution through vengeance killing (*ari*). Genealogical and other oral and written historical data I have collected for Gbaya clans in the Mbere Department indicate that payments of persons to settle inter-clan disputes were relatively common even during the colonial period (see Christiansen 1956: 188–91 for a case from the 1930s), and the notion of the collective responsibility of co-resident clansmen remains prominent in Gbaya conceptions of justice even in the present day.

In addition to the clan-based political organisation of pre-colonial Gbaya society, I have already described in Chapter 2 how the political and economic influences of the Ngaoundere state and of 'Hausa' traders contributed to the greater political centralisation of certain groups in the western Central African Republic during the last few decades of the pre-colonial period. In some cases, such as in the Mbum-dominated chieftaincy at Kounde or the Gbaya-dominated chieftaincy at Bertoua, the degree of political hegemony of these slave-raiding groups was sufficient to encourage processes of cultural assimilation or acculturation of politically subordinate groups which are still detectable today (see Burnham, Copet-Rougier and Noss 1986; Copet-Rougier 1987). At the same time, the political structuring of these chieftaincies, which was based in part on the ethnically differentiated model of state organisation current at Ngaoundere, Tibati and the other Fulbe states in Adamawa during this period, offered the more westerly Gbaya-phone peoples such as the Yaayuwee a new conception and experience of inter-ethnic relations. On the other hand, although I do not wish to pursue this point here, this nineteenth century development of incipient political centralisation among certain western Gbaya groups, as a result of their contact with the Fulbe states of Adamawa, must be set against a recognition of the novelty of this contact with state structures for Gbaya-phone peoples as a whole. Prior to the arrival of the Fulbe on the western margins of the Gbaya region in the 1830s, there is no evidence that the thinly scattered Gbaya peoples had ever previously been in contact with a state system.

However, these processes of political centralisation, cultural assimilation and inter-ethnic accommodation were abruptly curtailed by the advent of colonial rule, which not only broke the independent powers of the Fulbe states on which these processes of change ultimately depended but also, in ending the warfare functions of Gbaya clan territory groupings, undercut the principal purpose of these political formations. Gbaya clan territories therefore rapidly fragmented and disappeared in the early colonial period, but the Gbaya clan categories (*zu duk*) remained and continue to constitute the framework of Gbaya residential organisation up to the present day. I refer to the *zu duk* as clan *categories* to emphasise that they are internally undifferentiated groupings whose identities are defined by a concept of shared patrilineal descent, a clan name, an alimentary taboo, and a rule of clan exogamy. Gbaya *zu duk* recognise no founding clan ancestor. They are not corporate lineages, since they have no comprehensive internal genealogical structure, either putative or actual, which could serve to order the relations of *zu duk* members according to notions of genealogical distance. Gbaya trace only shallow genealogies which normally do not extend beyond the grandparental generation, and it is therefore the case that all male members of a Gbaya clan are ultimately of structurally equivalent status, aside from considerations based on relative age.

It has long been a commonplace in the anthropological literature to compare the concept of categorical clanship to notions of ethnicity or nationality since each of these cultural constructs specify little more than a shared sense of cultural origins based on presumptive common descent. For example, speaking of Western Pueblo Amerindian matriclanship, Fox (1967: 35; compare also Durkheim 1964 [1893]: 175–8; Comaroff 1983 or Schilder 1994: 53) argued, 'Clan membership is thus not an extension of lineage membership. It is a kind of nationality: one takes one's mother's clan.' In the Gbaya Yaayuwee dialect spoken in the Mbere Department (as in many other Gbaya dialects), the link between clanship and ethnicity is quite explicit, since the term *zu duk* is used to refer both to patriclanship and to ethnicity or nationality, with context indicating which level of social grouping is the relevant one. Thus, if I meet a Gbaya who does not know me and I ask him to tell me his *zu duk*, he is most likely to answer 'Gbaya' in order to indicate that he is not an Mbum or a member of some other ethnic group. But when I am speaking to a Gbaya who knows me and I ask about his *zu duk*, he will probably respond with the name of his patriclan since he is aware that I already know his ethnic identity. In other words, in terms of Gbaya linguistic usage, there is no explicit distinction drawn with regard to constitutive social processes between the (less inclusive) level of social grouping which I have called a 'clan' and the (more inclusive) level I have called a 'dialect tribe'. Both are termed *zu duk*, even though, analytically speaking, it is possible to show that the former is defined by a more immediate concept of shared descent while the latter is based on somewhat more vague notions of shared culture or dialect (although these too can be taken as indices of shared descent at more distant levels, if need be).

In discussing the nature of Gbaya ethnic identity during any of the earlier periods for which we have data, then, it is apparent that such consciousness was largely determined by the level of functional political organisation existing in Gbaya communities at the particular period in question, as well as by the character of the political organisation and ethnic consciousness of the other peoples with whom the Gbaya were in contact. During late pre-colonial times, Gbaya ethnic identities were defined primarily in relation to the relatively contingent clan territory groupings operating within the more politically amorphous dialect tribes. The larger-scale multi-ethnic chieftaincy structures that emerged among certain Gbaya groups during this period, as a result of contacts with the Fulbe state systems and their Mbum intermediaries, did not last long enough to bring about a radical transformation in Gbaya ethnic consciousness, although they did provide a favourable setting for cultural borrowing from these neighbouring societies.

Both these forms of Gbaya political unit disappeared at the start of the colonial era, and the Gbaya peoples soon found themselves incorporated, after a brief and turbulent interlude of German domination, into the various territorially defined administrative groupings of French colonial rule. The international frontier between Cameroon and the Ubangi-Shari (now the Central African Republic) henceforth separated a significant minority of the Gbaya-phone peoples in Cameroon from their fellows to the east. Within Cameroon, the administrative boundary between northern and eastern Cameroon divided the Gbaya population of the Mbere Department (formerly the Meiganga *Arrondissement*) from Gbaya living further south in the Lom-and-Djerem and Kadey Departments. For the most part, in discussing the various forms of Gbaya ethnic consciousness manifested in the present day, these colonially created units are the pertinent political arenas within which these cultural arguments are expressed. However, before narrowing our focus to the Gbaya of the Mbere Department, it is worth considering a bit more closely the Karnu Rebellion (*Koŋgo Wara*) of 1928 to 1931, a movement which briefly mobilised a broad range of Gbaya groups and neighbouring peoples and which today is increasingly being interpreted as foundational for a Gbaya ethnic identity that transcends local political boundaries.

Politically acephalous peoples like the Gbaya are not corporate groups; they lack a comprehensive internal organisational structure to co-ordinate the actions of their memberships. Moreover, as we have seen, during the late pre-colonial and early colonial periods the identity of the Gbaya as a broad ethnic category was only hazy. On the other hand, when we look at the emergence of Karnu's rebellion, we can say with a fair degree of certainty that the movement was conceived in opposition to what Karnu and his followers defined as dangerous external threats – specifically to the French and the Fulbe who had invaded their lands. But these outsiders were seen by Karnu and his followers as threats to whom? To Karnu's local village group? To some wider group of peoples sharing Gbaya cultural understandings or identity? To any local group, regardless of their culture, who felt threatened by the French and/or by the Fulbe? Answers to these questions must remain to some extent at the level of speculation in the absence of clearcut evidence, but we can learn a good bit about the character of Karnu's movement from a consideration of the key symbols he employed to mobilise support.

As Thomas Christensen and I have discussed in detail elsewhere (Burnham and Christensen 1983), the symbols associated with Karnu's movement were drawn almost entirely from the ritual repertoire available in his local Gbaya community of Nahing, but debate will surely persist as to whether Karnu also drew upon exotic, possibly Christian, sources (see Noss 1993: 213, 216). Although the original content of Karnu's message can convincingly be claimed to have been non-violent in character (despite the later bloody turn of events), it also undeniably contained explicit implications of resistance since it promised his followers an end to French and Fulbe domination. His message also contained symbolic elements that resonate of anti-witchcraft procedures, suggesting an equation of these threatening external forces with anti-social powers.

Who, then, did Karnu conceive to be his potential followers? To begin with, his message was directed to people living in his locality, in other words to fellow Gbaya of the *Bodoi* dialect tribe, who in any case were best equipped to understand the more esoteric references associated with the key symbols of Karnu's message – the small hooked sticks resembling miniature hoe handles, the stirring stick for manioc porridge and the leaves of various plants. Quite rapidly, however, as Karnu's fame spread, he developed a set of standardised procedures for the diffusion of his 'magic' to other groups, many of whom lived at considerable distances from Karnu's village. The symbols used in the diffusion of this message were widely utilised by other Gbaya-phone groups throughout this zone. But, considering the eventually very wide diffusion of the Karnu Rebellion, which extended beyond the Ubangi-Shari (now the Central African Republic) to areas in Cameroon, Chad and the Congo (Brazzaville) and to culturally unrelated peoples like the Mbum, the Mbai, the Kpana, the Yangere, the Mbimu and the Gundi, in addition to the many Gbaya groups,[4] it is apparent that the power of the message did not necessarily depend on a shared knowledge of Gbaya ritual symbolism or on any putative pan-Gbaya ethnic consciousness. Moreover, since Karnu was already dead by the time the movement reached its greatest extension and he could have had no prior knowledge of the diversity of peoples it would eventually touch, the multi-valencies, the ambiguities and the unintended consequences of Karnu's message merit as close attention as do more 'deeply symbolic' readings deriving from 'traditional' Gbaya culture. The only feature that the diverse peoples who participated in the rebellion had in common was their desire to resist domination.

Whatever their meaning(s) in the past, the Karnu events are there for the appropriating today, and the range of uses to which they have been put is wide. (See Burnham and Christensen [1983] and Noss [1993] for more details on this point.) For the Gbaya of the Mbere Department, I would argue that stories of the Karnu Rebellion serve as what I term 'ethnically constitutive histories' – accounts that valorise elements of history which help to define and underpin current ethnic identities. The Karnu Rebellion is seen by the Gbaya today as early evidence of a broadly defined Gbaya ethnic consciousness that transcended clan boundaries, which at the same time offers a model for more equal and empowered Gbaya relations with other groups. From this perspective, the symbols of Karnu's movement are seen by the Gbaya as quintessentially Gbaya symbols.

The emergence of this 'ethnic reading' of the Karnu legend has been noteworthy during my twenty-five-year period of contact with the Gbaya. In the late 1960s, I still found old men who were hesitant to speak of their role in the rebellion of forty years ago. Some were still bitter about the deaths of their kin at the hands of the French and viewed the experience not as one of empowerment but one of defeat. A decade later, the new cinema in Meiganga had been named after Karnu and the story was told in a much more positive light. In 1993, Karnu was again on everyone's lips, but it was in the context of stories about the violence of 1991 and 1992, when 'the Gbaya warriors sang the songs of Karnu just as in the old days' before wreaking vengence on the Fulbe attackers.[5]

These versions of the Karnu story, despite their implied references to a pan-Gbaya ethnic identity, are essentially rooted in the political situation in the Mbere Department. Other Gbaya in other regions tell different Karnu stories and up to 1993, as mentioned above, I could detect no trace of a pan-Gbaya political movement that transcended colonially created political boundaries. Therefore, it is appropriate now for us to narrow our focus and concentrate on the Gbaya within the political framework of the Mbere Department, since the social forces of ethnic differentiation at work in this district are largely particular to this setting and are significantly different from those affecting other Gbaya populations in Cameroon and the Central African Republic.

THE GBAYA WITHIN THE MULTI-ETHNIC SOCIETY OF THE MBERE DEPARTMENT TODAY

Nowadays, the Gbaya of Mbere Department live primarily in numerous small mono-ethnic villages lining the roads where they practise a mixed economy centred on the cultivation of manioc and maize. In fact, for about six months of each year, these rural villages stand largely vacant while many of their inhabitants take up residence in temporary encampments adjacent to their fields scattered throughout the bush. The remainder of the Gbaya population of the Mbere Department resides in the few larger multi-ethnic villages and towns of the district but, even in these larger settlements, many Gbaya practise farming as their principal occupation.

The size and composition of most Gbaya settlements today reflect the effects of the administrative policy of village *regroupement*, a practice which began in the colonial period but one which is still actively pursued by the present government. The government's aim is progressively to increase the average size of Gbaya villages and when opportunities present themselves, such as the construction of the new Meidougou to Ngaoundal road in the mid-1970s, pressures are exerted to encourage small villages to coalesce into larger units. We should note in passing that this is but one of many examples wherein the present government, just like its colonial predecessors, operates what is notionally a uniform and non-discriminatory administrative policy in a differential manner in relation to the various ethnic groups of the Mbere Department. Although in practice it is hard to conceive how this could be otherwise (since, for example, the social ecology of the pastoral Mbororo necessarily implies a different mode of village organisation from that of the agricultural Gbaya), such administrative policies are frequently viewed by the ethnic groups concerned as evidence of ethnic favouritism on the government's part.

With regard to the issue in question, Gbaya complain that government *regroupement* policies within the Mbere Department are applied only to them and, during President Ahidjo's long period of rule when the Fulbe were in the ascendant, the Gbaya were fond of citing this as evidence of ethnic discrimination. As will be discussed later, the pendulum has swung somewhat in the other direction under President Biya's regime, and it is more the Mbororo who now feel out of government favour.

As just mentioned, most of the rural Gbaya villages in the Mbere Department are mono-ethnic in composition and are composed of several clan-based residential quarters known as *ndok fuu* (a term borrowed from the Mbum language). Here and there, one encounters a non-Gbaya family or two living in these small Gbaya villages. These families are usually headed by Fulbe or Fulbeised men. Typically, these men may originally have made contact with their Gbaya neighbours while working as a paid herdsman in the area. Having resigned this job, they may have decided to remain in the locality to try to build up their personal cattle herds, while perhaps carrying out some petty trade on the side. Fulbe who live among 'pagans' in this way (known as *'fulɓe baamle'* in Fulfulde) are low in the status hierarchy in Fulbe society. Their Gbaya co-villagers, while usually maintaining courteous relations with them on a day-to-day basis, are likely also to make disparaging remarks about their social status behind their backs, calling them *bara mbisa* (slaves of the Mbisa).[6] Although some of these Fulbe may continue to reside for a decade or more in Gbaya villages, most of them are evidently attempting to accumulate sufficient wealth to be able to move to a more Fulbe-dominated context with their social status enhanced. (This is indeed what eventually transpired for several of these men whom I first met in 1968.)

Such occasional non-Gbaya residents aside, the quality of social relations in the smaller Gbaya villages is very much conditioned by the norms of reciprocity associated with Gbaya clanship. The *ndok fuu* group, which on average contains about two dozen members, is the major focus of every Gbaya's communal identification within the rural villages of the Mbere Department, although these units are subject to relatively frequent shifts in membership over time and cannot be classified as corporate groups. In previous publications, I have referred to *ndok fuu* as 'contingent' groups, seeking to emphasise thereby that the Gbaya do not view them as presumptively perpetual structures because of their high rate of residential mobility.[7]

Despite their contingent character and the fact that the membership of an *ndok fuu* often consists of families who share clan affiliation but are unable to trace patrilineal connections, the *ndok fuu* is normatively conceived of by the Gbaya as a cohesive kinship unit in which familial values should prevail. Gbaya norms stress the importance of close co-operation between co-resident clansmen in most of their daily activities and emphasise that an individual's welfare is closely connected with the wellbeing of the *ndok fuu* as a whole. *Ndok fuu* members should stand together in disputes; for example, should an *ndok fuu* member receive a fine in a government court, his co-resident clansmen will often assist with its payment. *Ndok fuu* members also participate in a complex web of generalised reciprocity on a daily basis – sharing uncooked food, partaking in communal meals and exchanging numerous small gifts. But despite such extensive distributions of the production of members of the clan-based residential group, such exchange is viewed as a sharing of individually owned produce, and thus a reaffirmation of the norms of generosity between co-residents, rather than a distribution of collectively owned *ndok fuu* property or a redistribution of wealth within an intra-village hierarchy. For Gbaya *ndok fuu* members hold no property as a corporate group; there are no communal granaries, no communal lands, and no communal moveable property. And since agricultural land is not scarce and there are no institutionalised mechanisms through which one member of a Gbaya village can gain control over the labour of another, Gbaya villagers are not hierarchically differentiated according to their access to the means of production.

One can draw analogies between the multi-clan structure of today's Gbaya villages and the multi-clan composition of the pre-colonial Gbaya clan territories. The long-term cohesion of modern Gbaya villages is not appreciably greater than that of the fluid pre-colonial clan territory groups. However, any tendencies toward stability and cohesion that do exist at the level of the modern Gbaya village derive largely from the external pressures exerted by the administrative policy of *regroupement* (and related infrastructural developments) whereas in the pre-colonial period as we have seen, co-operation between the different clan fractions making up a clan territory reflected the need for mutual defence. Political leadership in today's regrouped Gbaya villages is as tenuous and problematic as the artificially regrouped village structure is unstable, with few indigenous mechanisms available to underpin the authority of the village headman – an office created in the colonial period. Public disputes between individuals and/or village sections emerge, often couched in the language of witchcraft or other supernatural powers, to signal breaches in norms of reciprocity or outbreaks of political competitiveness. In these circumstances, members of a Gbaya village may seek to escape the ill will of a particular set of co-resident clansmen or the inhabitants of a neighbouring residential quarter by shifting residence to a different village, often one occupied by other fractions of their own clan.

In my 1980 Gbaya monograph, which was based primarily on data collected between 1968 and 1970, I developed an analysis linking the reliability of Gbaya subsistence agriculture, the norms of *ndok fuu* reciprocity and the contingent character of these residential units with processes of wealth levelling and ethnic boundary maintenance in Gbaya rural villages. Looking back after two decades and, judging by the light of several more periods of field research, this analysis still seems to me essentially correct and, in the present day, remains applicable. Briefly summarised, my argument was that inside the boundary symbolised by the Gbaya residential quarter and its manioc-based subsistence activities, economic risks are minimised. Subsistence reliability is supported by the norm of *ndok fuu* reciprocity, which is also used in practice by its members as a barometer reflecting the state of inter-personal relations in the unit and the likelihood of imminent group dissolution. The expectation that personally owned resources should be freely shared with other group members on a day-to-day basis constitutes an effective levelling mechanism within *ndok fuu*, and failure to adhere to norms of reciprocity is likely to attract the malevolent attentions of witches or the curses of fellow clansmen.

> Inside the boundary, the Gbaya hold the reins, minimising risks and controlling their daily lives in their local communities to a more or less satisfactory degree. Outside the boundary exists a non-Gbaya world which, although Gbaya interact with it from time to time, is full of dangers and opportunities over which the Gbaya have little control. Gbaya conceptualise this boundary essentially in ethnic terms, explaining their relative lack of success in the market economy by reference to documented or alleged cases of ethnic favouritism and discrimination . . . In this multi-ethnic setting and in the context of the contingent *ndok fuu* residential groupings, the structural features at the core of the Gbaya system have become morally reified and act as prominent symbols and tests of 'Gbaya-ness'. The great commitment of the Gbaya to *kam*, their 'national' manioc dish, to collectively eaten meals, and to living for half the year in the bush may be more easily understood in these terms. (Burnham 1980a: 281)

This public commitment to sharing within the residential quarter does not mean, of course, that individual Gbaya do not attempt to accumulate wealth within the rural village context. Rather, their efforts, which are viewed ambivalently by fellow villagers, are seldom crowned with success due to a tendency to dissipate capital through (almost mandatory) gifts. The alternative of attempting to dissimulate one's wealth through lying and secrecy is a strategy which is fraught with the risk of witchcraft attack. As a consequence, although Gbaya agricultural activities provide them with a generally reliable subsistence base, their efforts to carve out a profitable niche in the local trading or cattle economy have not been highly successful. This has not been due as much to limitations operating within their system of agricultural production as it has been linked with their failure to find a means of parlaying the profits from their income-earning activities into effective strategies for capital growth.

For example, many of the methods of capital accumulation available in the Mbere Department are effectively precluded for the Gbaya both by the ethnic boundary mechanisms operating in the regional market economy as well as by the social demands of participation in Gbaya life. As we have discussed briefly in Chapter 3, successful Fulbe or Hausa merchants in the Mbere Department generally operate mono-ethnic business consortia which dominate regional trade in cattle and kola nuts. A similar situation obtains within the Bamileke community in Meiganga which is heavily involved in trade in second-hand clothes, motor parts, hardware, dry goods, bottled beverages and several other lines. Many Bamileke living in Meiganga hail from Bapwentou, the home town of one of the original Bamileke migrants in the 1950s; others come from Bafang. Virtually all of the younger Bamileke men now trading in Meiganga first arrived as a result of sponsorship by older migrant fellow townsmen, who offered them initial employment within their trading firms while they found their feet. These younger men gradually constituted a personal business capital by small-scale trading on the side and by participation in rotating savings societies (*tontines*), eventually setting up in business on their own (cf. Miaffo and Warnier 1993).

The contrast between the collaborative business norms of these migrant groups and the markedly individualistic approach of Gbaya who attempt to trade could not be more striking. For example, a group of Hausa butchers are likely to share a single business licence (*patente*) while Gbaya butchers seldom do so – each man buying his own. Effective modes of sharing collectively owned property, as opposed to the sharing of individually owned property, do not exist in Gbaya society, and the commercial results of such a situation are plain to see. There are almost no Gbaya-owned stores in Meiganga, and virtually the entire commercial centre of this 'Gbaya' town has been taken over by non-Gbaya who have gradually bought out the original Gbaya landowners.[8] Indeed, as we shall discuss in Chapter 7, acrimony over the alleged Fulbe takeover of 'downtown' Meiganga played a part in stimulating the violence in 1991 and 1992.

On the other hand, the few relatively affluent Gbaya businessmen known to me have achieved their success by associating themselves with Muslim trading milieux. In one well-known case, the Gbaya businessman in question, having made his early career as a servant for European employers in Douala and in other cities far from the Mbere Department, accumulated much of his capital via cattle investments. As soon as he was able, he ratified his status within Meiganga's Muslim commercial community by making the pilgrimage to Mecca, a trip he has made several times subsequently. He also further distanced himself from Gbaya circles in Meiganga town by conducting a long-running dispute over land rights with the Lutheran church. Gossip flew about in the Gbaya community concerning the purportedly evil methods he had used to acquire his wealth; he was nicknamed '*Al Hajji Gbɛɛ Zu*' by his Gbaya opponents, to suggest that his wealth derived from murdering people through sorcery. The businessman himself shrugged off such gossip as typical Gbaya jealousy of success. At the same time, he continued to assert his Gbaya ethnic identity, saying that he wanted to prove to the Fulbe that Gbaya could prosper in business.

Concern for ethnic boundary maintenance impinges directly on Gbaya economic activities in other spheres in addition to the commercial sector. Opportunities for piece-rate wage labour are relatively plentiful in the Mbere Department, thanks to the culturally defined attitudes of the Mbororo and high-status Fulbe to occupations other than cattle herding. Although many Gbaya men, especially in their younger years, undertake agricultural labour, house construction and other tasks for Mbororo and Fulbe employers, the servile implications of this work make it unpopular. Gbaya who do engage in it prefer to travel away from their village so that they will not have to suffer the unspoken opprobrium of their fellow villagers. In contrast, 'Congo' labour migrants from the Central African Republic do not have the same compunctions about working for Mbororo or Fulbe employers and respond readily to these employment opportunities.

An interesting exception to the general Gbaya distaste for working for Fulani employers occurs in the context of bond friendship (*soobaajo*) relations established between Gbaya and Mbororo men. As part of their *soobaajo* link, the Gbaya will perform services such as house building or fencing for his Mbororo bond-friend, and the men's wives will regularly exchange milk products for manioc and other Gbaya agricultural produce. The Mbororo herdsman will give his Gbaya *soobaajo* gifts of cattle from time to time – for example, animals that are judged to be too weak to endure the dry season transhumance. By placing their performance of labour services within the moral framework of a longer-term relationship of generalised exchange, Gbaya men are able to interpret their *soobaajo* relations with the Mbororo as more status equivalent and therefore more acceptable than wage labour for Fulani employers.

On a day-to-day basis in small Gbaya villages (during the wet season at least), interactions with Mbororo women exchanging dairy products, as well as with Mbororo men passing the middle of the day sitting under a tree or sun shade, are a Gbaya's most frequent experiences of inter-ethnic contact. Such contacts between Gbaya and Mbororo, which are often accompanied by light-hearted banter and jokes, contribute to the generally easy relations between the two ethnic groups. Even during moments of tension provoked, for example, by Mbororo cattle damaging Gbaya crops, these relations can serve as a basis for the informal settlement of disputes. Unfortunately for the Gbaya, such *soobaajo* links have become less frequent in recent years and, particularly in areas such as the northeastern margins of the Mbere Department where Mbororo and Fulbe are especially numerous, Fulani prefer to employ labourers for cash on piece-work rates.

Although thus far I have been discussing the phenomenon of levelling and social control largely with reference to its effects on economic success in Gbaya society, I should emphasise that I see these processes as of more general importance in conditioning Gbaya attitudes toward inter-ethnic relations. It is noteworthy, for example, that in the several Gbaya villages where I have resided for extended periods over the past twenty-five years, the numbers of Christian and Muslim Gbaya have been roughly equal, and it has not been at all uncommon to find members of the same Gbaya family practising different religions. Within the Gbaya village or kin group context, religion is typically treated as a matter of personal choice and is not normally a subject of inter-personal dispute or discrimination.[9]

But for Gbaya living in the larger multi-ethnic towns or having substantial involvement in social fields extending beyond their rural village, choice of religion takes on greater politico-symbolic weight, since it will be noted and commented upon by their associates, both Gbaya and non-Gbaya. As mentioned in the previous chapter, Gbaya converting to Islam in an urban context are likely to be accused of utilitarian Islamisation – one of the charges levelled against Al Hajji Gbee Zu mentioned above. As Schilder (1994: 214) noted, we must not view Islamisation as equivalent to Fulbeisation, even though (as I described in the previous chapter) Islamisation is clearly a prerequisite for passing into the Fulbe ethnic category. I have encountered several Gbaya living in northern towns and cities who were practising Islam while continuing to declare themselves to be ethnically Gbaya. However, to the extent that their children were being raised as Muslims in a predominantly Fulbe cultural setting, this younger generation has a greater likelihood of Fulbeisation.

The only possibility of escape, then, from the social constraints of the rural Gbaya village is to move into a multi-ethnic, usually urban, setting.

Here the Gbaya migrant can be free of the day-to-day demands of clanship-based reciprocity, although if periodic return visits are made to the home village, there are still occasional days of reckoning when major gift-giving will be required. At the same time, as argued above, moving from one's natal Gbaya village and living in town leads to an accentuation of a Gbaya's day-to-day experience of inter-ethnic relations and a closer contact with the assimilative processes of Fulbe ethnicity. But any such close association by a Gbaya with Fulbe-dominated social settings will be strongly disparaged by other Gbaya, who label such individuals as *bara mbisa* (slaves of the Mbisa) – one of the ways of talking about Fulbeisation in the Gbaya language.[10]

Previewing our discussion in Chapter 7 of the emergence in 1993 of the Gbaya elite association, MOINAM, it is interesting to note that one of the dissatisfactions expressed by this association concerning the status of the Gbaya ethnic group within Cameroon society related to what we can call the 'ethnic invisibility' of Gbaya living outside their home region. Gbaya are said to no longer name their children with distinctively Gbaya names and to no longer speak Gbaya in public, multi-ethnic contexts. Indeed, it is primarily the Christian missions, rather than any distinctively Gbaya social form, that offer a mode of communal organisation to the Gbaya that stands as an alternative to Fulbeisation in the urban society of northern Cameroon.

Thus, both the culturally generated levelling processes at work within Gbaya society as well the ethnic boundaries erected by other groups act as strong brakes on Gbaya success in the market economy of northern Cameroon. In effect, when combined with the political marginality of the Gbaya which I will discuss more fully in a moment, these socioeconomic forces contribute to what I term the 'encapsulation' of the Gbaya ethnic group within the Mbere Department – a lack of effective articulation with centres of modern economic and political life within Cameroonian society.

Such mechanisms of levelling and social control, which manifest themselves as constraints on wealth creation and weak authority structures, are not unique to Gbaya society, of course. They have been noted among politically uncentralised peoples elsewhere in Cameroon and, more widely, in many peasant societies around the world. Peter Geschiere's study of the Maka, a people living to the south of the Gbaya in eastern Cameroon, contains many relevant comparisons in its discussion of the problematic position of the Maka village chief, the 'victim of the tension between "traditional" and bureaucratic principles of authority' (1982: 207). Geschiere's analysis is particularly insightful in his discussion of the role of Maka witchcraft and sorcery beliefs in providing both a theory of political and economic success and an ultimate control over emergent hierarchical tendencies. Among the Maka, from the late colonial period onwards, the most successful route for individuals to escape the constraints of village life and make their way in the outside world has been via western education. The first generation of Maka elites, including those whom Geschiere (1982: 427) terms 'intellectuals' (in preference to the more usual *évolués*), were able to do so through their contact with the Presbyterian mission – obtaining primary school certificates and possibly normal school qualifications and then using their educational advantages to gain access to government employment in the post-colonial period.

The story is not greatly different among the Gbaya of the Mbere Department, although the more limited educational provision available in northern Cameroon, both during the colonial period and subsequently, as well as the dominance of the Muslim Fulbe within the state sector during most of the same period, have meant that the development of a modern Gbaya elite has proceeded more slowly. But before discussing the constitution of this Gbaya elite, we must consider in more detail the social impact of the Christian missions within the Mbere Department, since I would argue that the Protestant Sudan Mission, joined in the post-Second World War period by the Catholic Mission, has provided the major non-state institutional focus for the development of collective Gbaya identity and political leadership in recent decades.

THE CONTRIBUTION OF THE MISSIONARY FACTOR TO GBAYA ETHNIC CONSCIOUSNESS

As explained in Chapter 2, one of the principal sources of collective organisation and leadership for the Gbaya during the last seventy years has been the Protestant Mission. From its arrival in Mboula in 1924, the Sudan Mission focused its work in the Mbere region particularly on the Gbaya, having judged them to be ripe for conversion due to their oppositional and subordinated position vis-à-vis the Muslim Fulbe of Ngaoundere. Up until the foundation of the Meiganga *Arrondissement* as an independent administrative unit in 1929, Gbaya government-appointed chiefs and elders were constrained to maintain links with the Fulbe overlords at Ngaoundere (not without obtaining certain benefits, of course), and Islamic influences were strongest among this 'traditional' Gbaya political leadership. As a result, Christian conversion proceeded most rapidly to begin with among women, younger men and children – the non-powerful members of Gbaya society who were little involved in Fulbe-dominated public affairs (see Christiansen 1956: 178, 186). Even in recent years, conversion to Christianity has not normally been very common among adult Gbaya men, and the male members of Gbaya Christian churches have mostly grown up in the faith. (However, a recent exception to this trend has been the spate of adult male Gbaya conversions following the outbreaks of violence in Meiganga in 1991 and 1992.)

Originally a 'faith mission' that received no regular financial support from a parent body, the Sudan Mission suffered from straitened circumstances during its first several decades, and this meant that its missionaries maintained a lifestyle which was relatively close to and integrated with that of their Gbaya hosts. There was little money available for the construction of churches, schools and dispensaries, and the early mission work was devoted mainly to direct evangelism, with limited teaching of literacy in Gbaya to give access to the Scriptures.

Over the years, the educational policies of the Sudan Mission have been of considerable significance in establishing the conditions under which the Gbaya have confronted the changing opportunities offered in the wider society of Cameroon. The missionaries' emphasis on literacy in the Gbaya language, which has involved great effort in translating the Bible and other literature and culminated in the foundation of a church translation bureau in Meiganga in the 1970s, has been much appreciated by the Gbaya population. It is not just that Christianity is another 'religion of the book' – long a boast of the Fulbe about Islam in contrast to the 'pagan' religions of their neighbours. The transformation of the Gbaya language into written form by the missionaries was also seen by Gbaya of all religious persuasions as making a strong statement about the equal worth of their culture in the face of Fulbe judgements to the contrary.

On the other hand, the missionaries were very slow to set up French-language schools to teach the national curriculum, and this foot-dragging was not simply the result of a lack of financial means. Even after the Sudan Mission secured its financial base by joining the Evangelical Lutheran Church in 1952 (later the American Lutheran Church Board of World Missions [Christiansen 1956: 228, 266–7]) and more funds for private school education became available from the French colonial government at about the same time, many of the conservative Sudan Mission workers continued to oppose mission involvement in the national French-language school system on the grounds that it would divert attention from the primary work of evangelism. Given the small amount of funding made available by the French administration for public primary education throughout northern Cameroon during all but the last few years of colonial rule and the relatively late arrival in the Mbere Department of the French Catholic mission with its more active involvement in education based on the national curriculum, the Gbaya, like the rest of the population of the region, were destined to enter the post-colonial period with relatively few individuals possessing even a rudimentary western-style education.

Despite the conservatism of the older American mission workers, the Sudan Mission's decision to affiliate with the American Lutheran Church did ultimately lead to a great expansion in the range of the mission's institutional activities as well as to an increase in the standard of living enjoyed by the missionaries. Missionaries were now paid a regular salary and vehicle allowance, and better schooling was made available for their children. Many new mission buildings were constructed, and the quality of missionary housing was improved. During the 1950s, a hospital was built and staffed at Garoua Boulai. A system of mission primary schools teaching the national curriculum was finally established. And in 1958, a theological seminary was founded at Meiganga to train African pastors.

Whatever the exact motivations for this significant expansion of the mission's programmes and physical plant, the fact remains that from the 1950s onward, the Sudan Mission was progressively transformed into a much more complex and bureaucratic organisation. By the late 1960s, most of the missionaries spent most of their time working in administrative posts, assisted by small groups of educated Gbaya pastors and other local employees. The mission station in Meiganga grew into what is virtually a small town of its own today, with the spacious landscaped mission grounds surrounded by residential neighbourhoods housing many of the mission employees and other Gbaya Christians – all of which are situated on a separate hill away from the centre of town.

A major factor in these changes was the establishment, in 1961, of an independent Lutheran church organisation under local African leadership, the Evangelical Lutheran Church (EELC) of Cameroon and the Central African Republic. This umbrella body, whose creation owed much to secular pressures at the time of Cameroonian independence to Africanise local institutions, groups into one body the different ethnically distinct Lutheran congregations created by missionary work in various parts of northern Cameroon and adjacent districts of the CAR. The Gbaya church in the Mbere Department is the largest of these ethnic congregations, but other missionised ethnic groups such as the Duru, the Mbum, the Vute, the Dowayo, the Chamba, and so on, in Cameroon, as well as various Gbaya groups in the CAR, are also represented. Subsequent to the foundation of the independent EELC, the American and Norwegian[11] missionaries of the Sudan Mission have continued their work in Cameroon, although the administrative convention now followed is that the foreign missionaries formally receive a 'call' to work from the African church.

Financially, the 'independent' EELC remains heavily dependent on overseas sources of support. Not only were the mission institutions that were in existence prior to 1961 – such as schools, hospitals and the theological seminary – greatly beyond the financial means of the African church to support on its own, but even more such developments, including an agricultural extension project, a youth organisation, a women's centre, a communication centre, and a translation centre, have been subsequently established with external funding. As one of the leading Gbaya pastors remarked disarmingly to a visiting official from the American Lutheran Church's home office, the overseas churches are like 'the fuel pump of a car' which enables the African church to run.

These institutional developments have created a rather paradoxical situation for both the missionaries and the African church. Since its creation, the EELC has on the one hand gained access to substantial external funding sources in addition to the American Lutheran church. These include the Lutheran World Federation in Geneva, NORAD (Norwegian government overseas development funding linked with the Lutheran church), and German Lutheran Church overseas development support, all of which have funded additional capital-intensive activities. Some of these projects, such as the tractor ploughing and agricultural credit schemes funded by the Lutheran World Federation, were clearly ill-adapted to local agricultural and social conditions. But they were the outgrowth of the community of interests between a foreign church body eager to validate its developmentalist credentials and local Gbaya church officials eager to have more money flow into church coffers while obtaining access to modern technology and facilities.

On the other hand, due to the earlier lack of commitment on the part of the Sudan Mission to western-style education or to the development of new sources of income for the Gbaya people at large, the present generation of Gbaya church leaders have neither the necessary education nor the experience to carry out successfully the substantial administrative functions that are now the responsibility of the local church. Nor does the Gbaya Christian population at large have the economic wherewithal to assume even a significant minority of the financial burdens associated with their church's institutional activities. The EELC therefore inevitably finds itself in a perpetual situation of dependency and mutual incomprehension *vis-à-vis* the foreign missionaries. On the other side of the coin, while most missionaries acknowledge that the EELC's future success in winning converts is likely to depend in substantial measure upon a continuing inflow of external funding, they find it frustrating that so much of this money flows into the wrong hands.

Much of this concern and debate over the functioning of the Gbaya church is focused on the leadership role of the Gbaya pastors. The early Protestant missionaries, with their conservative understanding of church affairs, were slow to move toward the creation of an African pastorate. It was not until 1955 that André Garba was ordained as the first Gbaya pastor, despite his lack of formal educational qualifications, on the basis of his 'faithful Christian life and outstanding service as an evangelist and church leader' (Christiansen 1956: 219). As already mentioned, the mission founded a theological seminary in Meiganga in 1958, but the first decades of its operation have been handicapped by the inadequate educational level of its recruits. The curriculum was ill-adapted to local conditions, as for example when theology students without primary school certificates, some of whom had only a mediocre knowledge of French, were asked to learn Greek.

Another basic problem has been the low level of salary paid to Gbaya pastors once they have qualified. This has often been a bar to high quality recruitment from within the small pool of potential Gbaya candidates with adequate educational qualifications; there have usually been more lucrative jobs on offer during much of the post-colonial period. Then too, the marked disparity between missionary incomes and those of Gbaya pastors is also an embarrassment and source of friction, although many missionaries consider themselves to be making financial and material sacrifices in their own lives and therefore expect the same of the Gbaya pastors. In other words, although the missionary argument that the independent Gbaya church cannot afford to pay more to its pastors is objectively quite true, it ignores the fact mentioned above that the mission was unwilling, throughout much of its history, to assist significantly in the economic development of Gbaya society and to establish thereby a sound economic basis for the true independence of the Gbaya church. The tangible results of this early neglect are today all too obvious and include continuing problems of recruitment to the seminary, frequent cases of unauthorised use of church funds by pastors and other church officials, pressures on catechumens awaiting baptism to work unpaid in the fields of some pastors, evangelists or catechists, and inadequate pastoral contact between certain Gbaya pastors and their congregations.

Despite all these difficulties, it is undeniably the case that some Gbaya pastors exercise prominent and often high-quality leadership within the Gbaya community of the Mbere Department at large. This is of particular importance given the fact, discussed above, that Gbaya society has never had any indigenous organisational structures capable of pursuing collective interests over the longer term. However, as a result of the Sudan Mission's policy which has been pursued from the start of focusing their efforts explicitly on the Gbaya, the Gbaya Protestant church is now assuming such a role within Gbaya society. Thanks to the regular round of comings-and-goings associated with church services, church conferences and committee meetings, Gbaya pastors are well placed to take the lead in community affairs – an opportunity available to few other Gbaya within the Mbere Department. Moreover, with the increased flow of external development funding coming into the Gbaya church in recent years, Gbaya pastors and other senior church leaders are in a position to play a broker's role within the Gbaya community and to represent both church interests, and Gbaya interests more generally, vis-à-vis local and regional government agencies concerned with social affairs and economic development. And during and after the violent outbreaks of 1991 and 1992, certain Gbaya pastors and other key church leaders played central and often controversial roles in inter-communal relations.

This community leadership function of the Gbaya pastorate is one of the principal factors that has maintained the competitive advantage of the Protestant church over the Catholic church within the Mbere Department in recent decades. Despite the generally superior reputations of Catholic versus Protestant mission schools, the lack of Gbaya priests or a locally independent

Catholic church organisation has precluded the development of an ethnically rooted Gbaya Catholicism. Although from time to time French Catholic missionaries in the Mbere Department have been quite active politically in attempting to protect the interests of local Gbaya communities against perceived government injustices, this has not contributed as substantially to a self-sustaining Gbaya ethnic politics as has the Protestant mission influence.

Although this is not the place to discuss at length the many changes that have taken place in Gbaya religious beliefs and practices over recent years, it is appropriate to note several developments in Gbaya Lutheran worship which relate to the church's contribution to Gbaya ethnic identity within the Mbere Department. As the Gbaya pastorate has progressively replaced the missionary pastors in officiating at Gbaya church services, it is noteworthy that the character of the service, particularly in the main Lutheran church in Meiganga, has changed. From an early phase, still under the direction of the older generation of missionaries, in which the service was based on a direct, and largely unmediated translation into Gbaya of the traditional American Lutheran form of worship, the Gbaya service passed through a period in the late 1960s and early 1970s during which some of the younger missionaries introduced a modified liturgy incorporating elements drawn from Gbaya culture.'This step, despite its evident concern to enhance intercultural communication, was greeted with mixed reactions in Gbaya congregations. Although the younger generation of Gbaya Christians certainly applauded the use of Gbaya musical instruments and melodies, some of the older generation were worried that these changes signalled a decline in the rigour of church practices. Indeed, many of the older Gbaya Christians had interpreted the early missionaries' strict moral code, which forbade drumming and dancing in church along with polygamy and many other Gbaya customs, in essentially political terms. As one 'pillar' of the Meiganga church explained to me:

> Even the [Muslim] Fulbe respect Protestants [by implication, more than they respect the Catholics, whom he considered to be less strict in adhering to the moral code of their religion] because they have so many rules to follow. That is why we keep the rules strict even today.

In modern-day Gbaya services under the direction of Gbaya pastors, the incorporation of new liturgical forms based on Gbaya culture has not proceeded much further, but shifts of emphasis have taken place which offer substantial opportunities, within the context of services which now last as long as three hours, to attend to what may be termed 'communal' concerns. A prominent economic dimension has found a place, and ample opportunities are now available for congregation members to display their generosity publicly. Likewise, time may now be devoted to discussing secular issues of interest to the Gbaya community in general – relating, for example, to ethnically based voting strategies or to plans for economic development projects of benefit to the Gbaya community.

This communalistic orientation in Gbaya Protestantism is also visible in a variety of other ways, especially within the large congregation in Meiganga town where Gbaya collective political interests are seen as most clearly in competition with those of other ethnic groups. Despite the substantial increase in the population of non-Gbaya Protestants in Meiganga since the replacement a decade ago of the Fulbe-dominated Ahidjo regime by the southern Christian Biya government, it is noteworthy that there has been no real effort to coalesce the Gbaya service with the French-language Lutheran service; the Gbaya service still remains the much more prominent one in Gbaya eyes. Even in relations with other Gbaya Lutheran congregations from the Eastern Province of Cameroon or from the Central African Republic, there is a marked competitiveness as the Gbaya of the Mbere Department strive to obtain the lion's share of the resources available.

Although there is much evidence that the relatively orthodox and conservative moral code of the Lutheran church does not adequately respond to certain Gbaya religious concerns (in remaining opposed, for example, to offering communion to polygamists and discouraging charismatic practices such as faith healing or exorcism), there have been no moves toward the foundation of a breakaway Gbaya church of pentecostal or similarly more expressive or syncretist persuasion.[12] Competing Protestant denominations such as the Seventh Day Adventists, the Full Gospel Church, or the True Church of God, which have expanded rapidly in adjacent districts of the Eastern Province of Cameroon including among some southern Gbaya-phone groups, have made no inroads at all among the Gbaya of the Mbere Department. Given what we have said concerning the Gbaya Lutheran church's role as the primary organisational vehicle for Gbaya ethnic interests within the Mbere Department, this is hardly surprising.

GBAYA POLITICAL MOBILISATION AND LEADERSHIP IN THE POST-INDEPENDENCE PERIOD

In other parts of Cameroon, indigenous structures of chieftaincy often afforded a basis for local political mobilisation in the late colonial and independence periods as well as a bridge to modern elite status. There has, however, never been any question that the Gbaya canton chiefs (who might now perhaps be termed a 'traditional' political elite despite the creation of these posts by the colonial government) would manage to exercise effective leadership in the modern setting or become founding members of a modern Gbaya elite. Aside from the fact that these chiefs have seldom been able to speak adequate French for effective participation in the modern state sector, they also occupy rather minor administrative roles in the governmental hierarchy and do not possess sufficient political power and legitimacy to exercise significant leadership outside their own cantons. Gbaya canton chiefs are tolerated and utilised by the Cameroon state to the limited extent that they suit its purposes, but they have never been able to stamp their mark on the course of regional or national political affairs.

Even for the Gbaya populations of their cantons, the ethnic allegiances of their canton chiefs can be rather ambiguous at times. As we have seen in Chapter 2, Gbaya conceptions of formally institutionalised chieftaincy were much influenced by their pre-colonial links with the Ngaoundere state via the tributary political formations at towns like Kounde, Mboula and Bertoua. These Fulbe Muslim models have been retained in large measure up to the present day. Thus, Gbaya canton chiefs in the Mbere Department are typically Muslim, inhabit large walled compounds entered through elaborate entry huts, and seclude their wives (in principle at least). They maintain a suite of courtiers and retainers (some of servile, Fulbeised status), as well as a (Fulbe) imam of the town mosque, which is always located adjacent to the chief's compound. On ceremonial occasions, Gbaya canton chiefs travel on horseback, dressed in ample turbans and multiple robes, and are surrounded by musicians and praise singers who proclaim their high status and deeds using conventional Fulfulde and Hausa phrases.

Apart from the distaste expressed by some Gbaya for the Fulbeised style of their canton chiefs, there is also the issue of their legendary cupidity for bribes. Maintaining their court retinues and displays is expensive, and Gbaya canton chiefs do not receive large salaries from the government. Judging from some cases that I have been able to observe, Gbaya canton chiefs appear to be particularly inclined to seek 'gifts' of livestock from Mbororo herders living in their cantons, and there is a widespread feeling among Gbaya villagers that this is the basis for a perceived favouritism of Mbororo herders in crop damage cases.

Whatever the failings or ethnic ambivalence of the Gbaya canton chiefs, the acknowledgement by the Cameroon state of the 'traditional' Gbaya right to the canton chieftaincies of the Mbere Department remains an important guarantee of local political status for their Gbaya followers. And, as we shall see in later chapters, it is an ethnic emblem that the Gbaya have defended fiercely against some recent attempts to overturn it.

In the colonial and post-colonial histories of many of the indigenous peoples of Cameroon, the emergence of modern elites has tended to be most closely associated with salaried government employment and less frequently with involvement in business, although as recent writers (Bayart 1989: 112 et seq. and Geschiere and Konings 1993) have emphasised, the two domains are often linked within a single individual's career through the practice of 'straddling' (chevauchement in French). However, the history of the development of the Gbaya elite of the Mbere Department, while not totally contradicting this familiar scenario,[13] displays certain differences which reflect the mode of articulation of the Gbaya with the larger regional society of northern Cameroon. As we have already discussed in this chapter, few Gbaya have been able to participate successfully in commercial activities and this avenue to elite status remains largely blocked. Access to salaried positions within the Cameroon government has also not been easy, both because of the low level of Gbaya education as well as the dominant position of the Fulbe and their preferential access to influential state posts in northern Cameroon during all but the last decade. Since the advent of the Biya regime, northern administrators have largely been replaced by southerners, with no major improvement for the Gbaya in the Mbere Department who continue to fill, in the main, junior administrative or clerical posts.

A significant proportion of the first generation of Gbaya to obtain primary school certificates preferred to enter the army or the gendarmerie, where they have remained in the more junior grades for the most part. This employment has also inevitably caused them to be posted outside their home region and to have little day-to-day involvement in local public affairs. The Gbaya, like many other non-Fulbe ethnic groups of northern Cameroon, were a popular source of military recruits during Ahidjo's long period in office. Evidently, as I have already mentioned in Chapter 2, they were viewed as more politically congenial to the northerner-dominated regime than soldiers from southern or western Cameroon (cf. Schilder 1994: Appendix 2). As a result, a disproportionate number of northern Cameroonian gendarmes, including Gbaya, perished or were confined to the state maximum security prisons following the active involvement of the *Garde Républicaine* after the abortive pro-Ahidjo *coup d'état* in 1984.

The first Gbaya to gain access to a politically prominent post within the Cameroon state did so via the legislative elections to the colonial Territorial Assembly (ATCAM) in the run-up to independence and, thanks to the Gbaya electoral majority in the Mbere Department constituency, Gbaya candidates have regularly been successful in local elections since that time. Such elected posts include those of deputy in the National and (before its abolition) East Cameroonian legislative assemblies, the leadership of the departmental branch of the unitary national political party structures (UNC and then RDPC) before the recent advent of multi-party elections, and the mayoralty of the commune of Meiganga. This first generation of elected Gbaya officials had quite weak educational qualifications (as indeed did President Ahidjo himself), having spent their early careers as primary schoolteachers, interpreters or other minor functionaries in the colonial administration or Christian missions.

The most prominent of this early group of modern Gbaya elite was Ninga Abraham Songo, a Protestant mission-educated native of Dir, a village in the western part of the Mbere Department that was the site of one of the early mission stations. After an initial period of employment as an auxiliary teacher in government primary schools, he was elected to the Cameroon

National Assembly as the first deputy for the Meiganga *Arrondissement*. In 1974, he was chosen as president of the Adamaoua Departmental Section (covering the *arrondissements* and districts of Meiganga, Ngaoundere, Banyo, Tignere, Mbe and Tibati) of the Cameroon National Union (UNC), then the sole national political party. This appointment coincided with his decision to convert to Islam, a step which caused a furore in Meiganga. Gbaya Christians angrily claimed that Songo had been bribed to convert by the reward of the political party post, and their outrage was heightened when certain local Fulbe ostentatiously attempted to distribute kola nuts to them in a (taunting) celebration of Songo's Islamic baptism. Songo remained in these posts until the Biya-Ahidjo conflict in the early 1980s and the transformation of the UNC into Biya's new national party, the RDPC, when he retired under a political cloud due to his overly close association with the Ahidjo regime. In the dying days of the RDPC one-party state period, his political career gained a new lease of life when he was elected as mayor of Meiganga, having rallied to the Biya regime. However, his political reputation has been compromised once again during the rise of multi-partyism in the 1990s, as a result of recriminations in the aftermath of the communal violence of 1991 and 1992 in Meiganga.

The up-and-down career of Abraham (now Ibrahim) Songo illustrates clearly the conflicting pressures experienced by Gbaya political elites in the early post-colonial period. In order to gain access to significant power in the national or even the regional arena, they have had to forge alliances with the dominant political forces within the Cameroon state. For most of the post-colonial period, this implied a close association with Fulbe and Fulbeising northern elite circles – too close for the taste of most Gbaya. On the other hand (and quite ironically given the Gbaya resentment of the longstanding Fulbe political domination within the north), these alliances of convenience placed the Gbaya in the '*nordist*' camp, at least as seen by supporters of the Biya regime, at the time of the attempted coup in 1984.

THE CHANGING CHARACTER OF GBAYA ETHNIC IDENTITY

While Gbaya ethnic consciousness can neither be said to be the invention of colonial administrators nor of anthropologists, *pace* Amselle (1990), the preceding sections have documented the substantial historical transformations of this identity from the pre-colonial period to the present. In the mid-nineteenth century, the Gbaya ethnic label, although sometimes employed in quite a broad sense, was more frequently applied to localised political formations as part of a sub-ethnic or 'dialect tribe' appellation. A more expanded Gbaya ethnic consciousness was reinforced by the effects of contacts with the Fulbe states of Adamawa, whose system of differential incorporation based on Islamic legal precepts encouraged the development of a form of ethnically based indirect rule among peripheral pagan groups like the Gbaya.

During the half-century of French colonial rule, especially in the last few decades when colonial administrative surveillance in the Meiganga *Arrondissement* had become more intensive, ethnically based differential incorporation ensured that Gbaya ethnic identity was a prominent issue in most domains of their public life. At the same time, the demarcation of colonial state and regional boundaries tended to differentiate and focus Gbaya identity formation within the different administrative units in which they now lived. Against this, it can be argued (as most Gbaya now do) that the Karnu Rebellion constituted an active attempt at resistance through the mobilisation of a pan-Gbaya ethnic consciousness, although doubts may be cast on whether participants actually conceived of their actions in quite such expansive terms at the time.

As the last decades of colonialism gave way to the post-colonial period, Gbaya ethnic identity construction became progressively more bound up in relations with the modern state. Competition for the many resources that the Cameroon state could provide has often been the focus of inter-ethnic rivalries and, as we have seen, neither the Gbaya 'traditional' chiefs nor the weakly developed Gbaya elite have been able to offer much in the way of leadership or clientelist linkages for their people on the regional or national level. The Lutheran mission has functioned as an organisational base for Gbaya ethnic consciousness but its impact has been restricted primarily to the Mbere Department. Although numerous commentators have suggested that a principle of sharing the spoils according to 'ethnic dosage' has been a fundamental one in post-colonial state affairs, this principle has applied only to ethnic groups that have been able to make their presence felt on the national stage. The Gbaya, who have remained weakly articulated with the political centre, 'encapsulated' by their ethnic boundaries and the logic of their cultural system, have been largely ignored. Alternatively, they have been forced to forge unpalatable alliances with Fulbe political elites or to shift ethnic allegiances altogether through Fulbeisation.

THE MBORORO ETHNIC CATEGORY: DISTINCTION AND EXCLUSION?

The Mbororo ethnic category occupies an interesting structural position within the larger society of Adamawa. Fulfulde speakers, who are often cited as a reservoir of Fulani linguistic and cultural traditions, the Mbororo are at the same time looked down upon by many Fulbe for their modes of customary behaviour, which are judged to be excessively rustic[1] and, more importantly, frequently un-Islamic. Although Mbororo herds are the economic base on which is built the reputation of much of Adamawa as a rich pastoral zone, most Mbororo still display a materially impoverished lifestyle and have not been able to utilise their cattle wealth to establish a position of political dominance within the region. In several respects, of course, such a structurally peripheral position is typical of many pastoral nomads, whose seasonal and longer term patterns of mobility are neither appreciated nor really understood by more sedentary people – including modern state officials. The structural opposition between Fulbe and Mbororo has deep historical roots and yet might seem surprising in view of the fact that both groups draw such a strong distinction between themselves, as Fulani, and all the other surrounding peoples, who are collectively considered to be '*haaɓe*' (subject non-Fulani pagans).

In this chapter, I will examine the implications of the fact that although the Mbororo are often thought of by outsiders as a fully integrated segment of a larger and culturally quite uniform Fulani ethnic group, in truth these pastoral nomads stand in an ethnically segmented and often oppositional relation to the politically dominant, sedentary Fulbe of northern Cameroon.[2] As we shall see, not only does this create strong feelings of political marginalisation among the Cameroonian Mbororo but it also induces, in certain social settings, a process of emulation oriented toward certain aspects of the religiously prestigious Fulbe lifestyle. Paradoxically, the Mbororo, who may be considered from one perspective to be archetypically Fulani, are nonetheless subject under certain conditions to a process of Fulbeisation.

ETHNIC TERMINOLOGY AND MBORORO MIGRATORY GROUP STRUCTURE

Although up to this point I have been using the term 'Mbororo' to refer in an undifferentiated manner to the large and heterogeneous category of pastoral Fulani, it is appropriate now to introduce a more refined categorisation of Mbororo subgroups, as well as to clarify my usage of such terms as 'clan' and 'migratory group' in this context. As Dupire noted in her massive work *Organisation Sociale des Peul* (1970), a fundamental problem facing an ethnographer of the Mbororo is to portray the subtle interplay of group formation practices characteristic of this people. Descent, intermarriage, residential propinquity and patterns of leadership all combine as elements in the constitution of Mbororo local groups. Or, as Dupire (1994: 268, my translation) has recently expressed it, 'Agnatic, affinal and residential relationships mutually engender one another.'

And so, although shared patrilineal descent may appear at first glance to be the primary referent of the many 'clan' (*lenyol*) and 'sub-clan' (*suudu*) labels which Mbororo use to divide their social universe – Dabanko'en, Doga'en, Ringi Maggi'en, Bogoyanko'en, and so on – it is not difficult to demonstrate that neither are Mbororo clans socially cohesive and unified collectivities nor are the local groups to which these clan labels are applied constituted on the basis of descent alone. For example, I have encountered encampments of the Bogoyanko'en *lenyol* in several widely spaced localities – near Zaria and near Yola in Nigeria as well as in the Mbere Department of Cameroon. These fractions drawn from the same clan had never encountered each other in their lifetimes, had no idea of each other's whereabouts, differed substantially in modes of dress and other customs, and obviously did not constitute a corporately organised group. As also emerges from this example, an Mbororo clan as a whole is not a culturally uniform unit, since the different fractions of a single clan are likely to have experienced quite different cultural influences and transformations in the course of their separate histories.

Furthermore, despite the common Mbororo practice of referring to local political groupings by clan names, careful examination of the social compositions of these 'clan' units typically reveals their memberships to be of heterogeneous 'descent group' origins. Dupire (1970: 304–11 *et seq.*; see also Dupire 1981) provides numerous such examples drawn from her fieldwork, but to take one of my own, the Ringi Maggi'en migratory group centred around Djohong in 1973 included membership drawn from the Bogoyanko'en, Akosanko'en, Sajanko'en, and Balewanko'en clans, in addition to the Ringi Maggi'en themselves. At that time, these segments of different clan origins were incorporated to different degrees within the political formation dominated by the Ringi Maggi'en clan fraction, according to the length of time they had been associated with it. The Bogoyanko'en, the most recently attached, paid taxes through a Ringi Maggi'en *ardo* (leader) but had not intermarried with them. The Akosanko'en were more fully integrated with the Ringi Maggi'en through intermarriage, but it was still commonly recognised that they were a group that had 'entered' (become incorporated in), as the Mbororo say, the Ringi Maggi'en. The other two clan segments were treated as fully integrated sub-clans of the Ringi Maggi'en, and my informants were in some doubt over the notion that they had 'entered' the Ringi Maggi'en at an unknown date in the past. Typically, such elements of differing descent are drawn together during the course of their pastoral movements, as their migratory routes happen to parallel each other over several seasons, and they may join the following of a single Mbororo *ardo* as they find that their political and pastoral interests coincide.

As Dupire has demonstrated, intermarriage plays an especially significant role in the fusion of such disparate social elements into a more cohesive group. Clan endogamy is highly valued by all Mbororo groups, but new social elements may be progressively incorporated into a local political formation by intermarriage. Although initially defined as clan exogamy, further intermarriage will lead in time to the progressive redefinition of the boundaries of the preferentially, endogamous group and the in-marrying segment will come to be seen as a sub-clan of the larger clan grouping (Dupire 1970: 304; see also Conte 1983: 192–5). To highlight these points, Dupire (1970: 224–5, 241–4, 576) has chosen to discuss Mbororo local group formation in terms of the concepts of 'endo-exogamy' and 'migratory group'. She emphasises thereby that these putatively endogamous local groups, although identified by 'clan' names, are formed by a complex process of fusion, through intermarriage, of social units of different putatively descent-based origins into locally collaborating politico-cultural entities, during the course of their concurrent migrations. Dupire has also described how the development of these local political formations is often linked with strategies through which Mbororo groups seek to exercise dominance over a zone of favourable grazing or other valued resources. This has been the case with the Ringi Maggi'en around Djohong, who progressively asserted their dominance in this part of the Mbere region from the 1940s onward.

Above the clan level, Mbororo recognise several broad groupings of clans, based on perceptions of presumed distant common descent, common history and/or cultural uniformity which carry what are, in effect, sub-ethnic group labels that are widely used in daily parlance. Thus, many of the migratory groups that were involved in the Lompta episode described in Chapter 2, and which subsequently moved to inhabit what is the Mbere Department today, form part of the grouping known as *Jafun*. This is an Mbororo sub-ethnic grouping whose constituent clan fractions display certain cultural uniformities which are said to date from a long period of common residence, beginning at least several centuries ago in an area around Kano in Nigeria and continuing along their migratory route with lengthy periods of residence in Bauchi and Yola. Among these common cultural practices are the keeping of the large, long-horned, red zebu cattle (*bodeeji*), the competitive baton-beating contests among young men (known as *soro*) associated with a particular set of marital customs between linked clans, and a distinctive form of the Mbororo infant naming ceremony (*indeeri*) involving the plunging of the child into the rumen of a newly slaughtered cow.[3] Other Mbororo sub-ethnic groupings of Adamawa, certain details of whose cultural practices contrast with those of the Jafun, include the *Wodaaɓe* (so well known from the works of Dupire and Stenning), the *Daneeji'en*, and the *Ba'en*.

As a result of their early arrival in Adamawa, compared with that of other Mbororo groupings, and their close association with the Fulbe states that dominated this region, the Jafun and other linked clan groupings have been influenced to a significant degree by the more orthodox Islamic values of the Fulbe. More than any other Mbororo group living in Adamawa today, the Jafun have tended to change their cultural practices towards this behavioural model; in other words, they have tended to Fulbeise.[4] For example, quite early after their arrival in Cameroon, they gave up the baton-beating contests of the *soro*, reportedly in response to Ardo Idje's strictures against this practice as being un-Islamic (see Chapter 2). Today it is only the oldest Jafun men who can proudly point to the large scars on their chests as evidence that they underwent this test of manhood.

The early arrival of the Jafun clans in Adamawa gave them advantages in the political domain, as we have seen in Chapter 2 in relation to their dominance at Lompta, but it did not mark the end of Mbororo migration into this region. Mbororo clans of various groups with differing cultural and historical origins have continued to seek out the excellent pastures of the Adamawa plateau right up to the present day.[5] Especially during the decades of the 1950s and 1960s, for example, large numbers of Mbororo arrived in the Mbere Department from the area around Jos in Nigeria, bringing with them the small, white, short-horned zebu cattle, known as *daneeji*, that are popular in that region. These new arrivals differed markedly in dress and dialect from the longer established Mbororo in Cameroon, having lived for many years in close proximity to Hausa peoples from whom they adopted many cultural influences. The longer-established Jafun of Adamawa called these new arrivals '*Aku'en*', a slightly mocking ethnic label derived from their usual greeting, and tend to view the Aku as rustics in comparison to themselves (see Dognin 1981: 148). In response, these newly arrived Aku groups labelled the longer resident, more Fulbeised Mbororo as '*Jafun'en*', including within that term a number of clan fractions that do not in fact claim Jafun descent origins. We therefore have two different meanings for the sub-ethnic label 'Jafun' in common use within the Mbere Department today – Jafun in its broad sense, which refers to long-resident, Fulbeised Mbororo of diverse origins versus Jafun in its narrow sense, which refers to those clans claiming a common Jafun descent.

JAFUN POLITICAL LEADERSHIP IN THE MBERE DEPARTMENT

As we have seen in Chapter 2, the Jafun clans of the Mbere Department have become more sedentarised over the course of the twentieth century. During the long eight-month wet season, Jafun families live in fixed cattle camps on sites to which they return over successive years following their dry season transhumance. Senior Jafun men and their close families may live in these camps all year round, sending most of their herds on the southward transhumance in the care of their sons and paid herdsmen. Some of these Jafun settlements were originally established on land that had been farmed by their slaves; towns such as Fada and Ngaouwi, which today house ethnically heterogeneous populations under the leadership of Fulbeised Jafun *ardo'en*, owe their origins to this process.

Aside from the fact that the existence of such a settled village focus obviates the necessity of aged Mbororo following the herds on transhumance, while offering the opportunity for an involvement in agricultural production through the employment of hired or servile labour, this sedentarisation also has certain political advantages. Although Gbaya canton chiefs continue to be recognised by the Cameroon government as the *chefs de terre* in the Mbere Department, the sedentarised *ardo'en* of the Mbere upland zone have enjoyed some degree of success in pressing their claims for parallel and equal political status. Within the last few years for example, Ardo Laabi, the very influential Jafun leader at the town of Ngaouwi, has finally succeeded in his long struggle to gain recognition for his town as a district independent of the Djohong *arrondissement* and the Gbaya canton chief located there. In addition, the fact of their permanent settlement in the Mbere area has given these Jafun *ardo'en* and their followers privileged access to some of the more favourable grazing lands of this excellent pastoral region. On the other hand, sedentarisation has also exposed these Jafun to substantial pressures to Fulbeise, a phenomenon that I will be discussing in more detail later.

As explained above, it is within the political field of the migratory group that competition for Mbororo political leadership is played out. As Dupire emphasised (1970: 516–7), a migratory group is seldom unified under the leadership of a single *ardo* but is normally divided into several '*fractions politiques*' or followings of competing leaders. There are no formalised principles of succession to the position of *ardo*, nor are there a fixed number of *ardo* offices to be filled. As Dupire explained (1970: 516, my translation and my parentheses):

It is in the image of their cattle that the eastern nomads conceive of the organisation of their political groups: the *ardo* [a term which derives from the verb *arda* – to be at the head] places himself at the head of his group [the members of which are termed *tokkuɓe*, from the verb *tokka* – to follow] just like the lead cow of the herd . . . When, after a long migration, the enlarged human herd at last reaches the security of a new grazing area, other herd leaders present themselves.

In fact, this pastoral metaphor glosses over the often keen competition between brothers, uncles or cousins to constitute a following and to be recognised as an *ardo*.

The leadership capacities of an aspirant to the position of *ardo* are judged by his potential followers according to a variety of criteria, many of which are subsumed under the general notion of *pulaaku* – virtuous and intelligent behaviour according to the 'Fulani way'. Although Mbororo groups now living in the Mbere Department no longer recognise a guardian of *pulaaku* as a separate office (cf. Stenning 1959: 200–2 or Kirk-Greene 1986), the emphasis on the need for proper observance of this behavioural code has not diminished, and *ardo'en* are expected to provide guidance in this regard – both in their personal conduct and in settling disputes among followers.

More specifically, an *ardo* should ideally enjoy a reputation for substantial knowledge of animal husbandry, including control of the technical and magical knowledge which is felt to contribute to herding success. An *ardo*'s large, well-conditioned herd is concrete evidence of such pastoral prowess and is also of great use as the basis for the generosity which leaders are expected to display. It is commonly the case that famous *ardo'en*, having owned many cattle in their middle age, use up all their cattle wealth in making gifts to their followers, or to government officials with whom they seek to curry favour, and end their days as any other aged man – dependent on their sons for sustenance (see Stenning 1958: 98–9).

On the subject of cattle, it is appropriate to open a parenthesis here and discuss further the question of the importance of cattle breeds in demarcating sub-ethnic categories among the Mbororo. Jean Boutrais has noted, in several publications (1978; 1983; 1986; 1988) concerning changing pastoral practices in Cameroon and adjacent areas of the Central African Republic, a tendency for Mbororo groups to modify the breed composition of their cattle herds as they become more sedentarised. He has argued with particular reference to the Jafun of Adamawa that their distinctive long-horned *bodeeji* cattle have been replaced almost entirely by crossbred stock and/or by the *gudaali* cattle breed of the sedentary Fulani – in keeping with the greater sedentarisation of Jafun groups in Adamaoua in comparison with, for example, the more recently arrived 'Aku' Mbororo groups. Thus, Boutrais (1978: 52, my translation) writes:

Since the Aku herdsmen are less involved in sedentarisation than the

Jafun, they remain more faithful to their characteristic cattle breed –
the short-horned white zebu known as *daneeji*. In contrast, one no
longer encounters pure *Mbodeeji* [*sic*] cattle except on the heights of
Tchabbal Mbabo.

During a visit to the field in 1987, therefore, I was interested to try to verify
this claim. In general, while I found it to be true in broad outline that
increasing sedentarisation has encouraged the Jafun to incorporate *gudaali*,
and crossbred cattle to a lesser extent, into their herds, Boutrais's statement
above exaggerates the extent of this tendency. Thus, according to a cattle
sample census (N = 350 cattle) carried out in 1985–6 by government veterinarians, the cattle population in the Mbere Department contained 44 per
cent of the *gudaali* breed, 20 per cent *bodeeji*, 19 per cent *daneeji*, 11 per
cent *gudaali* x *bodeeji* crossbred, and 3 per cent *bodeeji* x *daneeji*.[6]

Moreover, looking at the question of cattle breed preferences more closely,
I discovered a further socially significant process at work. I found that some
senior, politically aspiring Jafun men were actually keeping two separate
herds – one composed of *gudaali* and/or crossbred cattle and the other of
pure-bred *bodeeji* stock. When questioned, these men acknowledged that
the *gudaali* and crossbred cattle are better suited to the more sedentary
lifestyle they live today. The *gudaali* in particular subsist better on the
overgrazed pastures around the permanent Jafun wet season camps and give
better yields of both milk and meat. However, these Jafun leaders said that,
out of pride and concern for their reputations, they would always keep a
separate herd of *bodeeji* stock, despite the greater problems posed by the
need for longer transhumances and lower economic yields, since this breed
is so closely linked with their ethnic identity as Jafun.[7] One Jafun *ardo* I
questioned, for example, stated that a Jafun would be ashamed to be thought
to have left behind his *pulaaku* to such an extent as to have totally changed
his cattle breed.

Excellence in cattle husbandry and similar evidences of leadership capacity
have formed the basis of recognition of Mbororo *ardo'en* for many generations,
but of great importance too has been a leader's ability to relate effectively to
the state administrations within whose territories the Mbororo live. This
was true in pre-colonial times in relation to the Muslim states of Adamawa
as well as in colonial times in relation to the colonial powers and the associated
native authorities, and it still remains true today with regard to the independent state of Cameroon. The principal concern during much of this period
has been the question of cattle tax and the *ardo*'s ability to protect his
followers from excessive tax demands. Indeed, during the latter part of the
colonial period and on up to the present, the collection of government head
tax and cattle tax and the official government recognition of *ardo'en* have
become closely intertwined in the context of the government's attempts to

administer the Mbororo separately from the other populations of the Mbere Department.

As explained in Chapter 2, the core of this separate administrative system is the so-called *rôle supplémentaire* (or *supplétif*) – a separate census and taxation roll designed for mobile or transient populations. Whereas settled agricultural populations like the Gbaya are annually censused and head-taxed, village by village, on the *'rôle primitif'* using their village and canton chiefs as tax collectors, mobile populations such as Mbororo herders and itinerant, non-Gbaya traders pay their taxes directly to the sub-prefecture where they are recorded on a separate census roll – the *rôle supplémentaire*. The French colonial administration was particularly wont to justify these arrangements as a veterinary measure to segregate Fulbe and Mbororo herds, although such ethnically segregated taxation procedures were in fact general throughout the north.[8] After independence in 1960, the Cameroon government has maintained this same structure, although in view of the provision of the Cameroon national constitution which prohibits any recognition of 'tribal' divisions in the structures of government, the fact of this continued ethnic segregation in local administrative practice is heavily glossed over.

In order to facilitate the collection of tax among the Mbororo, the sub-prefect appoints certain Mbororo *ardo'en* as designated tax collectors for their followings, who are required annually to deliver the head taxes and cattle taxes assessed on their group to the sub-prefecture. Not all *ardo'en* recognised by the Mbororo are recognised by the government as 'official' *ardo'en* (*ardo'en bariki* in local parlance, *bariki* being derived from the pidgin English word 'barrack' and referring to government buildings), and there is strong competition among *ardo'en* for such recognition. Aside from the mere cachet of the government title, *ardo'en* also value this appointment, despite the tiresome collection duties it entails, because it places them in the role of protector of their followers *vis-à-vis* the government. In this connection, they make every effort to curry favour with the tax assessors to minimise the taxes levied on themselves and their followers. In addition, should one of their followers fall on hard times or a young man be struggling to establish himself and his family as an independent herding unit, an *ardo* may well intervene and pay the man's taxes himself as a gesture of generosity and personal reputation building.

The annual tax census and assessment day in a populous Mbororo district, held during the wet season once the Mbororo have returned from transhumance, is usually enlivened by considerable political intrigue, as Mbororo vie for favourable tax assessments and perhaps for eventual recognition by the government as *ardo'en bariki*. The assessor and his assistants set up a desk in the open air in front of the chief's compound in one of the Gbaya canton chieftaincy centres or in an important market village, and senior Mbororo men from the surrounding countryside descend on the village *en masse*. An *ardo* may arrive followed by a younger man dragging a recalcitrant ram as a 'gift' for the tax assessor. More covert strategies, one of which is discussed in Chapter 6 in the case of Al Hajji Maudo, may entail even more substantial 'gifts' of cattle to the tax assessor or even to the sub-prefect. Indeed, the temptations of bribery associated with the competition between Mbororo leaders, who often make liberal use of their cattle resources for such purposes, led to the downfall of at least one sub-prefect in the 1970s and contributed to the reputation of the Meiganga *Arrondissement*, during the Ahidjo years, as a prime posting for government officials seeking personal wealth. On the other hand, the higher echelons of the Cameroonian territorial administration are well aware of these temptations, and the 1980s witnessed various attempts to alter the modalities of Mbororo tax collection, as yet without much impact.

Despite the continuing quest for more influence within the Cameroon political system by senior Mbororo men, exemplified by their liberal use of cattle resources in the context of the *ardo'en bariki* competition, these efforts have not been notably successful, and Mbororo leaders frequently express feelings of frustration about their powerlessness and marginalisation. During my fieldwork in 1987, such sentiments were manifested in an especially clear manner when one prominent Jafun *ardo* went as far as to welcome gendarmes from the Central African Republic to his village, which is located on the Cameroon side of the international frontier, and to permit the raising of the Central African Republic flag there. According to gossip that circulated widely in the Mbere Department after this incident, the *ardo* had taken this step because he felt that Mbororo are given a greater political role in the CAR and had been offered the post of *chef supérieur* of the Mbororo living in the neighbouring district of the western CAR. True or false, this rumour was widely believed by Mbororo to whom I spoke, since it accorded so closely with their own opinions.

Trying to view the situation objectively, one might argue that the differential incorporation of the Mbororo population within the regional political structure of northern Cameroon has both advantages and disadvantages for those concerned. The separation of the Mbororo, under their own chiefs, from the rest of the multi-ethnic society in a region such as the Mbere Department permits them to remain relatively free of the administrative control of local *haaɓe* chiefs (that is, the Gbaya canton chiefs), but it has also established the conditions for substantial economic exploitation by officials of the regional territorial administration. One must also point out that the Cameroon government has tended to recognise the separate existence of the Mbororo ethnic category when it has suited them, as for example in the collection of taxes, but has refused to recognise this separate identity when it hasn't suited them – as for example when it rejected a Catholic missionary's plan for 'mobile schools' for transhumant Mbororo groups, on the grounds that the Cameroon constitution forbids ethnically segregated provision of facilities. Some progressive Mbororo *ardo'en* feel that their people suffer from a lack of educated Mbororo in key positions (since very few Mbororo youngsters go to school even today), and they also feel that their influence is limited with the regional government due to their ethnic compartmentalisation within the regional system. Ultimately, Mbororo interpret this as one more manifestation of what they see as the traditional relationship that has always obtained between nomadic and sedentary people.[9]

THE FULBEISATION OF THE JAFUN MBORORO

Leaving for a moment the question of the present relations of Mbororo groups with the Cameroon regional and national administration, I want to look in more detail at the cultural and political meanings of the fact that older, politically aspirant Mbororo men tend to establish permanent homes in sedentary agricultural settlements while the younger members of their migratory group remain mobile. We can easily see that the motivations for this are deeper than the mere fact that older men cope with the transhumant lifestyle less well than younger men. In any case, this sedentarisation normally takes place well before infirmity has set in. From Mbororo leaders' point of view, aspirations in the political domain, which imply a close liaison with sedentary Fulbe-dominated social milieux, necessitate changes in their life-style because, from the Fulbe point of view, numerous features of the mobile life of the Mbororo are considered to be conducive to immorality or to outright paganism (*yaafi*). And for the Fulbe, proper political leadership is necessarily carried out within a framework of Islamic values.

I have already briefly mentioned the Jafun stick-beating contests between groups of young men, known as *soro*, which are condemned by orthodox Muslims particularly because of the extensive use of magical practices to ensure physical protection in the contests and to attract the sexual favours of the female spectators.[10] My Jafun informants in the Mbere Department recounted that the *soro* was banned by Ardo Idje in the 1920s after their period of residence at Lompta (described in Chapter 2) – an interesting tradition in view of Idje's own evident tendencies toward sedentarisation and Fulbeisation in the latter part of his political career in the Ubangi-Shari (see Dupire 1970: 243–4). On the other hand, Jafun groups who have been less subject to Fulbe power, such as those presently resident in the Benue river valley near Garoua, still practise the *soro* and are, in general, less Fulbeised in their culture (see Bocquené 1986: 357).

Another prominent source of Mbororo immorality, in the Fulbe view, is the great freedom of movement and association enjoyed by Mbororo women, both married and unmarried. This occurs most frequently in the context of the Mbororo women's daily milk-marketing activities when they visit, usually unescorted by their men, the villages and markets of neighbouring cultivating peoples. Indeed, Mbororo gender roles and marital practices in general are anathema to orthodox Fulbe Muslims, who consider the long-drawn-out process of Mbororo first marriage (*koobgal* – to be discussed more fully in a moment) to be immoral. In a number of respects, then, sedentarisation offers senior Mbororo men the opportunity to conduct their lives in a more orthodox Islamic manner.

Thus, from the late 1960s onward, many senior Jafun men living along the Djohong road began exerting pressure on their wives and daughters to give up the selling of milk in the villages of neighbouring farmers. They also progressively transformed the age and sex structures of their cattle herds from a milking herd structure to one oriented more toward beef production, primarily by keeping a larger proportion of steers.[11] The starch staples for the family diet would henceforth be purchased in bulk for cash derived from cattle sales. A parallel tendency has not been observable, however, among the more recently arrived Aku Mbororo, whose daily subsistence continues to be derived from exchanges of milk products for agricultural products by the women of the household.

These divergent orientations toward Fulbe models of a proper mode of Muslim life, which have been visible within Mbororo societies inhabiting Adamawa at least since the time of Ardo Idje, continue to provoke active debate among the Mbororo of the Mbere Department today (compare Stenning 1959: 229 *et passim* and Bocquené 1986: 356–7). And it is in this context that the stories of Ardo Idje serve as legitimation for the progressive Fulbeisation of the Jafun. The major themes of this history as recounted by Mbororo today focus on Idje's cleverness as a leader and his heroic resistance to Fulbe domination, as well as his suppression of quintessentially Jafun customs such as the *soro*. From the Jafun Mbororo perspective, the Idje story is iconic of the possibility of a more orthodox adherence to Islam without the need to subordinate themselves to Fulbe power or to lose their Jafun identity. Just as the Gbaya now tell the story of Karnu in ways that contribute to a modern (re)construction of Gbaya identity, so too has the Idje story become an ethnically constitutive history for the Jafun.[12]

In view of the emphasis on Islam in my discussion of the process of Fulbeisation, one might well ask, 'Why bother with coining a separate term – "Fulbeisation" – for what could simply be called "Islamisation"?' My answer to this question is that we are dealing here with two contrasting but intertwined cultural logics – the one Islam and the other *pulaaku* – that co-exist within the process of Fulbeisation (cf. Mohammadou 1969: 73–80). According to the discourse of Islam, there is a single standard of moral and religious comportment which, if adhered to, makes all Muslims, be they Fulani or others, equal in the sight of Allah. *Pulaaku*, on the other hand, is an ideology of racial and cultural distinctiveness and superiority that ranks the Fulani above all other ethnic groups. But within the practice of *pulaaku* in daily life, as we have already explained, different Fulani groups are wont to claim that *their* modes of behaviour are the purest version of the 'Fulani way' (*laawol pulaaku*). Thus while Jafun elders may wish, primarily for political reasons, to lead a more Islamically orthodox life, they are not prepared to accept that the settled Fulbe adhere to a superior version of *pulaaku*.

Within the context of Fulani society, these two cultural logics – one exclusivist, the other inclusivist – have been intimately interacting for centuries. At the time of the *jihad*, as Last has noted on the basis of a study of the contemporary manuscript sources (Last 1989: 6; see also Burnham and Last 1994), Islamic reformers like Usman dan Fodio (Shehu Usumanu) attempted to downplay the discourse of Fulani distinctiveness in favour of arguments that all good Muslims should be considered as a single social whole, undivided by distinctions of ethnicity, or servile versus free status. And yet, as the history of the Fulbe states of Adamawa clearly demonstrates, the culturally hierarchical discourse of *pulaaku* remained strong – as it still does today.

The co-existence of these two cultural logics, within the complex social process which I have labelled 'Fulbeisation', continues to generate apparently contradictory tendencies in Mbororo society. On the one hand, Mbororo continue to express disdain for the sedentary Fulbe because of their loss of *pulaaku* – labelling them with the pejorative term '*huya'en*'.[13] As Issa and Labatut write (1974: 61, my translation):

> if it is true that this cultural wisdom, [i.e. *pulaaku*] is, above all, the basis of Fulani social identity, one can understand that the Fulbe, who are sedentarised and strongly Islamised, have lost much of their Fulaniness – especially those living in towns. *Doovi'el ngalaa pulaaku* – sedentary people do not have *pulaaku*, as the nomads often say.

On the other hand, as we have seen, many of the Jafun who have long been resident in the Mbere Department strive to emulate the Islamically more orthodox Fulbe ways and to gain closer links thereby with Fulbe-dominated centres of power.

Such 'Fulbeised' behaviour on the part of senior Jafun men may place them in an ambivalent position with regard to their juniors, their political followers. These junior men, who are nearer the start of their pastoral careers and who are likely to have fewer cattle than their elders, are interested in expanding their herds as rapidly as possible and in living a more mobile lifestyle, which they feel is more conducive to the health and reproductive increase of their cattle. They are also liable to attempt to structure their herds with a view more to milk production than to meat production, looking more favourably upon their wives and daughters continuing to trade dairy products for grain and other agricultural foods. Such milk sales can provide a significant proportion of food for family meals and thereby reduce the number of cattle a herdsman will need to sell for his family's subsistence. In these respects at least, if not always in others, some junior men may be committed to a more 'traditional' mode of pastoral life, which they conceptualise as proper adherence to *pulaaku*, in contrast to the Fulbeised behaviour of their leaders. Mbororo elders who have already attained affluence in cattle can afford to be open-handed with their wealth but for younger Mbororo men, a patient and frugal approach to cattle husbandry is the only route to economic success open to them, given their lack of western education or familiarity with other modes of livelihood.

While it is recognised that certain advantages may accrue to an *ardo*'s following from his pursuit of closer links with government circles, junior men are likely to judge that these benefits do not outweigh the losses the group may suffer resulting from reduced pastoral mobility, more frequent cattle sales and the like. And in more extreme cases, younger Mbororo men may strongly resent what they judge to be their *ardo*'s excessive vanity and profligacy, when for example he takes a full complement of four wives as an additional means of enhancing his prestige. (Such a case will be discussed in some detail in Chapter 6.) It is frequently on issues such as these that junior Mbororo men decide to secede from the following (*tokkal*) of one leader in order to join that of another. An Mbororo *ardo* finds himself, therefore, in an ambiguous position. His practice of orthodox Islam, with its related 'Fulbeised' lifestyle, leads to closer relations with influential Fulbe political circles and permits a degree of control over favoured grazing lands through sedentarisation, whilst support of 'traditional' standards of Mbororo *pulaaku* ensures the respect and continued political adherence of his juniors in the context of a more mobile lifestyle.

I do not wish, however, to overdraw this contrast in pastoral orientations between elders and juniors in the present-day society of the Mbere Department. Other social dynamics are also at work. Over the last few decades, it has been noticeable that some young Jafun men, particularly those who have inherited large cattle herds from their fathers (Mbororo men normally inherit from their fathers pre-mortem, at the time of their first marriage), are much attracted by a sedentary life. Living in town and leaving their cattle in the care of paid herdsmen, they may be tempted to disperse their wealth in profligate ways such as alcohol, drugs, gambling and prostitutes – a style of life that they consider 'modern'. Pursued to its logical conclusion, such a way of life leads to a total break with the Mbororo ethnic category and absorption into urban Fulbe society. Of course, their sedentarised elders, despite their own positive orientation to settled Fulbe society, do not approve of such ways since they are so visibly in conflict with the Islamic values that the elders are seeking to espouse. It is in describing such counterposed tendencies currently present in Mbororo society that I find it useful to have available both terms – 'Fulbeisation' and 'Islamisation'.

PLATE 1: The women's produce market in Meiganga, the scene of 1991 violence.

PLATE 2: Mainstreet Meiganga with passenger buses loading.

PLATE 3: Young Mbororo men – the modern generation (in Gbaya village).

PLATE 4: Gbaya chief addresses villagers during a tour of his canton.

PLATE 5: Fulbe village along the Mbere River valley.

PLATE 6: Two Mbororo women pass the mid-day hours in a Gbaya village after marketing their dairy products.

PLATE 8: Jafun Mbororo woman.

PLATE 7: Fulbe *mallum*.

JAFUN MARRIAGE AND ETHNIC BOUNDARIES

In several senses, therefore, the generations of elders and juniors in Mbororo society stand in a structural opposition. It appears likely that this structural opposition is a longstanding one, as is evidenced by the existence of a system of named age classes, with associated customary behaviours like the *soro* baton contests of the *sukaaɓe* age class or the ritualised anti-social behaviour of the *kori'en* age class. (See Bocquené 1986 for extended descriptions of Mbororo age class behaviour.) And it is clearly not a matter of chance that, over the years, it has frequently been precisely those Mbororo customs practised by the junior age classes, such as the *soro* and the licentious behaviour of the *kori'en*, that have attracted the special disapproval of Fulbeised Mbororo leaders such as Ardo Idje. During the twentieth century, in the context of the progressive Fulbeisation of the Jafun of Adamawa, the particular cultural foci of the structural opposition between generations have been subject to change and, following the abolition of the *soro* and the licentious sexual behaviour of the *kori'en* known as *koraaku*, other points of inter-generational dispute have emerged. And yet, even in the present day, the modalities of this opposition remain closely related, I would argue, to the ongoing process of Fulbeisation of the Jafun ethnic category within the society of northern Cameroon.

To illustrate these points concerning the persistent inter-generational debate over the proper practice of *pulaaku*, while at the same time analysing further the boundary mechanisms which continue to maintain the Mbororo ethnic category as a discrete structural unit despite the Fulbeising tendency which we have noted, I will now discuss some data on Jafun marriage collected during my several periods of field research in the Mbere Department.

The classic ethnographic works on the Mbororo by authors such as Stenning (1958; 1959) and Dupire (1962; 1970) have laid great stress on the analysis of marriage as a phenomenon of central importance in establishing and maintaining the boundaries of the Mbororo ethnic category in general and of Mbororo migratory groups in particular. This focus on the institution of marriage in Mbororo society is certainly warranted, since in Mbororo eyes, proper marital practice is integral to the perpetuation of *pulaaku*, the Fulani way of life – having fundamental implications for the maintenance of racial purity, the formation of political groups, the constitution of independently viable households, and the socialisation of children. This is especially true of the complex set of customs relating to the first marriage, which is commonly referred to by ethnographers of the Mbororo as *koobgal* marriage after one of the principal steps in the traditional first-marriage process.

Koobgal marriage is preferentially endogamous to the localised set of clan members living within a migratory group. Close cousin marriage is preferred, paradigmatically with the patrilateral parallel cousin, although in a clan in which endogamy has been practised at a high rate in previous generations, other forms of cousin marriage such as that with the matrilateral cross-cousin may be clan endogamous as well.

Mbororo informants cite a variety of interlinked rationales for their preference of clan endogamy:

1. The risk of dilution of *pulaaku* arising from clan exogamy;
2. the preservation of the racial purity of the clan;
3. the ease of relations with 'in-laws' who are also consanguineal relatives;
4. the retention of the clan's cattle within the clan.

As already explained, these rationales are strongly linked within the Mbororo cultural logic of *pulaaku* to form a compelling ideology which defines race, language and culture as mutually causal and supportive (see note 8, Chapter 3).

As Stenning (1959: 56–7) explained:

> *Kooggal* [sic] marriage maintains and fortifies moral virtues, but also, though in a somewhat negative sense, conserves the physical type of the clan. The desirable physical qualities of a Fulani are a light colour ['red' in Fulfulde], slight bone-structure, straight hair, thin lips, and, above all, a long narrow nose. Members of some Wodaabe groups in which there has been a high degree of endogamy take pride in what is often their distinctive facial likeness, and in commenting upon it say: 'We are all of one stock' (*Min iriiri go'o*). But, in general, Fulani can no longer correlate these desirable physical traits with lines of descent. Then the association becomes curiously reversed so that a man or woman possessing these features is regarded as being more likely to possess the moral virtues of a Fulani. A Wodaabe proverb runs: *Raara kine nana gikku* – 'See the nose, understand the character'. By definition, *haabe*, or non-Fulani cannot possess these qualities, for they do not follow the Fulani way.

Informants from dominant Jafun clans in the Mbere Department with whom I worked (such as the Ringi Maggi'en living near the village of Djohong, for example) expressed the same sentiments as Stenning's Wodaabe informants, commenting particularly on the notable similarity of facial traits and build of the men of these highly endogamous clans (while glossing over the fact that several current members of the Ringi Maggi'en have non-Fulani slave ancestry).

When I first began my ethnographic research among the Jafun of the Mbere region in 1969, the migratory group among whom I worked was a highly endogamous unit and for the generation of appropriate age for first marriage among the dominant Ringi Maggi'en clan fraction of this migratory group, clan endogamy and *koobgal* marriage were practised at virtually a 100 per cent level. The steps in the *koobgal* marriage procedure as practised by the Ringi Maggi'en at this period were numerous and complex, stretching from birth to early adulthood, and I have described these at some length in an earlier paper (Burnham 1991; see also Bocquené 1986 for a similar description of Jafun marriage).

The first stage in this *koobgal* marriage, that of infant betrothal (*naŋgardu*), was still visible in 1968 among the Jafun of the Mbere Department in its influence on the marriages of young adults, aged about fifteen years and older, since most of them had been betrothed to their first spouses according to this custom. However, by the late 1960s, new infant betrothals had largely ceased as a result of Fulbeisation tendencies and opposition by younger Mboro, which I will discuss more fully in a moment. Following betrothal in infancy, *koobgal* marriage is characterised by a very long series of stages, with the husband not achieving full rights of co-residence and, by implication, exclusive sexual access to his wife until after the final stage of the process (known as *baŋtal*) following the weaning of the couple's first child. Indeed, it is the long duration of the Mboro marriage process, with the consequent delay in the establishment of sexual control of a husband over his spouse, that is the major cause for disapproval of *koobgal* marriage by more orthodox Fulbe Muslims. In Fulbe marriage, by contrast, there is an emphasis on the rapid establishment of the new household at marriage, on the virginity of the bride, and on the early control of the new wife by the husband.

By the late 1960s, the opposition between generations in Mboro society was particularly manifest in a strong resistance by the younger generation against the custom of infant betrothal, resulting from a desire on the part of the juniors for the exercise of marital choice unconstrained by adult political considerations. This opposition was most clearly expressed in a great upsurge in the custom of *deetawal*, a sort of marriage-by-capture – which apparently had been a much less frequent practice prior to the decade of the 1960s.

Deetawal, which can be termed an elopement, involves the suitor kidnapping his beloved, with her full compliance, from the encampment of her father in the dead of night. The suitor signals his honourable intention to marry the girl properly by bringing one of his cattle to the outskirts of the girl's camp on the night of the *deetawal* and slaughtering it there – to be found the next morning by the girl's father. Given the prevalence of the practice of infant betrothal and of *koobgal* marriage at this time, *deetawal* normally implied that the suitor was eloping with a girl who had already begun the long *koobgal* marriage procedure with another man, and *deetawal* would often provoke an acrimonious response both from the prospective husband of the girl as well as from her father. By 1969, *deetawal* had assumed the status of a fad; young men were vying to outdo each other in the audacity of their exploits, and young women were competing to enhance their reputations based on the number of times they had been solicited for elopement. A marital practice which had formerly been practised infrequently had assumed great prominence as a symbol of the desire for freedom on the part of the younger generation.

The practice of *deetawal* was disapproved of by senior, politically influential men since, viewed from an Islamic perspective, this practice was seen as highly immoral and therefore opposed to the Fulbeising tendencies of the Mbororo elders.[14] Opposition of the elders progressively hardened, and the Fulbe imam in his Friday sermons at the Djohong mosque often touched on this question, saying that those who did such things would go to hell and that even those who ate meat killed on such an occasion risked this fate. By 1973, when I returned to Djohong for more field research, it was evident that the concerted efforts of Jafun elders had managed to put a stop to *deetawal* marriages. For example, in a highly symbolic and very public act, one of the senior elders, Al Hajji Dandi, even sold the meat from a returned *deetawal* cow killed by his son to neighbouring *haaɓe* villagers rather than permitting his family to consume it.

Although the custom of *deetawal* was therefore virtually abolished among the Ringi Maggi'en by the mid-1970s, it was also the case that the main cause of *deetawal* had disappeared by this time since both the custom of *naŋgardu*, infant betrothal, and of *koobgal*, child marriage, had been given up as well. The younger generation had won the battle with their elders for more control over the choice of their marital partners. It is interesting to note, however, that the decline of *naŋgardu* and *koobgal* during this period did not affect the tendency toward clan endogamy, which remained very high for first marriages among the Ringi Maggi'en.

A first marriage among the Ringi Maggi'en since the 1980s, as I have observed it during recent field visits, now commences only when both spouses have passed the age of puberty. After a relatively short preliminary phase in which the future partners make known their mutual desires to be married, the *teegal* ceremony is held, in which the marriage is formalised before a *mallum* by witnesses acting for the couple. However, after this ceremony, the Mbororo first-marriage process continues much as before, with a succession of further ceremonies and feasts stretching over several years until the new couple finally takes up permanent co-residence after the weaning of their first child. Nonetheless, in the eyes of the Jafun at least, there has, since the 1970s, been a progressively greater emphasis on the Islamic component of the marriage procedure, along with a concomitant rapid expansion in the amount of brideprice (*rubu*) paid. In 1973, the *rubu* paid by Ringi Maggi'en husbands stood at 20,000 CFA, whereas in 1986, *rubu* had reached the 300–400,000 CFA level.

The pattern of these changes in Ringi Maggi'en marriage over the past two decades corresponds very closely with the predictions made by Marguerite Dupire in her book *L'Organisation Sociale des Peul* (1970: 26 *et passim*) regarding the effects of sedentarisation and Islamisation on the marriage practices of pastoral Fulani. Dupire has analysed the marriage prestations of the pastoral Fulani as falling into four categories, the first three furnished by the husband's group and the fourth furnished by the wife's group:

1. Cattle (*kirsol*) killed and eaten by the two families;
2. cattle and other goods 'attached' to the wife and her eventual offspring;
3. gifts by the groom's family to the bride's family;
4. gifts from the bride's family to the groom's family and to the bride herself in the form of a dowry.

Dupire argues that the first two types of prestation are more important among less Islamised, nomadic groups and that the first and the fourth types are reduced in importance with greater Islamisation and contact with sedentary groups. The second prestation changes its significance and the importance of the third increases with greater Islamisation and contact with sedentaries. Dupire says that among the Jafun and Wodaabe of Adamawa, the amount of cattle killed (*kirsol*) has tended to diminish and the third type of prestation has taken on the character of a brideprice (that is, the *rubu*). She argues that the 'dowry' has become Islamised in conception, and notes that all gifts, except a few to the wife, are paid back in the case of the dissolution of the marriage.

It is transformations in the procedures of Mbororo marriage such as these that form a central part of the process of Fulbeisation and which reflect the conscious attempt of Mbororo groups like the Jafun to model elements of their lifestyle more closely on the 'Islamised' behaviour of the politically dominant sedentary Fulbe. Objectively, then, there has been a progressive assimilation of Fulbe elements into Jafun marriage but, as of 1987 when I last worked among the Mbororo, Jafun marriage customs were still viewed as distinctively Jafun Mbororo, both by themselves and by the Fulbe.

One would be warranted to ask, in view of the disappearance of the *naŋgardu* and *koobgal* stages of Jafun marriage, in what sense is '*koobgal*' marriage truly central to Mbororo ethnic identity? In answer to this question, I would argue that the analyses of Stenning and Dupire have given pride of place to *koobgal* marriage because of the question of the viability of the pastoral domestic group, which is reliant upon the cattle endowment received in the course of *koobgal* marriage for the provision of adequate cattle resources to establish its independence as a newly created family unit. This is clearly a prerequisite for the perpetuation of the Mbororo mode of pastoral economy, which in turn remains central to Mbororo self-definition as a distinct ethnic unit.

In this regard it is important that, despite giving up the infant betrothal and child marriage elements of so-called *koobgal* marriage, the Jafun of the Mbere Department have retained the distinctively Mbororo custom of endowing the new couple at marriage with sufficient cattle for an independent livelihood – a practice which stands in significant contrast to the sedentary

Fulbe practice of inheritance of cattle by the younger generation after the death of their father. In addition to this, as Dupire has particularly emphasised, endogamy remains important for the definition and maintenance of the political boundaries of Mbororo migratory or clan groups; by extension, one can argue that high rates of endogamy are also central to the maintenance of the boundaries of the Mbororo ethnic group as a whole. The practice of preferentially endogamous marriage within the clan is also intimately linked, in Mbororo cultural discourse, with the notion of *pulaaku*, since it stands in clear contrast to the dilution of a clan's putative cultural and racial purity associated with exogamous marriage. Thus, ultimately, the concepts of culture and race are closely inter-related, according to the logic of *pulaaku*, within the Mbororo conceptualisation of endogamy.

It is important to re-emphasise in closing this section on Mbororo marriage that endogamy within the clan or migratory group is not a prescriptive rule. Under certain social conditions, for example when a segment of a different clan is in the process of 'entering' into a locally dominant migratory group, exogamous marriage is favoured – thus Dupire's coinage of the term endo-exogamy discussed above. However, the fact that marriage practices are utilised strategically in this way (cf. Bourdieu 1977: 38 *et seq.*) does not negate or confuse the abstract positive value of endogamous marriage for Mbororo actors, which is continuously reaffirmed as an exclusivist logic by the naturalising and self-evident ontological beliefs to which it is linked within the ideology of *pulaaku*.

MBORORO IDENTITY: THE CULTURAL LOGIC OF A PASTORAL LIFESTYLE

Mbororo informants believe that their distinctive way of life is constantly endangered by the encroaching influences of surrounding societies. There is always the possibility of losing the cattle herds which are the basis of mobile Mbororo lifeways, and an Mbororo who is forced to settle, to cultivate or to trade for a living, risks becoming a Fulbe. Settling in a sedentary village also exposes an Mbororo to the risk of marrying a non-Mbororo, an act that automatically condemns him to a sedentary existence, since only Mbororo girls are trained and willing to live the difficult nomadic life. As I have explained, the Mbororo view inter-marriage as a dilution of cultural as well as racial purity, since possession of Fulani racial traits is thought to entail commitment to *pulaaku*. As a cultural discourse, then, Mbororo *pulaaku* manifests two significant dimensions – an in-built logic of superiority *vis-à-vis* other groups and an inherent concern about the risk of straying from the true Fulani way via acculturation and/or inter-marriage with other groups.

Our discussion of the ongoing debate concerning marital practices among the Jafun of the Mbere Department has documented the impacts and inter-relations of: 1) the notion of *pulaaku*, defined as a moral code of conduct;

2) the mode of competition for political power among Mbororo leaders within northern Cameroon, especially as influenced by its linkage with the Fulbe and Cameroonian state systems; 3) the inter-generational conflicts between elders and juniors in Mbororo society; and 4) the influence of Islam, in the context of the Fulbeisation process, particularly upon Jafun elders. Out of this complex of processes substantial changes in Jafun culture have been generated. But neither has their commitment to *pulaaku*, as an abstract moral concept, nor the firmness of the boundary between the Jafun and the Fulbe ethnic categories, as defined by either group, been significantly affected (although other Mbororo resident in the Mbere Department, such as the Aku or Wodaabe, may well consider the Jafun to have virtually become Fulbe).

Thus, for example, although certain customs, such as the Jafun system of cattle marking, the *soro* contests, *deetawal* marriage, and itinerant milk selling by their women, have become identified as iconically anti-Islamic by Fulbeising Jafun and are therefore actively avoided or opposed by them, other customs which orthodox Fulbe Muslims also despise, such as the widespread use in Mbororo rituals of the leaves of the *barkehi* tree (*Piliostigma reticulatum*, cf. *Bauhinia reticulata*) or the plunging of infants into the rumen of a newly slaughtered cow during their naming ceremony, have not received such iconic recognition by the Jafun. Such 'unmarked' customs therefore continue to be positively valued by Fulbeising Jafun as integral to their *pulaaku*, rather than being avoided as 'paganism' (*yaafi*). Once again, these examples can serve to remind us that ethnic differences are not a function of an ethnographer's objective assessment of cultural difference but depend on the subjective political weightings given to selected cultural elements by the actors concerned.

In contrast to the Fulbe ethnic grouping which is highly assimilative, the Mbororo category is markedly exclusivist. Its strong ethnic boundary, legitimated and reinforced by the ideology of *pulaaku*, is maintained by a distinctive pastoral social ecology and by normatively endogamic group formation processes. At the same time, as we have seen, Mbororo culture can by no means be said to be unchanging, and the continued distinctiveness of the Mbororo ethnic category cannot therefore be due to the persistence of '*traditional*' Mbororo culture, understood in any simplistic sense. Analytically speaking, we can say that Mbororo ethnic identity persists at an abstract categorical level despite historical variation in cultural content. For the Mbororo themselves, *pulaaku* as a cultural logic argues for the continuing possibility and necessity of living a proper lifestyle governed by Mbororo traits of character and good breeding.

From the 1930s onward, when the Mbere Department was demarcated as a grazing zone reserved for the Mbororo, their cattle have generally thrived on the rich pastures of this area. The resultant heavy concentration of herders in this region has led to the overgrazing of certain areas and, over the last two decades, outbreaks of trypanosomiasis and other cattle diseases have caused herd losses and some Mbororo out-migration. But it is in the nature of Fulani pastoralism that herders must cope with substantial risks of environmental fluctuation, disease, and so forth. At any point in time, some pastoral herding units may become destitute and be forced, temporarily or permanently, to sedentarise, to take up agriculture, or to work for others as paid herdsmen. But the loss (or eventual re-entry) of some such herding units to the category does not affect the pastoral ideal, any more than does the decision by certain rich elders to sedentarise and pursue political or religious goals defined by surrounding societies. The ethnic category persists despite actors' movements over the boundary.

6

SITUATION, AGENCY AND STRUCTURE
IN INTER-ETHNIC RELATIONS

As explained in the introductory chapter, during the early months of my first stay in the Mbere Department my research was focused on an analysis of the Gbaya society of the region, although I soon found that many of the social situations I was observing were multi-ethnic in character. Moreover, many of these inter-ethnic interactions displayed substantial amounts of repetitive patterning, indicating various degrees of shared, and largely taken-for-granted, behavioural expectations on the part of the different ethnic groups involved. For my Gbaya ethnographic project, I needed to make a pragmatic assessment of the significance of these institutionalised inter-ethnic relations for the Gbaya and used criteria based on the patterns of flow of economic resources and the constitution of political and residential groupings to determine the extent to which these phenomena should be incorporated into my Gbaya monograph (Burnham 1980a).

But the nagging question remained concerning a more adequate character-isation of the society of the Mbere Department as a whole. Was I observing a social field in which ethnic identities constituted such persisting cleavages as to ensure that, for the foreseeable future, the various ethnic segments of Mbere Department society would remain differentiated and opposed, meeting mainly in the marketplace or in the courts? Or was the Mbere Department a locus of ethnic redefinition and/or assimilation where a more homogeneous 'northern Cameroonian' regional society was in the process of emerging? It seemed to me, then as now, that such issues were of crucial importance for the future development of northern Cameroon, and Cameroonian society more generally, and it has been with such thoughts in mind that I have pursued my subsequent ethnographic work.

In the preceding chapters, I have attempted to answer a basic set of inter-linked questions with reference to each of the three major ethnic categories that inhabit the Mbere Department: 1) what is the nature of their ethnic boundaries and how permeable or firm have they been over time? 2) what are the major reinforcing ideologies, ethnically constitutive histories, and self-validating cultural logics that define the social orientations of actors to ethnic difference? and 3) what are the major political, economic and religious processes affecting the status of these ethnic categories within the multi-ethnic society of Mbere Department and northern Cameroon? This mode of ethnographic description, while providing a convenient framework for the presentation of data, has probably had the effect of emphasising in the reader's mind the boundedness of these ethnic units, viewed as discrete settings of primary socialisation and cultural transmission. In this chapter, as a means of rethinking this conceptualisation, I wish to shift focus to a more trans-ethnic perspective and to examine more closely the significance of multi-ethnic social situations as normal features of the daily life of the inhabitants of the Mbere Department. At the same time, in order to highlight issues of individual agency and situationally negotiated social meanings in such multi-ethnic settings, I want to open this chapter with an episode from one of my early periods of fieldwork and see where it leads us.

A WEDDING CELEBRATION

The various Mbororo life-cycle ceremonies constitute one of the common multi-ethnic interactional settings in Mbere Department society. These take place during the wet season when these herders have returned from their dry season transhumance and are living sedentary lives in their permanent wet season encampments. These rituals include infant naming ceremonies, Koranic school 'graduations' and marriage celebrations.

In 1973, I was living in one of the larger Gbaya canton chieftaincy towns in the Mbere Department. Although the town's population was predominantly Gbaya, it was also the home of substantial minorities drawn from the Fulbe/Fulbeised ethnic category as well as 'Congo' labour migrants from the Central African Republic. In the bush surrounding the town, there were also many wet season encampments of Jafun and Aku Mbororo, and it was one of the Jafun leaders, *Ardo Al Hajji Maudo*, who was the host and the groom at the marriage celebration I attended. (I use the title 'Al Hajji' here, rather than the more correct 'Al Hajj', since this is the colloquial usage in the Mbere Department.)

Prior to this event, I had only met Ardo Maudo on a few occasions on and off since 1969, but it is in the nature of Mbororo life-cycle ceremonies that anyone living in the neighbourhood is free to attend without invitation. I knew Al Hajji Maudo largely by reputation as one of three Jafun *ardo'en* in the vicinity who were in active competition for followers, a relationship which is consolidated when an Mbororo herder agrees to remit his head-tax to the government through the hands of a particular *ardo* as intermediary. Although informally recognised as the leader of an Mbororo migratory group for several years, Al Hajji Maudo had only recently achieved government recognition of his status as *ardo bariki* thanks to a clever ruse two dry seasons earlier. While he and his followers were sojourning for a few months of the dry season in a southern district, he had managed to convince a government tax collector that his migratory group had moved permanently to this area and that they should be censused and taxed separately. When his group returned to the Mbere Department at the start of the next rains, he was able to present this independent status as an officially documented *fait accompli* to the tax collector from Meiganga, whose acquiescence was reportedly sealed by a gift of livestock.

Al Hajji Maudo had recently constructed a new compound, complete with entry hut and enclosed in a fence of straw matting in the Fulbe style, less than a kilometre beyond the outskirts of town. This had provoked much comment in the neighbourhood, since Mbororo did not normally locate their encampments so near to Gbaya villages where there was substantial risk of their cattle causing crop damage. In fact, Al Hajji Maudo also maintained another encampment in the bush some five kilometres away where he kept his cattle in the care of his adult sons and two paid herdsmen. His decision to construct a substantial compound adjacent to town was widely viewed as an attempt to ensure that he would be available to act as a middleman between the town and the sub-prefectural authorities, on the one hand, and local Mbororo on the other – thus positioning himself to attract more followers. His present marriage to a third wife was also widely interpreted in this light. She was a young and quite beautiful recent divorcee who had been raised in a rather urban lifestyle in a nearby town where her wealthy Jafun relations enjoyed local political prominence. Al Hajji Maudo's marriage to her was seen by many as an attempt at status enhancement through an ostentatious display of wealth. Indeed, the bridewealth (*rubu*) that Al Hajji Maudo had paid was rumoured to be substantial – very much in the Fulbe manner (as discussed in the previous chapter). At the same time, the bride was said to have a rather flighty disposition, which had been aggravated by excessive urban contact, and predictions were already being made that she would soon divorce Al Hajji Maudo unless she should happen to become pregnant.

When I arrived at Al Hajji Maudo's compound during the forenoon, preparations for the feast were well under way. The actual marriage ceremony, conducted by a Fulbe *mallum* before witnesses acting for the bride and groom in the Gbaya canton chief's entry hut, had already taken place in the morning, and the canton chief had received the gift of a hindquarter of beef from one of the cows killed for the marriage feast. And now, quite anomalously for the groom at an Mbororo marriage, Ardo Maudo was very much in evidence, welcoming the more prominent male guests to his compound and ensuring that they were comfortably seated in the socially appropriate grouping.

Indeed, the spatial segregation of the participants at the wedding feast according to gender, age and ethnic group was one of the immediately noticeable features of the gathering. Inside the compound fence, a group of middle-aged and older women were congregated, actively involved in cooking the rice, manioc porridge and offal stew for the guests. About a dozen women, mostly Gbaya with a few Fulbeised women, were doing the heavier work such as pounding manioc flour or stirring the porridge; the Mbororo women, close relatives of Al Hajji Maudo, were supervising the food preparation and distribution. Also inside the compound near the cooking fires were a few Gbaya women, sitting beside washbasins filled with manioc which they had brought for sale. The younger, marriageable Mbororo girls, dressed to the nines, were standing in groups near the opening in the back of the compound fence, chatting among themselves, glancing furtively at the Mbororo youths standing in the bush to the west and joining only occasionally in the work of food preparation if prevailed upon by their mothers.

Two large cows had been killed for the feast and their carcasses were lying on piles of leaves inside the compound fence to the west. One of the cows had been pregnant and the foetus had been discarded along the path where the arriving guests could not fail to notice it. 'An act of conspicuous consumption and waste?' I wondered as I arrived, but several informants I queried later disagreed on this point. Forty metres outside the compound to the southwest of the entry hut, a large fire was burning and there a group of men were at work, cutting the meat into long strips and hanging it on racks beside the fire for smoking and grilling. This work was supervised by two of the adult sons of Al Hajji Maudo, although the most skilled operations involved in cooking the meat were carried out by Al Hajji Garba, an older man who had been purchased as a slave by the Mbororo when he was a boy but who was now assimilated to Jafun status. The heaviest work of butchering and of carrying wood was performed by some Gbaya men, while the wood for the fire had been chopped the previous day by Gbaya and Congo hired labour.

Also outside the compound fence adjacent to the entry hut was a cluster of Fulbe merchants who had spread their wares – cloth and clothing, cheap jewellery, enamel dishes, sweets, cigarettes, kola nuts, and so on. Not far away, along the path leading to the entry hut, was a group of three Fulbe and Hausa praise singers, who loudly announced the arrival of all the senior male visitors with litanies of praise in hopes of receiving gifts. Al Hajji Maudo's name figured prominently in their praises too, of course, as they contemplated the gifts of expensive gowns he had promised them. The guests were seated in their appropriate locations both inside and outside the compound. Two of the houses within the compound were occupied by senior Mbororo and Fulbe women, while the third house was occupied by senior Gbaya male visitors. The entry hut to the compound was at first occupied by a group of rather boisterous Mbororo young men until, late in the day when a rain shower passed, they were chased outside by senior Mbororo men seeking shelter. Outside the compound to the southwest, not far from the bonfire, several sunshades had been erected and were occupied by different age groups of middle-aged and elderly Mbororo men, segregated according to criteria of male age-based deference which are such a strongly marked feature of Mbororo society. Numerous Mbororo children were also in attendance, dressed in their best clothes and cavorting between the different groups of Mbororo guests, who would chase them away in mock anger if they became bothersome. Non-Mbororo male guests, aside from the Gbaya notables who were provided with a separate house, were also grouped ethnically here and there near the bonfire – Gbaya, Congo and Fulbe. Groups of Gbaya and Congo children were in attendance, but their attention was devoted mainly to the festoons of grilling meat, which they eyed hungrily. Al Hajji Garba, the master cook, had armed himself with a stick which he used quite liberally to keep them at bay.

Also near the fire was the Islamic prayer ground, at which the Mbororo and Fulbe men who were present carried out the afternoon prayers as a group. None of the Gbaya elders present took part in these communal prayers, despite the fact that several were Muslims.

Well to the southwest of all these activities and partly screened by intervening bush was a group of gamblers who remained occupied with their card game throughout the day, scarcely stopping to eat. Most of them were young Mbororo men, although the organiser of the game was a non-Mbororo Fulbeised man of indeterminate origins. Although in other areas around Al Hajji Maudo's compound the smells of grilling meat and simmering stews were pervasive, standing near the card game, one could detect the acrid odour of *tabajeeji* (hemp) which, although illegal, is a common accompaniment of such pastimes. It was also noticeable that the language spoken during the game was a polyglot argot of pidgin French and vehicular Fulfulde (cf. my discussion of *kambariire* and *bilkiire* in Chapter 3), which contrasted markedly with the *fulfulde laamnde* spoken in the other Mbororo groupings.

The distribution of the food was the high point of the day for most of the other guests and provided an opportunity for the expression of social stereotypes by the different ethnic groupings represented. The senior men, Mbororo and Gbaya in their separate groups, were served first and Al Hajji Maudo, in keeping with Mbororo perceptions of the Gbaya as gluttons who fail to control their appetites in public, made elaborate and very visible efforts to see that the Gbaya elders were fed copiously. The large servings were duly appreciated by the Gbaya men, who had spent much of the afternoon discussing the considerable wealth that Al Hajji Maudo had expended for this marriage. The Mbororo men, on the other hand, ate sparingly as enjoined by *pulaaku*, laughing all the while at the way the little Mbororo children attempted to cram as much food into themselves as possible – an indication that they had not yet reached the age of social awareness. The ravenous appetites of the Gbaya children, however, were interpreted by the Mbororo not as being due to immaturity but as resulting from a culturally deficient upbringing.[1]

As already mentioned, the feast drew to a somewhat premature and dampened close for most participants because of an afternoon shower but for the Mbororo youth, the main event of the day was only starting. In the late afternoon, the sharp beating of an armpit drum summoned groups of young men and girls to a clearing some distance from Al Hajji Maudo's compound where an evening of dancing began. Dancers drawn from opposing lines of boys and girls took turns in moving rhythmically across the intervening space while surveying the line opposite. At the last instant, with a studiedly casual gesture of the hand, each dancer would indicate his or her preferred partner and return rapidly to his/her starting place, yielding centre stage to the newly 'chosen' dancer advancing from the line opposite. The dancing continued until dusk when the youth departed for their cattle camps.

STRATEGIES AND UNCERTAINTIES; INTERPRETATIONS AND STRUCTURES

In the twenty years since Al Hajji Maudo's wedding feast, I have returned to the area on four occasions and have had the opportunity to follow his fortunes and those of the town near which he was living. When I first met him in 1969, Al Hajji Maudo had struck me as far from subtle. Hardly a political virtuoso among Mbororo *ardo'en*, his machinations seemed rather too obvious. But, looking back, one can see that a conjuncture of historical developments, some of which he could not have foreseen, contributed ultimately to the realisation of many of the goals that were only a gleam in his eye in the late 1960s. Degradation of pastures, especially through the spread of the weed known locally as 'Bokassa grass',[2] and several outbreaks of cattle disease in the region where Al Hajji Maudo made his wet season camp, soon drove away his major political competitors for the *ardo bariki* post. Although Al Hajji Maudo also lost both some cattle and some followers from these causes, by 1980 he was virtually unchallenged as *ardo bariki* within the local political field.

Al Hajji Maudo's strategy in taking his third wife in 1973 did not pan out immediately as he had hoped, although the lavish marriage ceremony and its associated gifts to influential actors may well have had their desired effects. However, a further effort in this direction eventually proved to be quite successful. The third wife he had married in 1973 divorced him before the year was out, having not become pregnant in the interim. But he then married another young wife of similar background, set her up in the cloistered relative opulence of a walled compound in the centre of town, and proceeded to sire several children with her while using this more urban residence as a political base to monitor local developments.

This cantonal town has grown substantially in the two decades since 1973 and despite Al Hajji Maudo's increasing prominence as the pre-eminent Mbororo *ardo* in the area, he has also been confronted by the contradictions facing Mbororo leaders who choose to live in such a modernising and more sedentarised setting (cf. Stenning 1959: Chap 6; Dupire 1970: 520 *et passim*; Baxter 1975; Burnham 1975; 1979). Although he and his followers enjoy privileged access to the pastures surrounding the town, the resultant heavier usage of these grazing areas has hastened their degradation. Although Al Hajji Maudo maintains a close relationship with the Gbaya canton chief, the sub-prefect and other local officials, he is thereby more exposed to dispersal of his cattle wealth through frequent gifts and other forms of conspicuous consumption, as well as through the inevitable crop damage fines caused by his cattle which are pastured too close to town. At the same time, the strategy of maintaining the bulk of his animals in cattle camps under the care of younger relatives or paid herdsmen at some distance from town is also fraught with risks. Younger followers may be attracted to join the following of another *ardo*, or a paid herdsman may neglect his duties or even abscond with some cattle. I have had opportunities to observe all of these scenarios at one time or another during the twenty-five-year period I have been visiting the Mbere Department, and the frustrations engendered among various *ardo'en bariki* as they have experienced these contradictions have boiled over on several notorious occasions. I have already described in Chapter 5 the incident involving an Mbororo *ardo* and the Central African Republic gendarmes. There was also an unsavoury occasion in 1969 when an *ardo*, enraged by an extortion attempt, tried to stab the government official concerned and then fled across the international frontier.

For the ethnographer, an event such as Al Hajji Maudo's wedding is meat and drink and offers a myriad of descriptive and analytical possibilities. However, the twenty-twenty hindsight permitted by the extended case study may encourage a misleading sense of historical predictability which is surely inappropriate at the level of the event, if not necessarily at the level of structure. As just remarked, no matter how single-minded or goal-oriented an actor like Al Hajji Maudo may be, much of social life unfolds in conditions of uncertainty and although actors may be adept retrospectively in accounting for and interpreting past events in terms of conventional cultural understandings, the ethnographer should not be taken in.

This intrinsic uncertainty surrounding social action, along with the related issue of the competing accounts that may be offered by the different parties to a social encounter, can be highlighted by the use of various ethnographic methods. An early classic that helped to point the way in the analysis of social events, although marred by a rather reified notion of shared community between the different ethnic categories concerned, is Max Gluckman's 'Analysis of a social situation in modern Zululand' (1958). In this study, which is centred on a description of a public ceremony to dedicate a new bridge, Gluckman directs our attention to the various and possibly opposed meanings, both conventional and potentially emergent, held by the different actors and ethnic categories in attendance. Clifford Geertz (1973: 9–10) raises similar issues in his well-known essay 'Thick Description: Toward an Interpretive Theory of Culture' when he offers us a multi-cultural vignette about the theft of some sheep, featuring Moroccan Berber tribesmen, Jewish traders and French colonial administrators. In this context, he suggests that the appropriate interpretive approach is to sort out the:

> structures of signification . . . and [to determine] their social ground and import. Here, in our text, such sorting would begin with distinguishing the three unlike frames of interpretation ingredient in the situation, Jewish, Berber, and French, and would then move on to show how (and why) at that time, in that place, their co-presence produced a situation in which systematic misunderstanding reduced traditional form to social farce. What tripped Cohen up, and with him the whole ancient pattern of social and economic relationships within which he functioned, was a confusion of tongues.

Geertz continues:

> The point for now is only that ethnography is thick description. What the ethnographer is in fact faced with . . . is a multiplicity of complex conceptual structures, many of them superimposed upon or knotted into one another, which are at once strange, irregular, and inexplicit, and which he must contrive somehow first to grasp and then to render.

There are obviously numerous possibilities for 'thickening' the ethnographic description of Al Hajji Maudo's wedding feast – by focusing, for example, on the many social implications and the multiple layerings and contrasts of cultural understanding of the occasion. Willing informants were certainly not lacking to comment on issues such as the political strategies being pursued by Al Hajji Maudo, the romantic intrigues of the Mbororo youth, or certain marked departures from 'proper' Jafun *pulaaku* in the conduct of the feast. Indeed, I have made use of some of this material in earlier publications and in Chapter 5 of this work. But, in the context of my present focus on the lived experience of multi-ethnic relations, my main aim is not to peel away ever deeper layers of cultural meaning but to consider the significance of such multi-cultural events for the social constitution and historical trajectory of the Mbere Department. Putting the problem in another way, one must choose an appropriate balance between, on the one hand, an analysis of events like Al Hajji Maudo's wedding that emphasises the discreteness, internal closure and 'situatedness' of various culturally specific interpretations versus an analysis that actively addresses the trans-ethnic interactional conventions, the possibly emergent shared understandings across ethnic divides, and the processes of ethnic conflict, assimilation and dissolution within the wider setting of the Cameroonian state.

Of course, a third, currently fashionable post-modernist approach is also available which would have us simply document the individual 'voices' in this 'social discourse'. However, I do not feel comfortable with the excessive relativism of Geertz's interpretive anthropology, let alone more extreme post-modernist views, whose

> essential vocation . . . is not to answer our deepest questions, but to make available to us answers that others, guarding other sheep in other valleys, have given, and thus to include them in the consultable record of what man has said. (Geertz 1973: 30)

Geertz himself admitted that such ultra-relativism is a recipe for a purely academic anthropology (cf. Marcus 1986a: 77), one only really suited for the most cloistered of ivory towers, when he noted in the preceding paragraph of the same essay that:

> The danger that cultural analysis . . . will lose touch with the hard surfaces of life – with the political, economic, stratificatory realities within which men are everywhere contained – and with the biological and physical necessities on which those surfaces rest, is an ever-present one. The only defense against it, and against, thus, turning cultural analysis into a kind of sociological aestheticism, is to train such analysis on such realities and such necessities in the first place.

But, in keeping with Geertz's richly multi-layered essay style, one that we might call 'thick equivocation', he acknowledged the danger while still advocating it.

I myself am acknowledging that a dominant concern in my mind as I write these words (with Bosnia and Rwanda very much in the news) is to try to understand the major determinants conditioning inter-ethnic relations in conflictual situations like the present one in the Mbere Department, in spite of all the fashionable, well-rehearsed arguments against even the slightest whisper of causal analysis in social anthropology (e.g. Rabinow and Sullivan 1979). Interpretive anthropology has gone overboard in treating ethnography as an academic or literary artifice, a 'fictio' (Geertz 1973: 16), rather than as a perfectable method aiming to illuminate social reality (see Gellner 1992). The metaphor which likens the interpretation of social action to the 'inscription of social discourse' (Geertz 1973: 18–19, following Ricoeur) offers a perspective more suited to a stylishly disengaged literary criticism than to a discipline seeking to make some impact on political perceptions and actions in the real world. As Gledhill (1994: 190) writes, following Starn (1992):

post-modernist social theory's rejection of model-building and 'master narratives' encourages a complete jettisoning of modernist concerns about 'how and why' questions.

In the present case, some of the questions in my mind are: 'Why did the outbreaks of violence occur in the Mbere Department in 1991 and 1992?', 'Is such violence likely to recur?', and 'Is there anything that can be done to prevent it?'. I believe that social anthropology should position itself theoretically so that it can seek to address such questions, rather than to find reasons why it is philosophically impossible to ask them (cf. Gellner 1992: 29).

Getting back to Al Hajji Maudo's wedding and pursuing some further dimensions of this case as a 'social situation' in Gluckman's sense, it is enlightening to consider, at least briefly, the perspectives of other actors in the ceremony, particularly those from other ethnic groups. The dominant themes in an interview I conducted some days later with Mallum Haman, the local Fulbe religious specialist who had officiated at the wedding, were Al Hajji Maudo's untrustworthiness and his shallow Islam. The particular vehemence of this discourse was no doubt provoked by Al Hajji Maudo's failure to reward Mallum Haman for his services as handsomely as promised, but its substance also conformed closely to some common Fulbe stereotypes about the Mbororo. Thus, for example, as Ndoudi Oumarou explained (Bocquené 1986: 306–7, my translation) concerning Fulbe stereotypes of anti-Islamic behaviour among the Jafun Mbororo:

> Yes, around Garoua our [i.e. the Jafun] reputation as sorcerers and casters of spells is so strong that we are absolutely unable to get a true *mallum* or *moodibbo* to come and say the ritual prayers over a dead Mbororo. They despise us too much. They wouldn't touch one of our dead for anything in the world; they would be polluted.
>
> In such a case we have only one solution. We must resort to employing one of those *mallum'en* who are more or less charlatans – one of those whom we call, with a certain disdain, '*mallum'en bitiri*'. Those are the ones who circulate around the pastoral districts and sell their Writings and their magical recipes to the incredulous Mbororo. With some money, one can always make an arrangement with them, even if it is a case of a *suka* (youth) killed in a *soro* contest who is being buried with his long braided hair.

Such ethnic stereotypes, despite their evident over-simplification, have important structuring effects in multi-cultural settings like the Mbere Department, and the accusation concerning shallow Islam is one we have encountered before as one of the principal motivations for the Fulbeisation of the Jafun.

As for Mallum Haman, he had indicated to me in other chats that a major part of his income was indeed derived from providing Islamic religious services to Mbororo, including a large amount of Koranic charm writing. Much of the content of popular Islam in northern Cameroon, in Fulani and non-Fulani societies alike, revolves around the search for efficacity and Allah's blessing in everyday affairs via recourse to such religious specialists. But in inter-ethnic contexts, the 'shallow Islam' epithet is one that putatively pietistic Fulbe often direct against non-Fulbe Muslims. In this case, Mallum Haman had publicly signalled his low opinion of Mbororo as Muslims (while tacitly revealing their importance to his livelihood) by officiating at the marriage in the canton chief's entry hut but by absenting himself from the feast afterwards.

Another guest at Al Hajji Maudo's wedding celebration was rather more open about his economic motives. A Fulbe commission agent for one of the large cattle dealers in the district had discreetly made his presence known to the card players while at the same time enjoying the feast. Certain young Mbororo men in the game were notoriously addicted to gambling and, if afflicted by a bad run of luck, were not above selling one of their cattle to renew their stake – in which case, the agent would be at hand.

Indeed, running down the list of non-Mbororo participants at Al Hajji Maudo's marriage fête – the praise singers, the merchants, the Congo and Gbaya labourers, the Gbaya children clustered beside the festoons of meat – it was tempting for me at first to interpret all these interactions as single-stranded, economically motivated relationships. Such a view of ethnically plural societies has a venerable ancestry, such as Furnivall's contention (1939: 449; see also Boeke 1942) that the ethnically differentiated segments of such societies only meet 'in the market place'. Thus, taking the example of Jafun life-cycle ceremonies of which Al Hajji Maudo's wedding is just one instance, it could be argued that such ceremonies may be successfully accomplished almost regardless of the particular multi-ethnic context in which the Mbororo find themselves. If we set this ceremony alongside the many other such instances observable elsewhere in Adamaoua Province (or elsewhere in northern Cameroon, northern Nigeria or the Central African Republic, for that matter), we can see that the Jafun are able to organise such events according to what they define as a culturally acceptable format as long as certain minimum conditions are fulfilled (see Bocquené 1986: Chap. 8 *et passim*). Namely, it must be the wet season when their milk cows are productive and their migratory group has congregated in one locality, and they must be able to obtain starch staples and '*haaɓe*' labour from surrounding sedentary cultivators. The ethnic identity of the '*haaɓe*' – be they Gbaya in Cameroon, Hausa in Nigeria or Kpana in the Central African Republic, might not seem to matter to the Mbororo.

But such an interpretation would neglect the backcloth of history, common experiences and areas of shared understanding in these various multi-ethnic societies which renders a purely economistic explanation unacceptably monochromatic. Viewed solely from a situationally specific perspective, it is often difficult to detect the social effects of long periods of mutual accommodation between co-resident ethnic groups; one is liable to be more struck by the ethnic boundary mechanisms and ideologies of difference than by the gradual processes of cultural assimilation. However, Dupire has provided several examples, drawn from her fieldwork in the Mbere region in the early 1950s, of the mutual effects that Mbororo and Gbaya cultures have experienced as a result of their decades of cohabitation. For example, she points out (Dupire 1970: 31) that the Mbororo, in emulation of the Gbaya, had taken to calculating the amount of bridewealth to be reimbursed in the case of divorce according to factors such as the consummation or non-consummation of the marriage, the number of children born to the union, and so on. In addition, speaking of the mutual stereotypes and accommodations of Mbororo and sedentary peoples, Dupire (1981: 171, my translation) has pointed out that:

> One observes that positive stereotypes and neutral comments are all the more numerous when the sedentary population who is making them has more direct contacts with the nomads; such is the case, for example, between the Baya and the Bororo of Adamawa.

In a like manner, a purely economic analysis of ethnic relations in the Mbere Department would also neglect the important fact that Mbororo in Nigeria live in a 'Hausaising' social context while in northern Cameroon, the dominant regional culture is a Fulbeising one. So much of Al Hajji Maudo's behaviour that I have described has been a reflex of his efforts to cultivate a more 'Fulbe' image, especially in the religious and political domains, without totally alienating his Mbororo followers on whose support his status as *ardo bariki* depends.

This is not, of course, to deny the major importance of economic factors in the structuring of multi-ethnic relations in the Mbere Department. As discussed in earlier chapters, the Mbororo cattle herds are the most important source of wealth in the economy of the Mbere Department and during the twenty-five-year period that I have been visiting the region, there have been a series of marked shifts in local economic patterns consequent on Mbororo pastoral movements. For example, the pastures along the Djohong to Yarimbang road, which during the 1960s had held the highest concentration of Mbororo, emptied during the 1970s in response to overgrazing and an infestation of tsetse fly, while the area from Bad Zer to Dir on the Meidougou to Ngaoundal road witnessed a great expansion of Mbororo settlement. It was through this period of flux that Al Hajji Maudo had elected to sit tight while his competitors for the *ardo bariki* post had migrated away. Concomitant with these changes there have been expansions or contractions in the levels of economic activity at the different marketplaces that form part of the district-wide weekly rotational retail markets and the cattle marketing system (Burnham 1980a: 191–7).

Thus, over and above the annual cycle of wet season to dry season expansion and contraction noticeable in all marketplaces in the region, which is linked to the transhumant movements of Mbororo migratory groups, there have been longer term fluctuations in which the numbers of market traders present, and the quantities of goods sold in particular marketplaces, have varied by as much as a factor of five in the space of ten years. Linked to these population shifts in turn is a set of adjustments in the complex web of exchange relations in which all ethnic groups in the Mbere Department are implicated via the demand for non-Mbororo labour for house building, craft production, paid herdsman employment, etc., and for agricultural produce obtained through *soobaajo* exchanges and bulk food purchases.

In addition, the variations in the level of farmer-herder conflicts consequent on Mbororo movements have very ramifying effects (quite apart from the question of crop damage), given the politically significant compensation payments and bribes paid by the Mbororo to Gbaya canton chiefs and village headmen to settle these disputes. In many cases, these payments, which chiefs may attempt to legitimate by reference to the Islamic concept of *zakkat* (alms), constitute the most important source of revenue for Gbaya chiefs and are instrumental, in turn, in determining the degree of political influence enjoyed by such leaders. Indeed, just as the different ethnic categories present in the Mbere Department are woven together into a dense fabric of economic ties, so too are they linked together by a web of political relations. The Gbaya elders and headmen who attended Al Hajji Maudo's wedding feast were not there just to enjoy the food. It is also through such daily interactions, both formal and informal, that Gbaya leaders aim to strengthen their links with Mbororo leaders and to monitor the development or decline of Mbororo migratory groups in their neighbourhoods.

THE MBORORO AND THE CAMEROON STATE

One 'actor' who was not present at Al Hajji Maudo's wedding but whose influence was very manifest nonetheless was the Cameroonian state. It was the state which defined the general modalities of the *ardo bariki* competition toward which Al Hajji Maudo's efforts were clearly focused, although the details of this local political contest owed much to the involvement of the particular Fulbe sub-prefect of Meiganga of that period. As I have already explained, during the twenty-five years of President Ahidjo's rule, the state administrative and political party structures throughout the north were firmly in Fulbe hands. It was to this hegemonic state apparatus that Al Hajji Maudo was seeking to link himself as he jockeyed for position both within his local Mbororo migratory group as well as within the local inter-ethnic political arena. It was also in relation to this political strategy that Al Hajji

Maudo's 'Fulbeising' behaviour, which was evident in certain of the cultural features of his wedding celebrations, should be interpreted.

The Meiganga sub-prefect may not have been in attendance, but his presence was symbolically manifest not far down the road in the form of a rather novel, and much commented upon, octagonal *'case de passage'* (guest-house). This accommodation had been constructed a few years previously so that, during his frequent visits to the area to keep a close (and extortionate) eye on the numerous wealthy Mbororo inhabiting this zone, the sub-prefect could live in full comfort. Nevertheless, however substantial his demands for 'gifts' from Mbororo herders may have been, to use the character of the sub-prefect as an ethnographic device to personify the state in a situational analysis has its limitations. Equally, although Marcus (1986b: 169, following Knorr-Cetina 1981) suggests that the 'invisible hand' of macrosystems like the state 'may be represented as they are subtly imagined or registered within the ongoing life processes of an intensely studied and interpreted microsituation', this is unlikely to be a satisfactory solution for our present purposes either. However subtly Al Hajji Maudo (or any other Jafun *ardo*) may have imagined the Cameroon state, and however great his efforts to Fulbeise, we must now shift focus back to the macrostructural level in order to understand the position of the Mbororo within the multi-ethnic society of the Mbere Department and the resultant limitations on the political agency of actors like Al Hajji Maudo.

As we have seen in earlier chapters, these structures of marginalisation and disability have deep historical roots, which can be traced back to the relations that obtained between Fulbe and Mbororo in pre-colonial times. These relations of inequality, which fundamentally disadvantaged the Mbororo by restricting their access to loci of political and economic power in the wider society, were then perpetuated by the practice of indirect rule via Fulbe traditional state structures in the colonial period and were maintained into the post-independence period by special modes of tax collection and territorial administration applied to the Mbororo.

Mbororo leaders continue to resent strongly the lack of respect and the barriers to access to power that they experience in their relations with the local administration. But up to the present, the response of the Cameroon state to the blandishments and protests of Mbororo leaders has been pure tokenism. The Mbororo have had little success in being incorporated into the national elite. In part, this is due to the low level of western education among Mbororo in general, although even the few younger Mbororo men who have obtained western educational qualifications have only been given minor roles in the local political party organisation or have been used as intermediaries between their people and the local government. Their influence in regional and national centres of power has remained very limited. In the 1992 National Assembly elections for example, which will be discussed further in the next chapter, two Gbaya and one Fulbe were elected to the three Mbere Department seats being contested, regardless of the fact that the Mbororo are the second most numerous ethnic group in the department – well ahead of the Fulbe.

The change of national government has had little impact on the *de facto* situation of the Mbororo in the Mbere Department, despite steps by the Biya regime to do away with certain of the ethnically discriminatory practices of the Ahidjo period. The interviews I conducted in the Mbere Department in 1987 with the southern Cameroonian administrative appointees of the Biya government contained a consistent set of themes concerning the Mbororo – namely, that the department had previously suffered from a policy of administrative laissez-faire perpetrated in the self-interest of the Fulbe-dominated administration and that what was required now was rapid economic development. The Mbororo were portrayed as the Fulani group who were the most recalcitrant to progress, as evidenced for example by their preference for their traditional Mbororo cattle breeds as opposed to the improved Fulbe *gudaali* breed being disseminated by the state cattle-breeding station at Wakwa, near Ngaoundere. Moreover, their mobile pastoral existence ensured that their allegiance to Cameroon was weak. What was needed, according to these administrators, was the sedentarisation of the Mbororo and the modernisation of the pastoral economy of the Adamaoua Province through ranching schemes.

In fact, for as much as a decade before the Biya period, this area of Cameroon has witnessed the emergence of a trend which is possibly even more significant and immediately threatening to the livelihood of the Mbororo than their failure to gain positions within the government or national elite. I am referring here to the discriminatory treatment meted out to them with regard to their access to and tenure of traditional grazing lands, in the context of various pastoral development, ranching, agro-industrial, dam building, and land registration schemes promoted both by the Ahidjo and the Biya governments from the late 1970s up to the present (see Boutrais 1982; 1983; 1994).

The crux of the issue revolves around the preferential (and discriminatory) allocation of title to desirable grazing lands by official government agencies, without reference to the longstanding patterns of pasturage use of local groups, some of whom are Mbororo. In certain cases, those who have benefited are wealthy, often absentee, cattle owners and businessmen, who were well connected in government and elite circles. In another case, the government expropriated 35,000 hectares of grazing land for the first phase of the SODEPA 'ranching' project (Boutrais 1983: 121–3), a para-statal company created with World Bank aid whose future is now uncertain as a result of the World Bank-mandated structural adjustment programme. More recently, on several notorious occasions during the 1990s, the Biya government has even made attempts to expropriate some 100,000 hectares of grazing land on the west bank of the Djerem river (which is especially valuable in the dry season both to Mbororo and Fulbe herders) and to grant this land to a major French-based multi-national firm in settlement of an overdue government debt. For the moment, this most blatant of neo-colonial deals has been blocked thanks to the mobilisation of popular opposition in Ngaoundere and elsewhere by an association of (predominantly Fulbe) Adamaoua elites but, as I write, it is far from clear that the danger has been definitively averted.

In some cases during the Ahidjo years, it was prominent Fulbe or Fulbeised elites who benefited from these government-sponsored land grabs (Boutrais 1983: 129–30), with both low status Fulbe as well as Mbororo herders being dispossessed. More recently, under the Biya regime, even the local Fulbe elites have lost out. In all cases, however, the Mbororo have been uniformly excluded from these allocations, and this fact is interpreted by Mbororo herders as yet another manifestation of their second-class status *vis-à-vis* the centres of power within the Cameroon state.

To date, the most obvious response of the Mbororo in the Mbere Department to their disadvantageous situation has been their migration in substantial numbers to the neighbouring Central African Republic, whose policies toward the Mbororo are seen by them as more favourable. In fact, the Mbororo are also differentially incorporated into the Central African Republic state, via the mechanism of separate Mbororo cantons (Boutrais 1988). However, in the CAR, this differential incorporation might be said to work to the advantage of the Mbororo, since the Central African state is actively seeking to encourage the migration of the Mbororo to their territory via the abolition of cattle tax and the provision of free inoculations and other veterinary services. And all this in a setting where sedentary Fulbe are not numerous and exercise no political hegemony over the Mbororo.

VIOLENCE AND THE POLITICS OF DIFFERENCE IN GLOBAL AND LOCAL PERSPECTIVE

This book began with a brief account of the ethnic clashes that took place in the Mbere Department in 1991 and again in 1992 and posed the problem of developing an understanding of such incidents, seen both from a local as well as a more global perspective. Subsequent chapters have painted in the social background of these events and focused particularly on the cultural practices constitutive of the three principal ethnic groups resident in the Mbere Department and their patterns of historical transformation and mutual self-definition. Now I want to return to these episodes of violence and consider more fully their motivations and their significance for the subsequent political trajectory of the society of the Mbere Department, viewed as part of the north and of Cameroon as a whole. Whereas in the previous chapter, the case of Al Hajji Maudo's wedding led us eventually to pay special attention to the position of the Mororo with regard to other ethnic categories and to the Cameroon state, in this chapter I will be discussing these same issues with reference principally to the Gbaya and Fulbe ethnic categories, the Mororo having taken no part in the violence. A central challenge in this discussion is to find an appropriate analytical balance between the impact of national or regional scale processes versus that of locally situated cultural practices in channelling, constraining or enabling political agency within the Mbere Department.

Picking up the thread of the argument from earlier chapters, we can say that with no direct access to the political centre through well-placed elites and no effective organisational structures for expressing their voice, the influence of the Gbaya on regional and national events has been quite limited. President Ahidjo's insistence throughout his long period of rule that organisational initiatives in the public sphere be channelled through the UNC, the sole national political party, combined with Fulbe political dominance in Adamaoua as elsewhere in northern Cameroon, inevitably implied a stifling, or at best a Fulbe mediation, of the Gbaya political voice. Up through 1982, Gbaya elites seeking to enter the regional or national political arenas were constrained to form links with Fulbe elites in the regional administration and the UNC party, relationships which subordinated them to Fulbe influence while at the same time compromising them in the eyes of their Gbaya constituents.

The succession to office of President Biya in 1982 was viewed initially with some optimism by many Gbaya as offering potential to free themselves from this Fulbe domination. Educated Gbaya in particular anticipated greater access to public sector employment opportunities. Granted, Biya's new version of the national political party, the RDPC, was still the only organisational forum countenanced by the government. But Biya took rapid steps to break up the Fulbe political hegemony in the north, and the Gbaya had hopes of exerting more influence in regional and national affairs. However, the political upheaval and repression associated with the 1984 coup attempt, followed by the decline of the national economy over the next few years, severely dented these hopes and turned many Gbaya against the Biya regime. With the advent of multi-party politics and the creation in 1990 of the UNDP (Union Nationale pour la Démocratie et le Progrès – led by Ahidjo's formerly close associate and fellow Fulbe Bouba Bello Maigari) as the principal party representing northern regional interests, Gbaya found themselves back in a position where an alliance with the Fulbe might again offer some advantages.

As already described in Chapter 1, the first violent episode in Meiganga on 15 July 1991 occurred during the national 'villes mortes' campaign, which had been started in May 1991 by opposition parties including the SDF (Social Democratic Front), the UPC (Union des Populations du Cameroun) and the UNDP to protest against President Biya's prevarication in the face of public demands for constitutional change. The protests also focused on the continuing repression and imprisonment by the Biya regime of its political opponents. Although the Cameroon National Assembly had passed a law in December 1990 facilitating the creation of political parties other than Biya's RDPC, the opposition accused Biya of foot-dragging and manipulation of the political process to keep his regime in power. In this context, the concept of a national conference or constitutional convention with power to decide Cameroon's political future, which was receiving much popular support at that time in several West and Central African states, was strongly advocated by Biya's opponents as the best way of moving rapidly toward a democratic society in Cameroon.

Demonstrations and violent protests had been a feature of Cameroonian political life for some years prior to the villes mortes campaign, especially in larger towns and cities like Douala, Bamenda, and Garoua. In Adamaoua Province, a crowd had burnt the RDPC headquarters building in Ngaoundere, and in Meiganga there had also been incidents when government buildings were ransacked and files burnt. In common with the rest of the Fulbe-dominated north of Cameroon where the UNDP was the dominant party, the *villes mortes* general strike was widely supported throughout Adamaoua Province.

However, although the *villes mortes* strike closed businesses and government offices in Meiganga town, the ethnic cleavage between Gbaya and Fulbe ensured that the political opposition was not fully unified. The Gbaya population found themselves in their usual quandary as they sought an effective role in regional and national political affairs. Should they ally themselves with the regionally dominant Fulbe, thereby potentially gaining greater access to important loci of power, or should they assert their ethnic distinctiveness and resist Fulbe blandishments?

One issue which tended to favour a Gbaya alliance with Fulbe political interests was the fact of the continued detention in the harsh state maximum security prisons of numerous northerners, including both Gbaya and Fulbe, who had been implicated in the failed *coup d'état* in 1984 (Amnesty International 1984; 1985; 1986; 1987 and 1989). From time to time, President Biya had publicly announced that these prisoners would be amnestied but, up to the time of the *villes mortes* general strike, this promise had not been kept. Indeed, one of the early successes of the *villes mortes* protests was achieved when the Biya government liberated most of these prisoners (Amnesty International 1991a and 1991b).

A Gbaya and Fulbe political alliance was also promoted on the basis of shared feelings within Adamaoua Province that the region had not been receiving its fair portion of the national cake, especially after 1987 when the period of economic crisis and austerity had set in strongly. It was in the context of these dissatisfactions that the initially trans-ethnic Adamaoua provincial elites association (ARA) came to prominence as a regional political force.[1] This association began to organise local social development initiatives using funds collected from its members. It also pressed for increased educational and other opportunities within the national system for natives of Adamaoua while at the same time protesting against cases of government corruption or expropriation affecting the province (as discussed in the previous chapter). A large majority of the membership of the Adamaoua Elites Association were supporters of the UNDP. The *laamiido* of Ngaoundere on the other hand, in common with many other superior chiefs throughout Cameroon, was constrained by the central government to manifest at least public support for Biya's RDPC, and this provoked widespread and sometimes violent protest against him.[2] Similarly, in the Mbere Department, the Gbaya elites who had been elected on the RDPC ticket during the days of the single party regime (such as the departmental deputy to the National Assembly, Adamou Emmanuel, and the mayor of Meiganga *commune*, Ibrahim Songo) were also discredited.

This then was the regional and national context within which the first episode of inter-communal violence occurred in Meiganga on 15 July 1991 but, as is usually the case with an event which hits the national headlines, there were particular local contextualising factors which generated much of the meaning for the persons involved. For example, in my subsequent interviews with participants on both sides of the conflict, a common element in many of their accounts has been a focus on urban Fulbe 'youth' as the instigators of the violence. On the evening of 14 July, there had been a series of altercations between Fulbe and Gbaya 'youth' in some of the bars in one of the downtown quarters of Meiganga, which culminated in several motorbikes of the Fulbe being set on fire. Gbaya informants claimed that young Fulbe men had been acting in an overbearing and insulting manner toward Gbaya patrons of these bars – flaunting their wealth and calling the Gbaya unclean, pagan, monkey- and insect-eaters. Familiar taunts were also voiced to the effect that the Gbaya were of no economic or political importance in Meiganga, having sold most of their land in town to well-to-do Fulbe and other merchants, and that the Gbaya canton chief of Meiganga consequently did not have a legitimate claim to rule and should be replaced by a Fulbe chief.

It is important to remember that, over the past decade or so (and especially in the relatively more liberal political climate fostered in northern Cameroon by the Biya government), there has been an influx of Mai'ine and other Fulbe agro-pastoralists into the Mbere Department, and disputes over Gbaya chieftaincy rights have become more common. Historically, although the Mbere Department had been removed during the colonial era from Ngaoundere's domination and reserved for the Gbaya and Mbororo, some Fulbe continue to argue that the Mbere Department is a part of Adamawa and therefore a Fulbe domain.

While many of my Gbaya informants placed emphasis on these ethnic insults and on the purported Fulbe plot to take over the Meiganga chieftaincy, senior members of the Fulbe community whom I interviewed tended to lay blame on the capacity of wayward youth to cause trouble in the context of the *villes mortes* campaign. Proponents of this view pointed to the growing use of narcotic drugs (especially hemp and amphetamines) in urban settings and the increase in unemployment among urban school-leavers. Some also recalled that inter-ethnic confrontations between youths had been a feature of Meiganga urban life as early as the 1970s, sometimes focused on the town football league which was then comprised of ethnically based teams. Government officials in the provincial and departmental administrations also tended to lay blame for the violence on the influence of drugs among urban ne'er-do-wells.[3]

Although the violent outburst on 15 July followed the historic fault line which has defined Fulbe-Gbaya opposition for more than 150 years, the large loss of life clearly shocked leaders in both communities and quite genuine efforts at reconciliation were subsequently made on both sides. At the same time, in UNDP circles, it was commonly claimed that RDPC agents had played the ethnic card and encouraged the Gbaya market women to refuse to support the *villes mortes* strike. Many Gbaya seem to have interpreted the violence in essentially local terms, as we have seen above, citing particularly the Fulbe-Gbaya ethnic competition within Meiganga concerning the canton chieftaincy. In any event, this violent episode did little to increase enthusiasm for Biya and the RDPC in either the Gbaya or the Fulbe camp, and the UNDP enjoyed a sweeping success throughout Adamaoua in the legislative elections of 1 March 1992. In the Mbere Department, the UNDP easily won all three parliamentary seats available, having fielded two Gbaya and one Fulbe as candidates.

It was only one month later that the second spasm of Fulbe-Gbaya violence erupted following the dispute over the end of Ramadan at Meidougou. The spark that ignited it was a local factional struggle over succession to the village headmanship – a type of dispute which has long been commonplace in Gbaya society (Burnham 1980a: 108–12). However, the social setting of the headmanship dispute was a village which has been transformed over the past two decades from an essentially mono-ethnic Gbaya village of several hundred persons into a growing multi-ethnic town of some commercial importance, due to its location at the crossroads between the major north-south national route and the recently paved spur road linking westwards to the rail depot town of Ngaoundal. In this setting, what would previously have been a factional contest solely between Gbaya could ramify and draw in non-Gbaya Muslim supporters, and this in turn could engender accusations that the Fulbe were plotting to take over the village chieftaincy, as they were also suspected of doing in Meiganga, some seventeen kilometres away. Local events were reinterpreted as having more general significance in the light of a globalising discourse about political parties, the *villes mortes* campaign, Gbaya-Fulbe ethnic opposition, and the historic Fulbe hegemony in northern Cameroon.

The spark therefore fell on the tinder prepared by the 1991 Meiganga clash and caused an even larger conflagration. Despite having voted for the same party in the recent elections, it is clear in hindsight that elements in both ethnic camps had been preparing for a second battle all the same. Rumours abounded that certain Fulbe *mallum'en* were preparing charms to render their fighters invulnerable to iron weapons. For their part, certain Gbaya had taken the precaution of fabricating homemade guns from lengths of pipe; these weapons are termed '*ibo*' by the Gbaya, who claim that the manufacturing technique was developed in Nigeria during the Biafran War. Once the fire was lit, both sides were eager to settle old scores. Indeed, for the Gbaya participants, the 'war' had historical resonances that long predated 1991. As one older informant proudly remarked, during the 1992 fighting he had heard once again 'the old Gbaya war songs that hadn't been sung since the days of Karnu'. Interestingly, his account tended to conflate the Karnu events (of 1928–30) with nineteenth century Gbaya resistance against the Fulbe of Ngaoundere. He went on to claim that whereas in the 1991 fighting it had been the older Gbaya men who were more involved, since it was they who knew about war, in the 1992 battle young men had played their full part, having received the necessary training in the old ways in the interim. For example, the fighters were said to have used the old Gbaya tactic of appearing to retreat, only to lure many Fulbe to their deaths in the fields and bush outside town.

PRESENT POLITICAL TRAJECTORIES IN THE MBERE DEPARTMENT

It is difficult to form an opinion as to the true voting patterns in the Mbere Department during the subsequent presidential elections of 11 October 1992, thanks to the blatant manipulation of the results by the Biya regime. And when I last visited Meiganga in 1993, a stay pervaded with a dismal atmosphere in the aftermath of the violence and the deception of the presidential election, my Gbaya acquaintances were uncertain what political stance now offered the best course of action to promote Gbaya interests on the regional or national stage. Judging from these conversations, it appeared to me that four options were conceivable. Firstly, there was the possibility of maintaining an alliance with Fulbe interests within the UNDP and the Adamaoua Elites Association in opposition to the Biya regime, a strategy ensuring the perpetuation of Gbaya subordination to the Fulbe while perhaps achieving limited benefits for themselves within Adamaoua regional affairs. However, this option had now been rendered even less palatable as an oppositional strategy since various prominent members of the UNDP had recently accepted ministerial posts in Biya's cabinet. Such co-optation of the opposition into the ruling party has been a well-established process in Cameroonian politics since the early days of Ahidjo's presidency and has much appeal to opposition leaders who must otherwise remain cut off from the financial resources and benefits of state office. However, the rank-and-file members of the opposition are not likely to benefit much from their leaders' change of allegiances.

Secondly, Gbaya could swallow their pride and join Biya's ruling RDPC. Some Gbaya had already taken this route, justifying their decision as a response to the recent Fulbe brutality, although it was also widely rumoured in the Gbaya community that large sums had been on offer from the RDPC to buy votes during the presidential election. In general during my 1993 visit, however, I found the RDPC option to be still quite unpopular among the Gbaya.

A third possibility which was being promoted by a few Gbaya was to join the MDR (*Mouvement Démocratique pour la Défense de la République*), a party whose principal power base lies in the Province de l'Extrême Nord among the non-Muslim *kirdi* peoples.[4] Although the MDR had joined the Biya government coalition following the legislative elections and could not therefore be seen as oppositional to the RDPC, its political strategy was primarily a regionalist one. In seeking to unify the *kirdi* throughout the north, wherein according to recent estimates they comprise more than 70 per cent of the population, the MDR was attempting to become 'master in its own house' by ending the Fulbe dominance of regional affairs. However, few Gbaya with whom I spoke seemed attracted to the MDR, since they did not see their interests as sufficiently close to those of the *kirdi*.

A fourth option, which seemed to me only a theoretical possibility and was not, as far as I knew, being actively organised or canvassed at the time of my visit to Meiganga in June 1993, was the Gbaya 'nationalist' strategy of founding a political organisation on overtly ethnic lines. Referring back to my short discussion on pp. 76–7 concerning the prospects for such a development, a passage that I had written in 1992 before my last visit, we can see what my understanding of the situation was at that time. I argued there that although the possibility of a pan-Gbaya ethnic movement was clearly envisioned in current ethnically constitutive histories like those concerned with the Karnu Rebellion (*Koŋgo Wara*), such an overarching organisational development was being counteracted both by the divisive effects of the colonially created regional and international frontiers as well as by the thinly veiled local particularism apparent among the Gbaya membership of the Lutheran Church (EELC) in the Mbere Department. Moreover, as regards their efforts to make their voice heard within the national political scene in Cameroon, and in contrast with numerous other ethnic groups in the country at that time, the Gbaya were quite unorganised up to 1993.

However, at about the time of my 1993 visit, this fourth political option was in fact taking shape as the small group of Gbaya elite in Yaounde began to formulate plans to set up a Gbaya ethnic association. A major stimulus for this move was the growing feeling among non-Fulbe members of the Adamaoua Elites Association that the Fulbe were dominating that organisation. According to this reading of recent events, Fulbe dominance was evidenced by the failure to adhere to the original organisational plan in which it had been agreed that the presidency of the association should rotate among the different peoples of Adamaoua, according to whichever town would host the annual conventions of the association. Then too, the provincial framework of the Adamaoua association had the effect of cutting off the Gbaya of the Mbere Department from the numerous Gbaya inhabitants of the Eastern Province, in towns such as Garoua Boulai, Betare Oya, Bertoua and Batouri.

The initial preparations leading to the creation of the new Gbaya association were carried out by the founding committee with some circumspection;

they feared either that there might be opposition from the government, or
from other quarters, due to the ethnic basis of the grouping or that one or
more political parties might attempt to co-opt the movement. For this
reason, the official (French) name chosen for the new organisation was
Mouvement d'Investissement et d'Assistance Mutuelle, a title with no outward
ethnic referent but which, when abbreviated as an acronym, spelled *moinam*
(in Gbaya, *moi* – to gather together; *nam* – kin). On 18–19 March 1994,
MOINAM successfully held its first convention in Bertoua, capital of the
Eastern Province, with the meeting being very well attended by both western-
educated Gbaya elite as well as by canton chiefs and village headmen from
all over the Gbaya-phone region of Cameroon. Although not officially publi-
cised, there were also Gbaya representatives present from the Central African
Republic.

The issues discussed at this convention ranged across the full gamut of
Gbaya ethnic concerns that have been described in this book thus far – a
fact of some reflexive significance which will be discussed further in a
moment. The central theme of the conference was that no one in Cameroon
could be expected to look after the interests of the Gbaya other than the
Gbaya themselves. Delegates noted that the division of the large Gbaya
population in Cameroon between the Adamaoua and the Eastern Provinces
significantly weakened their electoral clout. This contributed to the present
situation wherein the Gbaya of Adamaoua Province are dominated by Fulbe
interests and the Gbaya of the Eastern Province are upstaged by the so-called
'Belabo mafia' – non-Gbaya elites from the Belabo-Deng Deng area who
have profited from their contacts in Yaounde.

Other topics discussed revolved around similar issues of cultural authenti-
city and empowerment – themes so characteristic of ethnic movements. In
the economic domain, a system of annual dues was created and the monies
collected by this means, aside from supporting the organisational activities
of the MOINAM executive committee, were earmarked for promotion of
Gbaya education, Gbaya businesses, Gbaya music and musicians, as well as
other cultural manifestations and activities. The tendency among Gbaya
parents to give their children names that are not distinctively Gbaya – and
often (Muslim) Fulbe or Hausa – was deplored as a cause of weakened
Gbaya ethnic solidarity. When combined with an increasing avoidance of
speaking the Gbaya language when outside one's home area and a preference
for Fulfulde or French, this practice was said to make it difficult to identify
fellow Gbaya when elsewhere in Cameroon. Gbaya were at risk of losing
their cultural identity, and MOINAM should take steps to counteract this
trend. It was proposed that a Gbaya national holiday be created, with 11
December, the anniversary of Karnu's death, being mooted as a suitable
date. The celebrations for this holiday should be based on authentic Gbaya
rituals, adapted to make them acceptable in modern society. A proposal was

put forward as well to hold a conference on the life of Karnu and the *Koŋgo Wara* war, focusing on enhancing public knowledge, especially among Gbaya youth, of the role of Karnu in the 'fight against colonialism' and the promotion of 'African nationalism' (*Mouvement d'Investissement et d'Assistance Mutuelle* 1994). There was also discussion of the need to return to authentic cultural forms of Gbaya leadership, given that much of the present ceremonial and procedures associated with Gbaya chiefship are of Fulbe or European colonial origins.

Somewhat ironically, perhaps, the conference also considered the need to diffuse within the Gbaya community academic studies of Gbaya culture in order to 'fight against cultural rootlessness', especially among the Gbaya youth who 'no longer have available (Gbaya) cultural and historical points of reference' (*Mouvement d'Investissement et d'Assistance Mutuelle* 1994, my translation). In particular, the Reverend Thomas Christensen's *An African Tree of Life* (1990), a study of 'traditional' Gbaya ritual symbolism and its resonances with Christian belief, was singled out as a first candidate for translation (into French!), with works by others of us who have written in English about Gbaya history, society and language being also on this putative translation list.

The history of the creation of MOINAM and, especially, its concern to use the printed word to disseminate a sense of shared and 'authentic' Gbaya history and values, is doubtless a good example of what Anderson (1991) had in mind when he wrote of the role of 'print capitalism' in the 'imagination' of communities. But it is important to remember (*pace* Anderson) that in 1928 Karnu was able to mobilise a major social movement with prominent communalist attributes – one which Coquery-Vidrovitch (1988: 179) has claimed to be 'the largest peasant insurrection experienced by sub-Saharan Africa between the two World Wars' – in the total absence of 'print capitalism' or even of literacy. In non-literate societies, terms of social categorisation such as the Gbaya concept of *zu duk* (clan or ethnic group) offer potential for 'imagination' of communal ties beyond the boundaries of the face-to-face community.

For those of us in social scientific or missionary occupations who have written on Gbaya history, society, religion and language over the past several decades, the avidity with which an ethnic movement like MOINAM has latched on to our publications might give us some cause for reflection. This is not to imply that most of us did not undertake such publishing enterprises with our eyes open. For example, in the case of the symposium entitled *Contribution de la Recherche Ethnologique à l'Histoire des Civilisations du Cameroun* (Tardits ed. 1981), some forty social scientists collaborated to produce a series of papers documenting the social histories of many of the peoples of Cameroon. This material was intended to provide basic documentation necessary for the production of school textbooks which had tended, up to that time in Cameroon, to dwell more on the history of the colonising powers than on the history of African peoples. For this reason, our project was carried out with the enthusiastic approval of Cameroon's Minister of Education. At the same time, it should be recorded that some careful thought was given by the editorial committee to the choice of title for the symposium, particularly in connection with the decision to employ the word '*civilisations*'. Using the term in its plural form certainly coincided with the original conceptual framing of most of the participants' field researches, which were based on cultural and/or linguistic boundary criteria. On the other hand, given the prominent concern of the Cameroon government of the day for 'nation building' and de-emphasising ethnic distinctions, this title risked provoking official displeasure.

Returning to a point raised in the introduction to the present work, Amselle may feel the MOINAM case provides an apt illustration of his contention that (1990: 22, my translation):

> the invention of ethnic groups is the joint work of colonial administrators, professional anthropologists, and those who combine these two qualifications.

I would disagree, on the grounds mentioned in Chapter 1 and further discussed in the Epilogue, although I do think that it does illustrate the way in which ethnic conceptualisations are continually subject to reworking on the basis of the materials that come to hand, anthropologists' publications included.

GLOBAL VERSUS LOCAL PERSPECTIVES IN POLITICAL PRACTICE

This discussion of recent political developments in the Mbere Department draws our attention to several issues concerning the interaction, or imbrication, of global and local social processes within the Cameroon state-society interface. For one thing, the various strategies envisioned at present by Gbaya political actors differ quite markedly in their implications for future participation in the national political arena. Certainly, in all cases presently under consideration, one can agree with Gledhill (1994: 20–1), following Giddens (1985) and Asad (1992), that political actors in a locality such as the Mbere Department, however spatially removed from central positions of influence within the Cameroon state, must necessarily be orienting their political practice with ultimate reference to the state, to a greater or lesser degree. To paraphrase Gledhill (1994: 21), even struggles for cultural autonomy and against domination take place under conditions that have been shaped by that domination. However, certain political stances are much more local than global in orientation and draw on cultural repertoires that are firmly rooted in specific local histories.

Consider, for example, a political stance such as that of the MDR, the so-called *kirdi* party, which phrases its message first and foremost in regionalist terms relevant to the political situation in 'the north' – so long subject to Muslim and particularly Fulbe hegemony. The category '*kirdi*', like '*haaɓe*', has no meaning within Cameroonian political discourse other than in opposition to the '*Fulɓe*' and/or the 'Muslim' categories, with all their historical loadings. But, while building a strong regional constituency in an attempt to overturn Fulbe dominance in the north, the MDR also had the aim of exercising influence in the national political arena. Counting on the well-rehearsed principle of Cameroon politics according to which the ruling party will seek to co-opt its elite opponents by offering them a share in the state's spoils, the MDR leaders could reasonably expect that if they made a good showing in their northern constituencies, they would be offered posts in the new government – and this is what transpired. Indeed, one measure of the relative success of Biya's opponents in the 1992 elections is the ludicrously large size of his new cabinet, more than forty as I write, where space has had to be found for so many erstwhile opponents wishing to jump on the Biya bandwagon, however belatedly.[5]

In the case of MOINAM, its political message is conveyed in yet more culturally specific terms, even if this poses difficulties relating to issues such as restricted literacy in Gbaya-phone languages and the necessity of weeding out the 'alien' influences that have infiltrated 'authentic' Gbaya culture. Nonetheless, a globalising orientation in MOINAM's ethnic particularism is not hard to detect. As noted above, the prime movers in the creation of MOINAM have been western-educated elite – the first generation of Gbaya to gain much of a toehold within the higher echelons of Cameroon state employment. It is they who are asserting the need (and possibly, they might claim, their right) to define the content of a more self-conscious Gbaya culture geared to the demands of participation within the national political arena (cf. Gellner 1983 and Anderson 1991).[6]

Moving to an even more local frame of reference, for most of the Gbaya whom I interviewed concerning the outbreaks of violence in Meiganga in 1991 and 1992, the key issue was the purported attempt of 'the Fulbe' to take over the chieftaincies of Meiganga, Meidougou and elsewhere, while at the same time exercising an increasing control over the commercial economy of the region. From this perspective, present-day political action can be linked historically with the feats of the hero Karnu in fighting for Gbaya autonomy against the domination exercised by the Fulbe and the French, and national political affairs of the present day, such as the move to multi-party elections, are of distinctly secondary significance.

So whereas the ethnic violence of 1991 and 1992 does betray evidence of a greater articulation of social practices in the Mbere Department with outside forces, we must also keep in mind the other, specifically local, side of the coin. A major analytic requirement here is to determine the appropriate weighting to be given to social phenomena seen as reflexes of the organisation and functioning of the state (or other more global processes) versus social practices that can be better interpreted as relatively autonomous forces emerging from local and more culturally specific realities. Rather than being dictated to by general theories about the workings of the state in Africa, I believe it to be preferable in the first instance to approach each case empirically and to choose the analytical frame of reference most appropriate to the problem in hand. In this respect, I tend to agree with Schatzberg (1988: 142–3; see also Burnham 1991: 83) that:

> The state is also a fluid and contextual entity whose shape and internal configurations of power are constantly changing. Also changing, there-fore, is the line dividing state and civil society as the fortunes and boundaries of the state ebb and flow . . . Moreover, as Bayart suggests, perhaps this fluidity in the boundary between state and civil society renders the standard dichotomy too simple to be of much analytical utility . . . Interactions between state and civil society should be the object of empirical inquiry before they become the subject of deductive theorising. Outcomes of these interactions are not predetermined and vary significantly as the state ascends and declines.

In order to pursue these analytical issues, while seeking to clarify further our understanding of recent political events in the Mbere Department, I want now to consider in turn three themes that find expression within this social field.

REGIONAL REORIENTATION OF ELITES AND NATIONAL POLITICAL PROCESSES

As Geschiere (1986: 77, my translation) argued with regard to the Maka region during the first two decades after independence:

> The hegemonical project of the Ahidjo regime was scarcely able to integrate the popular modes of political action and, rather, limited itself to the incorporation of the regional elite – a process which had the effect of deepening the separation between this elite and the peasants.

This, indeed, appears to have been a widespread, if not universal, phenom-enon in Cameroon at that period – one which reflected both the relative strength of the state as well as the perceived threats to these elites arising from witchcraft accusations and other social levelling mechanisms specific to their particular cultures. Local elites were thus in an ambivalent position with regard to their home areas and didn't have too much need, in any case, to retain strong local roots to further their careers on the national scene – given the marked centralising tendencies characteristic of the Cameroon state during the Ahidjo period. As already explained in Chapter 4, although the Gbaya elite at this same period were fewer in number and rather less successful than the Maka elite in gaining access to the political centre, due both to their more limited access to western-style education and the domination of political opportunities within Adamaoua by Fulbe elites, the situation in the Mbere Department was still broadly similar to that described by Geschiere.

It seems relevant to open a parenthesis here to note that the overly broad categorical usage of the term 'elite' in much of the current literature on Cameroon can have unsatisfactory consequences when one is seeking to evaluate the political influence and social trajectories of such actors. Thus, for example, the tendency to consider anyone with more than a minimum degree of western education as an 'intellectual' and therefore a member of the regional elite, as did Geschiere in his 1982 book, might well have been appropriate for a period when secondary education was still relatively rare and jobs in the public administration still relatively plentiful. But now, with government employment being progressively cut back and many secondary school graduates counting themselves among the unemployed, persons who would formerly have expected to be able to join the elite of white-collar workers (more aptly referred to as 'tergalisés' in Cameroonian French, after a popular brand-name of cloth used for suits) find themselves hustling for a living in the cities or back on the farm in their home villages. A more nuanced concept of the 'elite' therefore seems required. However, rather than opting for an abstract and historically unsituated definition of the 'elite', it seems preferable to envision that different combinations of political, economic, educational, religious and prestige considerations are likely to be variably significant in defining elites in different local settings (cf. Bayart 1993: 176–9) and that the key questions to be addressed in each case are the means and extent to which such locally relevant social practices may be translated into public efficacity and prominence on the regional or national stage.

With the rise of multi-party politics and the weakening of the state over the last five to ten years, the balance of attracting forces between state centre and home region has shifted substantially for many members of the Cameroonian elite. Multi-party elections have enhanced the importance of local and regional constituency building for those with political ambitions, which in turn have been facilitated by the new-found legitimacy accorded ethnically based political organisations, even on the national stage. I am thinking here, for example, of such neo-traditional ethnic organisations as the 'Ngondo' of the Duala (Austen 1992) or 'Laakam' of the Bamileke, in comparison to which MOINAM of the Gbaya is distinctly parvenu.

This centripetal tendency in elite politics stands in marked contrast with the monolithically centrist and nationalist ideology of the UNC and the repression of particularistic tendencies so common during Ahidjo's day. At that period, as Chazan and her co-authors (Chazan *et al.* 1992: 201–2) have noted, the Cameroon state tried to follow a predominantly 'normative' strategy through emphasis on the construction of 'the nation' by suppression of non-party organisations and on national symbols. In more recent years, the weakening of the Cameroon state and the shrinkage of state sector employment opportunities, resulting from the economic crisis and the World Bank's structural adjustment programme, have encouraged greater attention to the pursuit of local-level economic activities in the private sector and emphasised the need for greater self-reliance in the supply of local social services such as schools and dispensaries. This more whole-hearted interest of elites in playing an active role in their home regions is also, no doubt, an expression of the pervasive discontent with the Biya regime, since political opposition can more easily be organised from a local base. These are the factors, then, that explain the current widespread emphasis in Cameroon's sociopolitical life on local or regional elites associations, indigenous non-governmental organisations and ethnic associations.

On the other hand, while one can detect a general trend toward a renewal of elites' interest in maintaining close ties with their home regions, this process cannot yet be said to explain much about the politics of daily life in rural areas of northern Cameroon like the Mbere Department. Neither does it go far in helping us to understand the violence in Meiganga in 1991 and 1992. This is because much of the content of social life in the Mbere Department continues to be generated by culturally specific practices rooted in local, ethnically defined social categories – practices in which elites must necessarily participate to the extent that they orient their activities toward the local political arena. Moreover the Gbaya, much like the Mbororo discussed in the preceding two chapters, remain only loosely articulated with the Cameroonian political centre, lacking well-developed elite networks or other means of effective access to the resources of the state. The Cameroonian state may have marked out the playing field but locally specific rules control much of the game.

Viewed from this bottom-up perspective, general theories about 'the state in Africa' are not likely to be of much explanatory power for the purposes of this book. For example, however useful Bayart's (1993) concepts of '*la politique du ventre*', 'the rhizome state', and 'the world of networks' may be in conceptualising the ramifying clientelist links radiating out from the political centre of an African state like Cameroon, these essentially top-down concepts give us limited grasp on local political realities. Bayart appears repeatedly to acknowledge the difficulty he experiences in attempting to make analytical space for locally grounded forms of political action within his general model of the African state. This is apparent, for example, in his references to 'the hollowness of the State' (1993: 258) or to the 'radical heterogeneity' arising from the fact that 'the social foundations of the contemporary state are geographically differentiated' (1993: 179). And yet, the need to accord adequate attention to local political realities is especially apparent during a period such as the present one in Cameroon, where the resources available to the state are diminishing under the combined pressures of the economic crisis, the structural adjustment programme and multi-party competitiveness. Less and less of value is presently flowing through the 'rhizomes' of the Cameroon state, even where they have managed to take full root in the rural areas. At the same time, in numerous zones of the political periphery in Cameroon, the Mbere Department among them, the state is finding it increasingly difficult to exercise effective political controls on a routinised administrative basis. There has been a rise in banditry – 'coupeurs de route' or 'jargina' as they are known in the north – or even, in the more extreme cases, chronic, low intensity warfare, such as that which has pitted the Kotoko people against the Choa Arabs over the last several years in the Province de l'Extrême Nord. In the latter case, the Cameroon state appears to have lost effective control over its armed forces, elements of which have engaged in vendettas and extra-judicial killings.[7]

Even leaving aside such drastic breakdowns of law and order, although they have become distressingly common in recent years, one can agree with Bayart (1993: 261) that African states such as Cameroon have:

> up to now . . . failed to achieve this ideal (of a total, well-policed state); the development of an 'integral State' from a 'soft State' . . . has not taken place despite advances in the technology of social control.

But, as we shall discuss more fully in a moment, Bayart goes on to argue that this 'incompletion' of the state can best be understood as a function of its character as a 'rhizome state' of personal networks and that analyses such as the one developed in the present book, which seek to give due weight to locally significant cultural differences via the concept of ethnicity, are fundamentally misdirected (Bayart 1993: 265).

ISLAM AND RELIGIOUS PLURALISM IN NORTHERN CAMEROON

If much of the recent literature on the state-society interface in present-day Cameroon has dwelt on the activities of elites as political entrepreneurs, there has been much less attention devoted to religious factors in this equation. However, within the Fulbe-dominated society of the northern Cameroon region, as discussed in Chapter 3, Islam is of central importance both in its close association with the traditional centres of political power as well as in its key role in the process of Fulbeisation. That being said, although the pre-eminence of Islam in the north has often appeared to outsiders as monolithic, Fulbe society itself is a potential factional battleground – factions which may express themselves in religious terms. For example, a Fulbe-dominated organisation such as the Adamaoua Elites Association, quite apart from its internal ethnic cleavages, also displays various competitive tendencies within its Fulbe membership – youth versus elders, progressive versus conservative, reformist versus more 'traditional' forms of Islam.

The politics of religious practice within northern Cameroon society is therefore expressed in several ways – in the well-publicised competition between Christianity and Islam for converts among the so-called '*haaɓe*' or '*kirdi*' peoples as well as in the cleavages generated by sectarian currents within Islam itself. While the jibes about monkey- and insect-eating that flew about prior to the violence in Meiganga in 1991 indicate that the longstanding opposition between Muslims and Christians played its part in these events, and we will examine this issue further in a moment, it is the phenomenon of sectarian divisions internal to Islam that I want to consider first since it illustrates how the society of the Mbere Department is increasingly becoming involved in more global ideological debates.

Let us remind ourselves of the relevant background to our present case. Although Islam developed in northern Cameroon from the pre-colonial period as both a religion of political domination (associated with the Adamawa *jihad*) and a religion of commerce, in the Mbere Department the commercial influence has always been in the ascendant due to its position on the periphery of Fulbe state power. As explained in Chapter 3, even in most of the centres of Fulbe power in Cameroon (Maroua and a few small other towns excepted), Islamic scholarship has remained relatively underdeveloped – in comparison, say, with the famous centres of Islamic learning in northern Nigeria (Paden 1973; Kane 1993; Burnham and Last 1994). This relative under-development of Islamic learning in northern Cameroon, in turn, must be viewed in the light of both pre-colonial and colonial history. As noted by Genest and Santerre (1982: 382, quoting French colonial archives, my translation), the French government's policy in its black African colonies was built on three principles: 'to support the Islam of the marabout, to hinder "Arabisation", and to moderate the influence of northern Nigeria'.

The commercial setting in which much of northern Cameroonian popular Islam has flourished has been conducive to a 'this-worldly' orientation of religious values, as well as a notable degree of heterodoxy. Adamawa, the traders' Eldorado of the pre-colonial period, retained this reputation throughout the colonial and most of the post-colonial period, supporting a large and heterogeneous population of Fulbeised Muslim traders. In the Mbere Department, the major economic attractions were the cattle wealth of the Mbororo and the smuggling and other opportunities offered by the proximity of the Central African Republic frontier. These economic opportunities began to diminish in the mid-1970s, with the decline in Mbororo numbers due to cattle disease among other factors, and this economic stagnation accelerated through the 1980s in tandem with that of the national economy. This same period witnessed the maturation of the first significantly large cohort of educated youth in Adamaoua, drawn from both the Fulbe and non-Fulbe communities, the result of the post-independence expansion in educational opportunities. For the better educated segment of these young men (and a few young women), western-style education had prepared them for white-collar employment, most likely in some part of the public services which were the main source of jobs. Even for those who had not achieved much western education, there was still a marked preference for 'modern' jobs outside of the 'traditional' trading sector dominated by their elders (see Boutrais 1994: 193). But many of these hopes have not been fulfilled and, for some of this disappointed generation, answers have been sought in religion.

As mentioned earlier in this chapter, my interviews with informants in Meiganga concerning the violent events of 1991 and 1992 contained frequent allusions to unruly youth. In addition to explanations of their behaviour that centred on drug use or unemployment, there were also several references to the involvement of certain *mallum'en*, who were said to have emphasised the religious justification for strong action by Muslims in support of the *villes mortes* campaign. This activity reflects a wider movement within northern Cameroonian Islam over the past decade or more in which reformist tendencies have grown in strength in opposition to the heterodox and 'this-worldly' popular Islam that has long predominated.

In common with other Muslim regions of West Africa, northern Cameroon has experienced, over the past decade or two, an increasing degree of religious influence from the Middle East, both as a result of Saudi Arabian petrodollar aid and the ideological currents stirred up by the Iranian revolution. In more urban settings, especially in northern Nigeria where they have reached a fuller development (Last 1988: 266–69; Gumi 1992; Kane 1993; Barkindo 1993), the reformist movements that these international contacts have stimulated have especially oriented their efforts in opposition to the politically and commercially powerful Muslim brotherhoods, such as the Tijaniyya, on the grounds that they encourage religious practices not in accordance with the authentic Islam of the *sunna*. In more general terms, and particularly relevant in the northern Cameroon context, reformists have also drawn legitimacy from the structural opposition between the modernism of the juniors versus the traditionalism of the elders. Beyond promoting Islamic and Arabic language education, disseminating reformist literature, and constructing mosques, these movements appeal to the disaffected youth to sweep away heterodox and venal popular Islam. In its place is to be (re)instituted true Islam which will be capable of competing against the ideological and political dominance of the western materialism of the Christian nations (see Brenner 1993).

Although certain sectors of the local Muslim community have been touched by their message, the Mbere Department has remained on the periphery of these reformist developments up to now. However, local Islam has also been buffeted over the past decade or more by internal cross-currents emanating from other sources. As described in Chapter 3, the influx of Mai'ine Fulbe, many of whom are adherents of the '*Tarbiyya*' brotherhood (the local name for Al Hajj Ibrahim Niasse's branch of the Tijaniyya), has injected another discordant note into the local scene. To some extent, Gbaya concern over retention of their local chieftaincy rights, which figures largely in local understandings of the recent episodes of violence, can be understood as a reaction against this in-migration of Fulbe agro-pastoralists and the accompanying crop damage and land claims, and expressions of Fulbe xenophobia. My discussions with certain members of the Fulbe community in Meiganga lead me to conclude that the arrival of the Mai'ine in the Mbere Department has not found universal favour within the Fulbe category either (see Boutrais 1994: 180).

This look at some of the sectarian tendencies within Islam, which have begun to impact on social life in the Mbere Department, can serve to make the point that the articulations of local society with the global do not always pass through the medium of the state, even though the state may make attempts to control or suppress them. For example, during the Ahidjo period, various sectarian religious movements, both Islamic and Christian, were subject to close surveillance or banned outright. Although such claims are hard to document, it is said that the Tarbiyya movement, many of whose adherents were relatively recent migrants from Nigeria, was one of the religious groups that attracted such official displeasure – possibly because Ahidjo, with his close links with Muslim business circles, found the 'traditional' Islam of northern Cameroon more congenial. Given the close proximity and strong historical links with Nigeria and the increasingly active interest of various Middle Eastern countries in diffusing Islamic doctrines in West Africa, such controls over the spread of Islamic religious beliefs and practices were never likely to be totally effective. However, to date, although these newer Islamic movements have joined with longer established Mahdist beliefs to enliven religious debates in northern Cameroon, they have yet to achieve the national political importance that they have in several other African countries (Brenner 1993).

AN EMERGING REGIONAL CULTURE FOR NORTHERN CAMEROON?

From time to time in this book, I have discussed the potential for the expansion of the Fulbe ethnic category, via the process of ethnic assimilation I have labelled 'Fulbeisation', so as to become the demographically preponderant ethnic group in northern Cameroon. The social practices and boundary markers that constitute the Fulbeisation process are linked together as a coherent set by a cultural logic which the members of this social category themselves term *pulaaku*. In its Fulbe variant (that is, as opposed to Mbororo understandings of this term), *pulaaku* prescribes certain minimal ethnic boundary conditions for admission to the broad Fulbe category, while at the same time establishing an internal hierarchy of status and cultural refinement. That this cultural logic has a strong assimilative potential when operating in the context of Fulbe political and economic domination has been repeatedly documented in ethnographic studies throughout the north (see Tardits 1981 and Boutrais *et al.* 1984 for useful summaries of much of this literature), and we have seen the particular influences of this ideology on the Gbaya and the Mbororo in previous chapters of this book.

Ethnic assimilation to the Fulbe category has tended to be more accentuated in urban settings and in areas that are directly subject to the power of 'traditional' Fulbe chiefdoms, and yet this process is by no means restricted to these milieux (see Burnham 1991: 83). The potential for Fulbeisation must be understood more generally in relation to the pervasive logic of Fulbe incorporative cultural discourse operating within the successive systems of ethnically based differential incorporation that have characterised the pre-colonial, colonial and post-colonial phases of northern Cameroonian history since the Adamawa *jihad*. Although certainly not 'primordial', and notwithstanding the fact that it may be employed by actors in a tactical manner in different social situations, the logic of Fulbe ethnicity, as a culturally linked set of social practices, has been a persistent phenomenon towards which, I dare say, most actors in northern Cameroon have had to take a stance for at least the last 150 years.

As my ethnographic case studies have shown, it would indeed be 'far too simplistic to reduce [the societal divisions of the north] to a contradiction between a dominant Peul (Fulbe) minority, uniformly Muslim, and the dominated *Haabé* or *Kirdi* pagan majority' (Bayart 1993: 45). On the other hand, Bayart's (1993: 46) conceptualisation of the north as:

> the hegemony of a block in power, cemented culturally by the Islamic way of life, but ethnically heterogeneous, since it is made up, in addition to the great Foulbé notables, of Hausa traders and converted 'elites' of Kirdi origin . . .

critically leaves out reference to the assimilative force of Fulbeisation in this 'historic equation'. The Fulbeisation process, although it was certainly very much aided by the long period of Fulbe political and economic dominance up through 1982, cannot be adequately conceived as being caused by the extension of clientelist networks of the 'rhizome state', since it is a cultural practice that affects the daily life of all the population of the north, not just the elites and their networks.

Working in northern Cameroon in the 1960s and 1970s, it seemed likely that Fulbeisation was on the way to creating a more uniform regional culture in the north. Ahidjo was in the ascendant and the Fulbe/Fulbeised society of northern Cameroon was his power base. Looking over the border at northern Nigeria, an analogous process of 'Hausaisation' was also at full steam. At this period, the main counter-current to Fulbe politico-cultural hegemony in the north was the Christian mission effort, which had made substantial numbers of converts among many of the non-Fulbe peoples, the Gbaya included. This competition was often played out in quite material terms and sometimes even degenerated into outright violence, as in rural Fulbe chiefdoms like Rei Bouba where Christian chapels were set alight from time to time. But it was also expressed in a competition of cultural orientations. In this connection, Christian conversion symbolised not just a rejection of Islam and Fulbeisation but also the choice of a more westernised lifestyle. As Schultz (1979: 201) noted for converts to Christianity in Guider:

> By opting for Christianity, a Pagan can advance while maintaining an identity separate from the Fulbe; he can surmount the cultural limitations of his Pagan group of origin without having to give up his identity as, for example, a Guidar or a Moundang; he can get ahead without having to go over to the enemy.

Such converts are more likely to dress in western-style clothing, to use French as a lingua franca, and to attend western-style schools. In short, conversion to one or the other of the two 'world' religions serves to draw the convert into one or the other of two globalising cultural discourses – worlds that extend well beyond the frontiers of the Cameroon state and offer different conceptions of both modernity and eternity. In this context, Gledhill's (1994: 23) point is apposite that:

> Though particular situations always reflect the interaction of the local and the global, local social and cultural histories now find expression in action in ways that are part of a common experience of modernity . . .

as long as the term 'modernity' is understood as referring to a field of cultural contestation rather than as an ethnocentric and evolutionist synonym for westernisation.[8]

Today, in retrospect, we can see that the Fulbeisation of northern Cameroon society reached its post-colonial apogee under Ahidjo and has lost ground subsequently under the Biya regime. In part, this decline has been due to the loss of the political and economic advantages the region had enjoyed under Ahidjo as well as the dismemberment of the formerly unitary territorial administration, centred in Ahidjo's home town of Garoua, into three separate provinces. The administrations of these newly created provinces are now frequently staffed by southern Cameroonian Christians, fundamentally reversing the practice under Ahidjo that had given marked preference to Fulbe/Fulbeised northerners. On occasion, some of these southern administrators have attempted to dismantle, although not always with success, the structures of ethnically based differential incorporation, such as the various formal or informal ethnically differentiated taxation systems (see earlier chapters and Schultz 1979: 17), that had long helped to underpin Fulbe dominance in northern regional affairs.

In part, the pace and character of Fulbeisation has also changed because of the opening up of northern Cameroonian society to a greater diversity of social forces, which have had varying impacts on the different social categories and groups that constitute this complex social field. This increased openness was facilitated by President Biya's relaxation of the controls on voluntary associations that had been a central tenet of the Ahidjo regime. This (relative) political liberalisation has culminated in the recent shift to multi-partyism, an innovation which had been supported by Biya in the early days of his administration but which was to become such a focus for his recalcitrance later on (see Amnesty International 1991a; 1991b and 1994a).

On the one hand, as we have seen in the case of an ethnic association like MOINAM (one of the many ethnic associations which are currently proliferating all over Cameroon), the move to multi-party politics and the political liberalisation measures of the Biya period have opened space for expressions of political interests phrased in more locally specific ethnic terms. For the Gbaya, like other non-Fulbe groups in the north, this amounts to an assertion that here is a people who can construct their own version of ethnic identity, adjusted to fit the modern political conjuncture, in a form that is unmediated by the hegemonic cultural projects of either the Fulbe or the Christianised évolué ethnic groups of southern Cameroon. To use Miller's (1994: 293) phraseology, they no longer have to see themselves as 'only second-rate versions of someone else'. On the other hand, as we have seen in our discussion of the competition between sectarian tendencies within Cameroonian Islam, the recently increased exposure to international Islamic discourses can promote either more globalising conceptions of Islamic religious identity within the Fulbe category itself – as in the questioning by religious reformists of the heterodoxy and particularism that have long characterised Fulbe Islam, or can lead to a greater exclusivism and xenophobia, as in the case of the Tijaniyya brotherhood among the Mai'ine Fulbe.

8

AN EPILOGUE ON ETHNICITY

Intellectuals must find it reassuring to be able to deconstruct ethnicity in the comfort of their studies. Attempts to deny the substance or the reality of the phenomenon are legion – for example, Bayart's phrase (1993: Chap. 1) 'the shadow theatre of ethnicity' quickly springs to mind. But out in the real world, ethnic politics, with its commonly attendant violence, shows little sign of vanishing. Benedict Anderson (1991: 5–6), commenting on similar academic treatment of the related phenomenon of nationalism, noted:

> unlike most other isms, nationalism has never produced its own grand thinkers: no Hobbeses, Toquevilles, Marxes, or Webers. This 'emptiness' easily gives rise, among cosmopolitan and polylingual intellectuals, to a certain condescension. Like Gertrude Stein in the face of Oakland, one can rather quickly conclude that there is 'no there there'.

Indeed, Anderson's (1991: 6) remarks concerning Gellner's (1964) attitude toward nationalism can easily be extended to the views of many writers on ethnicity:

> With a certain ferocity Gellner . . . rules that 'Nationalism is not the awakening of nations to self-consciousness: it invents nations where they do not exist.' The drawback to this formulation, however, is that Gellner is so anxious to show that nationalism masquerades under false pretences that he assimilates 'invention' to 'fabrication' and 'falsity', rather than to 'imagining' and 'creation' . . . In fact, all communities larger than primordial villages of face-to-face contact (and perhaps even here) are imagined. Communities are to be distinguished, not by their falsity/genuineness, but by the style in which they are imagined.

The strategies of argument that have been used in the deconstruction of ethnicity merit close consideration and evaluation since they are very influential and show little sign of disappearing. Pursuing for the moment the reasoning of Bayart, the most prominent commentator on the Cameroonian political scene, we can see that he does not go so far as to adopt the extreme position of Amselle (1990: 22), quoted in Chapters 1 and 7, but writes (1993: 42, my translation):

> The existence, even the irreducibility, of ethnic consciousness cannot be denied. It is not the expression of an elementary stage of development to be condemned by modernisation. Neither is it simply the result of the manipulations by colonists, imperialists or even the incumbents of the contemporary state.

However, he then continues (1993: 46–7):

> The very notion of ethnic group, at least in the form in which it is usually imagined, that of a given entity, going back over centuries and corresponding to a limited geographical area, does not square with fact. Anthropologists are now interestingly abandoning this aim . . . Ethnicity is a complex and relative phenomenon, not a stable combination of invariables, a static and atemporal structure.

The principal focus of Bayart's attack here, if it is not simply the opinions of writers in the popular press or those of ethnic actors themselves, appears to be the concept of primordial attachments – a notion that was widely held by earlier schools of social thought and which was particularly significant in the thinking of Parsonian modernisation theorists and fellow-travellers (Almond and Coleman 1960; Shils 1962; Geertz ed. 1963; Inkeles 1966). As an unhistoricised concept, the primordial view of ethnicity is much less prevalent in recent anthropological writing (as Bayart acknowledges) and although it deserves continued rebuttal, we should not throw out the concept of ethnicity with the bathwater of modernisation theory. Rather, we need to take this phenomenon seriously and analyse its historicity – its creation, its persistence, its transformations, its dissolution and its role in shaping events. As we have seen in the case of the societies of the Mbere Department, ethnic categorisations are subject to change, although they have the capacity in certain social contexts to persist, as logics informing social action, over substantial periods of time. Ethnicity is certainly not primordial, nor is it an attribute that somehow, necessarily, brands an individual for life.

In this regard, Bayart's (1993: 42–56) principal argument that ethnicity is 'consciousness without structure' is unsatisfactory. It is indeed an interesting fact, as Bayart notes, that numerous ethnic groups in northern Cameroon today can be shown to be comprised of populations of heterogeneous origins. It is possible to show, as I have discussed above, that the present 'Gbaya' population of the Mbere Department includes a considerable number of individuals of Mbum ancestry, and that many 'Gbaya' cultural practices are of Mbum origin. The logic of Gbaya 'categorical' clanship has certainly facilitated the incorporation of formerly non-Gbaya elements, as indeed have similar clanship logics in many of the so-called *kirdi* cultures throughout the north (Martin 1981; Adler 1982). And, as I have argued in earlier chapters, categorical clanship, although typically envisioning closer kinship among fellow clansmen than does the concept of shared ethnicity, is based nonetheless on a reasoning analogous to that defining an ethnic group. From this perspective, clanship is often better seen as sub-ethnicity rather than as super-lineage.

Bayart's response to such historical data which reveal a 'fusion of disparate elements' (1993: 47) within an ethnic category is to consider that this somehow renders ethnicity false, insubstantial or unauthentic. This or that population is not *really* what they claim to be – their name covers up a great heterogeneity of culture and descent! But of course, concepts of social categorisation and community are all ultimately based on actors' subjective cultural constructions. In other words, not just the 'ethnic group' but also concepts like 'state', 'class', 'elders', 'juniors', 'women', 'men', and so on, are all 'imagined' in Anderson's (1991: 6) sense.[1] In particular let me emphasise, since we will have occasion to consider this issue further in a moment, that the state is as much a cultural phenomenon – constructed as it is of conceptual notions such as laws, legitimacy, citizenship and boundaries – as is ethnicity. To claim otherwise is to fall prey to a reified structure-versus-culture opposition or to partake of outmoded Marxist arguments concerning infrastructure versus superstructure (see Sahlins 1976). Moreover, the state is not immutable. It is made up of heterogeneous, often overtly dissenting elements. And it is potentially fluid in membership and in territorial demarcation, both *de facto* and *de jure* – a fact with which one is increasingly being forced to come to terms in many African contexts.

But to return to ethnicity, to argue that it is 'consciousness without structure' or that it is not a 'substantial notion' (Bayart 1993: 56) is to neglect the many different ways, at different historical periods, in which ethnicity has been firmly institutionalised as a dominant social cleavage within the society of Cameroon. In earlier chapters, I have documented many instances of ethnically defined differential incorporation based on legal and administrative criteria, both *de facto* and *de jure*. There are also numerous ritual, marital and economic practices in which criteria of ethnic difference are taken for granted by the actors concerned as defining the logical/rational basis for their conduct. These institutional underpinnings, as is the case with all cultural practices, are of course not immutable; they are subject to situational manipulation, historical transformation and dissolution. But they are no more or less substantial or structural than other cultural forms.[2]

However, as discussed in earlier chapters, not all cultural knowledge is ethnically marked – that is, considered relevant to actors' ethnically phrased political projects. As Fredrik Barth (1969: 14) argued:

It is important to recognise that although ethnic categories take cultural differences into account, we can assume no simple one-to-one relationship between ethnic units and cultural similarities and differences. The features that are taken into account are not the sum of 'objective' differences, but only those which the actors themselves regard as significant.

For example, Jafun elders pursuing a Fulbeising strategy do not (as yet) define the use of the leaves of the *barkehi* tree, in infant naming ceremonies and other ritualised contexts, as 'paganism'; this is an element of Mbororo cultural practice which is not currently ethnically marked. Likewise, the present method used by Jafun in the Mbere Department to calculate the amount of bridewealth that should be reimbursed in cases of divorce – a cultural practice which seems to have been adopted in the 1930s or 1940s in analogy with divorce procedures among their neighbours the Gbaya (Dupire 1970: 31), is not acknowledged by the Mbororo as having a Gbaya source and is therefore not ethnically marked either. Indeed, it appears to have become an unquestioned element of Jafun *pulaaku*.

As for forbidding one's wives to sell milk in neighbouring sedentary villages, which is part of the Fulbeising strategy pursued by certain Jafun, this ethnically marked cultural prohibition has certain implications (Burnham 1987: 161; Smith 1974: Chap. 6) in relation to the type of pastoral economy being practised, which makes it a more appealing move for Jafun elders than for many junior men struggling to establish a viable herd unit. In other words, all Jafun individuals, through their socialisation, possess this cultural knowledge, which in the present historical setting has come to be ethnically marked. Jafun actors have a choice whether to follow this practice or not, and they may change their choice situationally in response both to material considerations such as their available cattle wealth as well as to considerations of ethnic identity. That being said, this social behaviour, whether ethnically marked or not, can be seen to have certain entailments for pastoral economic practices (such as its likely effects on the preferred age and sex composition of cattle herds). It is therefore likely to have objectively measurable effects on the success of different pastoralists who are attempting to subsist on their herd resources alone.

The existence of a diversity of cultural practices within a single ethnic category is a fact which has often been remarked upon. Within the Fulbe ethnic category of northern Cameroon, as we have seen, there are quite notable degrees of cultural and linguistic variation – debates over religious orthodoxy, differences over details of *pulaaku*, to say nothing of the very substantial degree of cultural variation among more or less assimilated 'Fulbeising' populations. However, these cultural variations can be and are all subsumed within the ethnic boundaries of the Fulbe category in many interactional contexts of Cameroonian daily life (although, as we have seen, they may often serve as criteria of social stratification within the category). I therefore find Bayart's suggestion (following Martin 1981) that we should avoid the concept of ethnic group and 'speak of a "population of Peul (Fulani) culture – more or less homogeneous – made up of heterogeneous groups"' quite unsatisfactory in its failure to capture the hegemonical implications of the politics of Fulbe ethnic difference in northern Cameroon society.

ETHNICITY, COLONIALISM AND THE STATE

Often linked with attempts to deconstruct ethnicity is the argument which claims that ethnicity is the product of colonialism. Admittedly, we lack firm historical evidence concerning the pre-colonial situation in many African societies; for example, I would say that Amselle's (1990: Chap. III) attempt to demonstrate the chimera-like quality of pre-colonial ethnic identities in southern Mali is reliant more on the absence than on the presence of contemporary evidence. But in areas of Africa where we do have pre-colonial, non-European written sources, as in the case of Shehu Usumanu's *jihad* discussed in Chapter 2, we often find persuasive confirmation of the existence of political projects phrased in terms of ethnic identity.[3]

Therefore, taken in its most extreme and literal form, the denial of the pre-colonial existence of ethnic identity can have no more than rhetorical value. But reading Amselle further, we find that he soon withdraws from these rhetorical heights and writes (1990: 38, my translation):

> Of course, each society, no matter how primitive, is the producer of a spontaneous ethnology in that it has need of a devalorised other in order to create its own identity or to establish its own *socius* . . .

Ethnic identities have not been created solely by colonialism, but it would be surprising if the colonial period had not been a particularly productive moment for ethnic political 'projects'. This is because ethnic discourses tend to be formulated with regard to the 'other' and colonialism represented a big political change in the 'significant other' for African societies. As we have seen in the case of northern Cameroon, as the colonial state developed, it drew upon many novel organisational resources – repressive modes of surveillance, policing and administration, modern means of communication and western education, which contributed to the redefinition and reinstitutionalisation of ethnic boundaries and to a generally greater pervasiveness of ethnic identity in daily life. In the case of the Gbaya in the Mbere region, for example, we have seen how French colonial administrative policies, such as village *regroupement*, the appointment of canton chiefs, and the assessment of head taxes and labour levies according to ethnic criteria, interacted with Gbaya cultural practices to generate a reformulated image of 'Gbaya-ness'. Likewise, the Gbaya involvement with the Protestant missionaries of the Sudan Mission has also been significant in the constitution of present-day

Gbaya ethnic identity. However, since this progressive restructuring of Gbaya ethnicity made use of the cultural materials to hand and was accomplished within the framework of the already existent Gbaya ethnic label, this more socially pervasive identity did not seem novel to the Gbaya actors concerned and has continued to be viewed as deeply rooted in tradition.

Reading Amselle (1990: 39) still further, we encounter the more nuanced argument that 'ancient or exotic societies' are characterised by supple modes of social identification and that the rise of more rigid modes of 'mono-identification' is linked with the emergence of the literate bureaucratic state. This is a more interesting hypothesis, one which closely parallels the argument of Ranger (1983: 248) who claimed:

> Almost all recent studies of nineteenth-century pre-colonial Africa have emphasised that far from there being a single 'tribal' identity, most Africans moved in and out of multiple identities, defining themselves at one moment as subject to this chief, at another moment as a member of that cult, at another moment as part of this clan, and at yet another moment as an initiate in that professional guild.

The processes of ethnic group construction do appear to receive a boost when linked with, or enunciated in opposition to, strongly institutionalised structures of centralised political power, as I remarked above. However, whether the situation prior to the rise of the literate bureaucratic state is best conceived as one of more supple identities or merely as one of more localised identities – i.e., more a question of demographic scale than of greater flexibility, is difficult to determine in many pre-colonial African contexts, *pace* Ranger, due to the paucity of data. Almost as a matter of definition, the 'tribe' as conceived under colonial rule is unlikely to have been prevalent in pre-colonial African societies. Nonetheless, it is likely to have been the case, as Despres (1984: 11) has argued, following Vincent (1974), that, 'The mask of confrontation in these societies is worn at the boundary of the jural community.'

Moving to the present day, it is virtually a truism that processes of ethnic identity formation and transformation, as well as political resistance movements, now take place with reference to state structures, since the state has become the ubiquitous frame of reference in modern times. For example, Bayart (1993: 56) argues:

> Ethnicity . . . is inseparable from the political process structuring the State. Unless it results in an irredentist or separatist plan – something surprisingly rare in postcolonial Africa – ethnic allegiances by definition form part of a 'universe of shared meanings', that of the State.[4]

But, in the light of my discussion of the cases of administrative weakness, declining legitimacy or outright breakdown of the state in Cameroon (which, of course, is by no means the most extreme case in Africa), it is worth asking ourselves just how pervasive is this domain of 'meaning' organised by the state. Viewed from the perspective of northern Cameroon, this domain appears to have been in the process of contracting for much of the last decade. Rather than firm borders, much of Cameroon is bounded by frontier zones, within which smuggling and banditry are rife. The growing economic weakness of the state, bankrupted by spendthrift policies and corruption in the oil-boom years and now under the thumb of a World Bank-mandated structural adjustment programme, has been the root cause of much of this decline, which has witnessed a stagnation or retraction of government services in many areas of daily life. Although the Cameroonian state has not descended to the level of the *Zairois* state (even though one now hears certain disaffected Cameroonian elites arguing rhetorically that it has), Schatzberg's (1988: 142) remark based on data from Zaire is still relevant:

> The state is also a fluid and contextual entity whose shape and internal configurations of power are constantly changing. Also changing, there- fore, is the line dividing state and civil society as the fortunes and boundaries of the state ebb and flow.

We have considered, for example, the role of several globalising religious discourses in opening spaces within the Cameroonian social fabric which the state finds difficulty in controlling. In the cases both of reformist Islam and of Christian development agencies like the Lutheran World Federation, we saw that during the Ahidjo regime, state repression managed to contain these influences. Thus, for example, in the early 1970s, the Ahidjo govern- ment refused an offer from the Lutheran World Federation of a piped municipal water system for Meiganga on the ostensible grounds that this was a service that should be supplied by the state. Needless to say, Gbaya Christians understood this refusal to be an attempt by the Muslim Fulbe to retain their hegemony. In other instances, as in the cases of the banning of various religious sects, both Christian and Muslim, state repression was more explicit.

On the other hand, even during the Ahidjo period, and even less so following the rather forced liberalisation of political life under Biya, the Cameroon state has been far from totally successful in insulating Cameroon society from such competing globalising forces. It is therefore too facile to see the state simply as a totalising force. Such a view conveniently obviates the need for in-depth analysis of culturally diverse local settings, their varying degrees and modes of articulation with the state, and their different experi- ences of and implications for globalising trends.[5]

Summing up his view on the analytical significance of ethnicity in modern African states, Bayart (1993: 49) asserts:

> Ethnicity cannot provide a basic reference point for postcolonial political

arenas, because it is itself constantly being formed and is largely mingled with the phenomenon of the State, for which it is supposed to provide the explanatory key.

I am certainly not arguing that ethnicity provides *the* explanatory key to the state. At the same time, as I have indicated earlier, I do not consider that Bayart's essentially top-down conception of the 'rhizome state', no matter how encompassing, gives us adequate analytical understanding of the political potential of the locally situated cultural logics that do play important roles in orienting actors' political practices. Moreover, I find it surprising, in view of Bayart's strong emphasis on the conception of the state as 'a historical process, a trajectory' which 'obeys a law of incompletion' (1993: 261), that he considers the historicity of ethnicity to somehow consign it to epiphenomenal, 'shadow theatre' status. No more for ethnicity than for the state should we conclude that, because a phenomenon is subject to historical change, it should not be our task to explain the role of these organisational forms in the transformation of African societies.

ETHNICITY, HISTORY AND THE CULTURAL STRUCTURES OF MEANING

Bayart's notion of 'consciousness without structure', in addition to reifying the analytical distinction between culture and social structure, also expresses his neglect or dismissal of the conceptual structure, and the structuring effects, of cultural consciousness. And yet, this is an area of anthropological research that has yielded numerous analytical insights in the study of ethnicity, and the closely related topic of nationalism, over the past several decades. Even Fredrik Barth, whose name has been associated for so long with the view that 'the critical focus of investigation . . . becomes the ethnic *boundary* [Barth's emphasis], not the cultural stuff that it encloses' (Barth 1969: 15), has moved to a position in more recent work where he stresses the importance of analysing the cultural content of ethnically plural societies. As he wrote in 1984 (Barth 1984: 77):

> we need to discuss not just the relations and reproduction of social categories but the conditions for the perpetuation of cultural traditions and ways of life. For this purpose we need concepts that allow us to inquire into the content and changing forms of these ways of life. Society-focused concepts of ethnicity and pluralism provide only oblique and too narrow templates for such topics.

Thus, for Barth, culture has now gained pride of place, seemingly almost to the exclusion of social boundaries! However, although Barth's earlier understanding of ethnicity was no doubt too single-mindedly focused on the question of boundaries, I would not agree that we now have to dispense with this useful concept in order to be able to devote adequate attention to the cultural content of ethnically defined units. Rather, in giving careful consideration to the historicity of ethnic groups and categories and the operation of cultural logics within these social practices, we can see the reproduction (or transformation) of ethnic boundaries as one of a number of effects of culturally defined ethnic projects.

In the present book, I have tended to gloss the various ways in which culture contributes to the ongoing structuration of social behaviour (and therefore to history) under the phrase 'cultural logics', although this has only served as a shorthand. People have very rich repertoires of cultural knowledge which are continuously implicated in the structuration of their social practice. Some of these may be so deeply ingrained as to be enacted routinely, in a virtually unconscious manner. Among the Gbaya, for example, their consumption of manioc porridge, whose name *kam* is synonymous for them with 'food in general', reconfirms each day their 'Gbaya-ness' through their culturally conditioned tastebuds. Gbaya who have not eaten *kam* during the day have not really eaten, no matter how much other sustenance may have passed their lips. On the other hand, for many other Cameroonian peoples, *kam* is a miserable dish fit only for the Gbaya.

Such culturally constructed knowledges and dispositions, supported by naturalising ontologies, may be taken as self-evident or god-given (Douglas 1975). For example, as Bourdieu (1977: 164) expressed these ideas:

> Every established order tends to produce (to very different degrees and with very different means) the naturalisation of its own arbitrariness . . . in the extreme case, that is to say, when there is a quasi-perfect correspondence between the objective order and the subjective principles of organisation (as in ancient societies) the natural and the social world appears as self-evident . . . The instruments of knowledge of the social world are in this case (objectively) [Bourdieu's parenthesis] political instruments which contribute to the reproduction of the social world by producing immediate adherence to the world, seen as self-evident and undisputed, of which they are the product and of which they reproduce the structures in a transformed form.

Bourdieu (1977: 165), like Sahlins (1981) and Kapferer (1988), has placed particular emphasis on 'the taxonomies of the mythico-ritual system' as sources of this self-evidence and legitimation. But the structuring effects of culture, which provides a set of appropriate 'reasons', historical precedents, and so forth to be drawn upon, are apparent in secular, quotidian realms as well, as in the Gbaya attitude toward *kam* just described.

These cultural orientations inhere in (as a result of the action of cultural logics in previous structurations) and are transmitted in various social forms. In addition to myth and ritual, these include language categories in all semantic domains, oral and written traditions or dogmas (such as concepts of natural law and other culturally specific ontologies, including concepts of racial descent), spatial arrangements (such as residential layouts and house plans) and other forms of material culture (including the cattle breeds discussed in Chapter 5, for example), taken-for-granted habits, tastes and manners, divisions of labour, work rhythms, and so forth. As Kapferer (1988: 29 *et seq.*) has argued, analysis of such taken-for-granted cultural dispositions which naturalise ethnic difference can help us to understand actors' often passionate support for ethnically phrased political projects – which excessively situationalist or presentist approaches cannot do. Indeed, attempts to deconstruct ethnicity, or to account for it solely through presentist or situational analyses, fail to give adequate consideration to issues of legitimacy, compliance and commitment – implying thereby that the social tactics of the moment have as much motivating power as 'god-given' moral certainties.

For example, we have seen that Mbororo ideals of marriage, which logically link a preference for endogamy with a racialist theory of cultural transmission, find day-to-day self-evident confirmation in the 'refined' manners of Mbororo actors which, according to the logic of *pulaaku*, are the natural and unique property of Fulani peoples. From this perspective, Mbororo notions of cultural refinement, glossed by terms like *semteende* – 'modesty', 'shame', 'reticence'; *munyal* – 'patience', 'self-mastery'; and *hakkiilo* – 'intelligence', 'foresight' (see Stenning 1959; Riesman 1977; Bocquené 1981), are asserted as so deeply ingrained as to be genetic in origin, and to be expressed in bodily attitudes, demeanour and tone of voice that are 'second nature'.[6] In short, 'proper' marriage produces offspring who display 'proper' behaviour. One is reminded of Ndoudi Oumarou's proud statement of his Jafun identity (Bocquené 1986: 309) as 'a son of the *barkehi*' who had been 'shaved with milk'. He was referring here to the distinctive Jafun naming ceremony when the infant's head is shaved using milk in which the leaves of the *barkehi* tree have been dipped, thus socially ratifying, through bodily inscription, the child's innate Jafun-ness.

Mbororo appear to experience little threat to this racial theory of cultural inheritance, despite the evident contradictions of this racial stereotype in practice, due to the confirmation of this 'naturalness' which is ingrained in so many domains of their everyday life. Equally, despite the great potential for multiplying genealogical connections and for situational manipulation of endo-exogamic marriage strategies that are inherent in a system of (so-called) 'patrilateral parallel cousin marriage' (which Bourdieu 1977: 30–71 and others such as Dupire 1970 and Conte 1983 have analysed at length), there is a strong sense of historical continuity in the Mbororo endogamic preference, which is logically implicated in the ongoing structuration of the Mbororo as a distinct pastoral social category.

The Jafun understanding of the continuity of their *pulaaku* traditions, despite the many evident social changes that have taken place, is well exemplified in their telling of the history of Ardo Idje which we have discussed in earlier chapters. Idje's quasi-mythic role in suppressing the *soro* stick-beating contests, which in earlier years had been a central element in Jafun *pulaaku*, can be seen by the Jafun of today as part and parcel of the leadership of an adept *ardo*, who heroically and successfully resisted the oppression of the *laamiido* of Ngaoundere and maintained Mbororo political and cultural independence from Fulbe hegemony. As Sahlins (1981: 7) remarked, 'the historical efficacy of persons, objects and events . . . arises in their cultural value.' In this regard, Idje's wise conduct as an archetypal Mbororo leader, although advocating change in Mbororo culture, may be said to have reaffirmed the core values of *pulaaku* by protecting Jafun ethnic difference and sense of superiority. In changing Jafun culture, Ardo Idje was also preserving its continuity.[7]

I am arguing, in relation to the old question of whether the event threatens the structure, that ethnically phrased political projects (both at the micro and the macro level) are continually open to (re)formulation, in relation to the available cultural materials and the current political situation – both of which are themselves subject to ongoing change. I am also arguing that, in the course of the lived, everyday experience of actors, the self-evident historical rootedness of ethnicity finds reassertion, both subtly and overtly, through the self-referring linkages of mutually supportive cultural meanings – conferring, in the great majority of situations, an ongoing sense of structure and continuity. We may often be able to demonstrate analytically that the cultural content and personnel of ethnic categories are changing (objectively speaking). Equally, the ethnic actors themselves may well be aware of such changes and may reinterpret these changes situationally, as appropriate. But, at the same time, the logic of tradition, combined with the day-to-day self-evidence inherent in taken-for-granted cultural dispositions, is available to validate a sense of continuity for the actors concerned.

In this regard, Hobsbawm and Ranger's (1983) popular notion of the 'invention of tradition', however appropriate in certain social contexts, can be positively unhelpful in other cases if it deflects our analytical attention away from the sources of social continuity and legitimacy which derive from actors' historically constituted cultural knowledge as expressed in their everyday practices. (Hobsbawm himself [1983: 1–2] seems to acknowledge this in his definitional contrast between 'invented tradition' and 'custom'.[8]) Of course, as Peel (1989: 199) noted:

> 'culture' must not be seen as a mere precipitate or bequest of the past. Rather, it is an active reflection on the past, a cultural *work* [Peel's emphasis].

Returning to the example of the rebellion mobilised by the Gbaya prophet Karnu against the French colonial state and the Fulbe of Ngaoundere, we have seen that Karnu's message drew largely upon the familiar symbolic repertoire of Gbaya culture and can hardly be said to have been 'invented' in the Hobsbawm and Ranger sense. Neither did literacy or 'print capitalism' (Anderson 1991) play a role in this mobilisation of Gbaya ethnic consciousness. Rather than speaking of 'invention' in such a case, it is better to understand Karnu's message as a creative synthesis of Gbaya cultural elements which spoke effectively (that is, in a culturally efficacious manner, even if the eventual great spread of the message was, to some degree, an unintended consequence) to the experiences of colonial domination of the Gbaya and other peoples of Cameroon and the Ubangi-Shari.

The situation is, of course, rather different in the case of the newly established Gbaya ethnic association MOINAM – which conforms closely to the ideas of Hobsbawm and Ranger, Gellner and Anderson concerning the role of modern elites in 'inventing tradition' and mobilising ethnic consciousness. Yet even here, as Peel (1989: 200) has argued in his discussion of the twentieth-century genesis of the Yoruba ethnic category as presently understood:

> However compelling the reasons for ethnic mobilisation – regionally uneven development, the expansion of nation-states, multi-ethnic urbanisation, etc., it still has to be worked at in cultural terms. The resultant ethnohistory or 'historicist argument' has been the standard means of intellectuals or ethnic missionaries to raise their fellows' consciousness. But despite the 'invention of tradition' that it may involve, unless it also makes genuine contact with people's actual experience, that is with a history that happened, it is not likely to be effective.

Likewise, Austen (1992: 285–6), commenting on the attempt in 1951 by the Duala chief Betote Akwa to get the French colonial government of Cameroon to authorise an official holiday associated with the neo-traditional Duala association known as 'Ngondo', observed:

> Contemporary modes of scholarship provide us with a familiar procedure for dealing with such a phenomenon, which is by no means peculiar to Africa (Hobsbawm and Ranger 1983) [cited by author]. First the historical claims of the tradition are subjected to an empirical test which can be expected (and the Ngondo case is no exception) [author's parenthesis] to reveal a great gap between the more immediate records of the past and its later reconstruction. Secondly, the process of invention is placed within its immediate context to explain why the past needed to be imagined in this particular way.

The problem with such an approach in African studies is that it can lead to the nihilistic position of reducing all historical claims about cultural identity to the more easily documented dialectics of colonial and post-colonial struggles (Amselle 1990) [author's reference]. A position like this is difficult for Africans themselves to accept, even when they are most steeped in post-modernist theory. It also presents serious personal and ethical problems for expatriate researchers who, by publishing such conclusions, may feel that they are betraying local informants and collaborators who believe in their own traditions and trust us to respect them.

But perhaps it is unnecessary to choose so sharply between nihilism and the acceptance of untenable accounts of the past. This essay will thus challenge the form in which the Ngondo tradition has been officially presented while treating seriously both the history of such contemplation and the objects other than historical narrative which constitute the tradition. The Ngondo tradition may not provide an accurate account of the events and institutions of the past, but it remains an important vehicle for connecting that past to present-day Duala experience.

As discussed in the previous chapter, the conceptions of Gbaya ethnicity advanced by MOINAM at its first convention cannot usefully be said to be invented but represent reworkings of Gbaya culture, adjusted to the sociopolitical situation of the 1990s, with meaningful connections to events in the past. What I am emphasising here, in common with authors like Peel and Austen quoted above, is the importance of taking the cultural content of ethnic projects seriously and not discounting this factor through excessively presentist analyses (Peel 1989). Although I would certainly not deny, and indeed have emphasised, the significance of the tactical manipulation of ethnic identities and categorisations in situations of cultural pluralism, these are not created situationally from nothing. There is a cultural stock of knowledge, ontology, myth, common-sense, and so on from which they are drawn and within which they are reproduced. Such cultural logics and self-evidence feed into the ongoing structuration of social behaviour in relatively predictable and socially shared ways. To claim otherwise may be theoretically fashionable in certain hermeneutic circles but often verges on the solipsistic – an attempt to deny actors' understandings of the cultural regularities and predictabilities of social life through a one-sided assertion of the uniqueness of each behavioural event.

As should also be evident from my preceding remarks, I do not think that it is helpful to introduce, in the excessively generalised way that Bayart (1993: 244 *et passim*) has done, the concept of 'creolisation' into the discussion of modern West African political culture. Used in this way, creolisation becomes synonymous with a notion of random cultural mixing – an analytically undifferentiated and unspecified creolised political culture flowing along the networks of clientage in the 'rhizome state'. This is a waste of a useful concept, for all cultures could be said to be 'creole' in this sense.

One does not need to be a proponent of a highly structuralist theory of linguistic creolisation such as Bickerton's (1981; cf. Romaine 1988) in order to support the view that creolisation processes reflect the operation of specifiable and generalisable regularities of language acquisition and borrowing (as opposed to a theory of random mixing). In referring to this linguistic work, I am not arguing that we should expect to be able to apply structural linguistic models to our anthropological materials in a direct or unproblematic manner. I am simply suggesting that linguistic theory offers anthropology a number of possibly useful metaphors for understanding cultural creolisation, and a notion of random mixing is not one of these, *pace* Hannerz (1987: 552).

My point concerning the potential analytic utility of the concept of cultural creolisation in certain specifiable social settings may be illustrated by contrasting the dominant cultural forms in two societies where I have first-hand fieldwork experience – Trinidad and northern Cameroon. As my colleague Daniel Miller (1994: 22) has described the Trinidad case:

> What emerges from a brief perusal of Trinidadian history is precisely the plurality of contributory forces and the difficulty of fitting contemporary Trinidad with a clear set of 'roots'. Few can claim ancestry with an original population, and although there are links with countries of origin such as India, no single group can claim the kind of hegemonic dominance which would permit a single historical trajectory to be transposed into a genealogy for modern Trinidad . . .
>
> Trinidad is then clearly a Creolised . . . society, which continues to have to define itself as much by its relations to other lands as to its origins. If it is to construct a sense of being 'Trinidadian' it has to do so under conditions of extreme difficulty. It is a society which has a strong sense of rupture, a radicalisation of the present with the concomitant effect that it cannot rely on a clear sense of custom or a morality that is defended as mere custom.

The contrast between this portrayal of Trinidad, seen as a 'rootless' creolising society lacking a taken-for-granted 'sense of custom', and the portrayal of Fulbe society with its strong sense of *pulaaku* (as described in Chapter 3 of this book) could not be more stark. While native accounts emphasising the positive value of Trinidad's creolising culture actively promote the notion of a creative and ongoing synthesis achieved out of cultural elements of diverse origins, the cultural logic of *pulaaku* asserts the importance of adherence to 'authentic' Fulbe cultural traditions. Despite the rapid assimilation of non-Fulbe population to the Fulbe category within the contested field of northern Cameroonian regional culture, Fulbe ethnicity is not therefore appropriately analysed as a creolising phenomenon despite the substantial degree of observable cultural mixing (and the fact that *fulfulde bilkiire* may appropriately be classified as a creole language).[9]

If one wished seriously to pursue the study of cultural borrowing, cultural *métissage* (Amselle 1990), or (to use an outmoded term) 'acculturation' (Redfield, Linton and Herskovits 1936), one would need to consider the role of cultural logics in these processes. But this is precisely what Bayart seems to be trying to avoid – judging from his disparaging references to the work of Augé, Sahlins and Bourdieu (Bayart 1993: 49, 248, 255 *et passim*) and his use of notions such as 'discursive cocktail' (Bayart 1993: 255).[10] Used in the way that Bayart does, the concept of creolisation serves as another rhetorical device to avoid locally grounded cultural analysis.

CONCLUSION

In this epilogue, as in the present work more generally, I have been arguing for the importance of devoting serious analytical attention to ethnicity as a political factor in modern Cameroonian society. Rooted in local cultural logics and practices, subject to historical transformations, ethnicity is no less significant for that. That ethnic difference may be judged a less legitimate basis for political action than, say, the state, and that it may serve to organise and promote shocking acts of violence in places like Rwanda, Bosnia or, to a much smaller degree, Meiganga, is hardly an adequate reason to neglect its substantive investigation.

I have analysed ethnic categories primarily in relation to their social boundary conditions and their cultural contents, while stressing the interactions between the two. I have also emphasised the historicity of ethnic identities, while at the same time considering the ways in which actors sustain a sense of cultural continuity, rootedness and commitment in the face of social change. In this connection, I have argued that ethnic discourses draw upon the legitimating power of self-evident ontological beliefs and actors' commitment to what they consider to be the core institutions of their societies.

It follows from my emphasis upon the cultural specificity of ethnic identities that I conceive of there being many different kinds of ethnic project. Ethnic discourses are based on different cultural logics, each with different implications for actors' practices and each displaying its own mode of articulation with the state and other more global processes. Some ethnic discourses are exclusivist; some are inclusivist. And some are more effective for political mobilisation than others.

At the same time, in a highly ethnically plural setting such as the Mbere Department, there will be many interactional settings in which inter-ethnic relations are routinised, taken for granted and, indeed, seen as necessary for events to run a successful course. In this sense, logics of inter-ethnic interaction themselves become relatively predictable structural forms. Analytically speaking, we must therefore try to develop an understanding of this complex layering and inter-penetration of cultural discourses and practices in daily life, recognising that multi-ethnic social situations are likely to be interpreted at several different levels and through different cultural lenses simultaneously.

The three major ethnic categories inhabiting the Mbere Department today illustrate these points nicely, since they display quite contrasting modes of ethnic identity construction and maintenance, which have been adjusted over time in response to their mutual co-presence. The Fulbe category has been highly incorporative from the nineteenth century to the present, although its mode of assimilation shifted markedly over this period. In the pre-colonial era, the Fulbe states created by the Adamawa *jihad* expanded their populations by the differential incorporation of conquered non-Fulbe groups, while retaining an exclusivist conception of Fulbe ethnic identity and not emphasising mass conversion to Islam. The new political, legal and economic environment of the colonial and post-colonial periods, however, encouraged the development of a more inclusivist definition of Fulbe ethnic identity, in conjunction with a greater emphasis on the universalistic doctrines of Islam. This inclusivist ethnic discourse exerted an especially strong influence during the Ahidjo period, when members of the Fulbe and Fulbeised categories enjoyed preferential access to the resources of the Cameroon state.

The Mbororo, for their part, have persistently maintained an exclusivist definition of their ethnic identity and have pursued their distinctive lifestyle on the margins of the successive state systems that have controlled northern Cameroon. Although, as we have seen, certain members of the Mbororo category are tempted to Fulbeise by the more orthodox Islamic discourses of the politically dominant Fulbe, this process has not weakened the Mbororo ethnic boundary. Following the dictates of their exclusivist ethnic logic, with little or no access to modern education and a correspondingly weak development of modern elites, the Mbororo have little capacity to express their voice in regional or national political arenas and remain a marginalised group despite their substantial livestock wealth.

The Gbaya too, if for different reasons, have remained quite peripheral to the centres of political power over the past 150 years. During this period, their ethnic identity appears to have become progressively more firmly defined as a result of their interactions with outside influences emanating from the pre-colonial Fulbe states, the European colonial powers, the Christian missions and the post-colonial Cameroonian state. Most recently, we have witnessed the emergence of the MOINAM organisation – a novelty for the Gbaya both in its explicitly political aims and its pan-Gbaya focus. Since MOINAM is a clear expression of a desire on the part of the Gbaya to lay their hands on 'their share' of the national cake, its members may well count the appointment in 1994 of the first Gbaya to serve as cabinet minister as an early mark of success. But over the longer term, one must express doubts about the likelihood of MOINAM's persistence and organisational efficacity, given the contingent character of any large-scale grouping in Gbaya society.

A key influence on the patterns of development of inter-ethnic relations in the Mbere region, which should not be underestimated, was the decision by the French colonial government in 1929 to define this area, on ethnic grounds, as a separate administrative unit for the Gbaya and the Mbororo, and to exclude settlement by Fulbe agro-pastoralists. This removed both populations, for the time being, from the direct influence of Fulbe incorporative ethnic processes, which in most other areas of northern Cameroon have been hegemonic. This segregated administrative arrangement also reduced the potential for inter-ethnic violence, which had been clearly signalled by episodes such as the Karnu Rebellion and Ardo Idje's struggles against Ngaoundere. When viewed from this longer term perspective, we can see that the recent violent confrontations in Meiganga cannot be considered anomalous but rather reflect historic social oppositions that colonial administrative policies had somewhat damped down.

It has only been within the last ten to fifteen years, as the thinly veiled, ethnically based differential incorporation of the Mbere Department's administrative system has begun to be dismantled, that significant numbers of Fulbe agro-pastoralists have moved in. This development has brought groups like the Mai'ine Fulbe, with their more exclusivist conceptions of Fulbe Muslim identity, into contact with the Gbaya and has had relatively predictable consequences in the form of increased ethnic tensions.

It is indeed ironic, if not totally unforeseen, that the liberalisation policies of the first years of Biya's administration created conditions that were conducive to episodes of violence such as those in Meiganga in 1991 and 1992. By attacking the longstanding system of differential incorporation in the north and facilitating the expression of a greater variety of cultural discourses and competing political projects, the Biya government took the lid off Pandora's box.

Some of the results of this increased political freedom seemed quite promising at first. Thus, for several years in the mid-1980s, the Adamaoua provincial elites association operated relatively successfully as a trans-ethnic vehicle for the promotion of regional interests. However, in the longer term, its multi-ethnic constitution has been called into question by the claims of some of its non-Fulbe members that it was being dominated by its Fulbe membership. The same concerns have impacted on the breadth of support for the UNDP, a party that had initially been constructed with quite a broad social base (while still capable of playing the Fulbe ethnic or Muslim religious card in situations where this was advantageous).

Thus, even in conditions where certain elites may conceive of their efforts at political mobilisation in regional or national terms, there is no guarantee that their constituents will not reinterpret their message in local terms. Culturally specific logics, sanctioned by ethnically constitutive histories and other sources of tradition, can act as relatively autonomous motivating forces. This appears to have been the case for many Gbaya in the Mbere Department, who interpreted the solid Fulbe support for the *villes mortes* campaign as a strategy to promote local Fulbe political interests.

Nowadays, with the centralised and authoritarian Cameroon state in retreat in the face of the onslaughts of the World Bank's structural adjustment programme and with multi-party elections the order of the day, the state has fewer political resources at its disposal to contain disorder or co-opt social forces emanating from the local level. It should be clearly recognised that the very steps that human rights groups and western donor governments presently deem to be necessary to promote democratisation in authoritarian African regimes are likely to engender increased ethnic particularism. That this is a recipe for increasing political instability there can be no doubt, although some may judge it to be worth the risk in the name of greater political freedom. But political freedom will remain a hollow phrase unless accompanied by peace, and unless African governments are in possession of the wherewithal to govern and to provide at least a minimum level of services for all their people, the prospects for peace look bleak.

NOTES

CHAPTER 1

1. Throughout the period of protests in the early 1990s leading up to the legislative and presidential elections in 1992, the Cameroon government made every effort to deny or play down the scale of the violence. This reached such a ludicrous point that the chief government spokesman, Information Minister Augustin Koumegni Konchou, came to be nicknamed '*zéro mort*' due to his repeated public disclaimers.

2. Throughout this book, I will employ the following conventions when referring to the Department of the Mbere and related geographic designations. I will use 'Mbere Department' as a shorthand reference to the Department of the Mbere which has existed since 1983 as an administrative subdivision of the Province of Adamaoua. The Mbere Department is administered by a prefect, whose offices are located in the town of Meiganga. The Mbere Department, in turn, is subdivided into two *arrondissements*, with their sub-prefectural offices located at Meiganga and Djohong. (However, at the date of my last visit to Meiganga in June 1993, a project was afoot to establish Dir as a third *arrondissement* to be cut out of the territory of Meiganga *Arrondissement*. The town of Ngaouwi on the Central African Republic frontier was also in the process of being recognised as an independent administrative district, answerable directly to the Prefect of the Mbere Department.) Between 1929 and 1983, on the other hand, the Mbere Department enjoyed only sub-prefectural status and the whole administrative entity was termed the 'Meiganga *Arrondissement*'. Finally, when referring to this geographical region as it existed before its separate administrative designation in 1929, I will use the phrase 'Mbere region', although it must be recognised that this area comprises some 17,000 square kilometres, large tracts of which lie quite distant from the Mbere river drainage. When I use the term 'Meiganga' on its own in this book, I am referring to the town of Meiganga.

3. As Jenkins (1994: 220) has aptly argued:

   > To describe ethnicity as 'possibly universal' opens up the argument about its supposedly 'primordial' character (Geertz 1963, reprinted 1973). The debate about whether or not ethnicity is 'situational' or 'primordial' seems futile; it confuses the ubiquity of a social phenomenon such as ethnicity with 'naturalness', implying fixity, determinism and some kind of pre-social power of causation.

4. Smith (1986: ix–x) explains the relationship between ethnicity and nationalism quite clearly in the following passage:

The aim of this book is to analyse some of the origins and genealogy of nations, in particular their ethnic roots. For while attention may legitimately be focused on the constant elements of 'nationhood' in the modern world and the universal trends that govern their formation, the variations between nations are equally important, both in themselves and for their political consequences. My belief is that the most important of these variations are determined by specific historical experiences and by the 'deposit' left by these collective experiences. Hence the importance attached here to the various 'myths' and 'memories', 'symbols' and 'values', which so often define and differentiate nations. These in turn require a study of pre-modern ethnic formations because it is here, above all, that we may trace the historical deposit of collective experiences and because 'ethnicity' has provided, in a very general manner, a potent model for human association which has been adapted and transformed, but not obliterated, in the formation of modern nations. The 'roots' of these nations are to be found, both in a general way and in many specific cases, in the model of ethnic community prevalent in much of recorded history across the globe.

5. In this book, I have used the spelling Adamaoua to refer to the present-day administrative Province of Adamaoua in Cameroon, which was established in 1983 with its provincial capital at Ngaoundere. I use the spelling Adamawa to refer either to the Adamawa Plateau as a geographical feature or to the pre-colonial political domain established during the nineteenth century *jihad*, whose capital was Yola (see Njeuma 1978 or Burnham and Last 1994).

6. Schultz (1979: 126) and Dognin (1981: 139–40) document the same usage of the 'Fulbe' and 'Mbororo' labels in northern Cameroon as that employed here. On the other hand, Lacroix (1965: 19) and Labatut (1973: 27) indicate that the term 'Mbororo' is considered to be pejorative among pastoral Fulani groups with whom they worked. I too have encountered pastoral Fulani who reject this term (see also Dognin 1981: 140) but, against this, one may set the autobiographical account of Ndoudi Oumarou (Bocquené 1986: 118 *et passim*), who proudly declares himself to be 'Mbororo'.

CHAPTER 2

1. The Mbum Mana, one of the major chiefdoms of the Mbum people, were not autochthonous to the Mbere region like the Mbum Mbere and Mbum Mbusa but originated from the region of the Faro river to the northwest of Ngaoundere. The Mbum Mana were conquered by the Fulbe early in the Adamawa *jihad* and, by the 1840s and 1850s, some of them were serving the Ngaoundere state as titled vassal chiefs (*arnaaɓe*).

2. *Gaimɔna* (referred to as 'Gamane' in German documents) was the nineteenth century name of the town of Bertoua (whose name derives from the famous Gbaya war-leader Mbartua). This Gbaya political formation lies more than 300 kilometres from Ngaoundere.

3. A full list of archival references is provided in the bibliography. In the text, archival references are abbreviated according to archive (AN = Archives Nationales, Section Outre-Mer at Aix-en-Provence; M = Archives of Meiganga *Arrondissement*, now the Mbere Department) and numbered sequentially as listed.

4. For ease of reference in this book, I sometimes anglicise the Fulfulde political titles '*laamiiɗo*' and '*arɗo*' as lamido and ardo.

 5. See, for example, the discussion of the Gbaya term 'ndɛm nam' in Burnham, Copet-Rougier and Noss 1986: 100 and in Copet-Rougier 1987.
 6. The term 'kambari' is used at Ngaoundere to refer collectively to members of non-Fulbe ethnic groups such as the Hausa, Kanuri and Choa Arabs who were Islamised before the jihad. Lacroix (1962: 78) says that the term is borrowed from Hausa and refers to a Muslim who has lived for a long time among non-Muslims.
 7. See Burnham 1975 for fuller details of the importance of mobility as a mode of resistance.
 8. As one can confirm by consulting any of the annual reports of the French government as mandatory power to the United Nations (Rapports Annuels du Gouvernement Français à l'Assemblée Générale des Nations-Unies sur l'Administration du Cameroun Placé sous la Tutelle de la France), head taxes throughout northern Cameroon were assessed at variable rates according to ethnic group.
 9. The development of western-style education proceeded very slowly throughout northern Cameroon, with Meiganga being no exception (Martin 1971; Martin 1982). For example, in 1957, only seventeen candidates from the whole of the Meiganga Arrondissement presented themselves for the primary school certificate examinations (Archive M5) and a secondary school was not opened in the region until 1980.
10. See Bandolo (1985: 68–70) and Schilder (1994: Appendix 2) for further details on the ethnic basis of military recruitment.
11. Given the substantially greater average educational level of southern Cameroonians, the Biya government has been able to appoint 'on merit' a much greater proportion of southerners to administrative posts in the Mbere Department and throughout the north. Such appointments are justified by their incumbents both as an ending of Ahidjo's policy of ethnic favouritism as well as a furtherance of the RDPC policies of 'renouveau' and modernist socioeconomic development.
12. As of my last visit to Meiganga in 1993, the towns of Dir and Ngaouwi were also in the course of being carved out within the Mbere Department as sub-prefecture and district respectively.

CHAPTER 3

 1. For a fuller discussion of the pre-colonial system of social stratification in the states of the Sokoto Caliphate, including criticism of Azarya's position, see Burnham and Last (1994).
 2. In emphasising firmly that the 'racial' basis of the classification of certain ethnic groups depends on cultural interpretations of human variation, I am drawing attention to the fact that such classifications are culturally relative and manipulable, rather than objective 'states of nature'. On the other hand, we must recognise that in cases where ethnic classifications are based on 'race' (that is, cultural perceptions of genetically controlled phenotypic differences) as opposed to other cultural traits which may be discarded within an individual's lifetime, the potential for and processes of ethnic redefinition and 'passing' are likely to be quite different.
 3. Apparently, this situation was much to Shehu Usumanu's and his close associates' regret, since they preferred to emphasise the Islamic basis of their movement.
 4. As Lode (1993) has documented at some length (and as the late Père Jean Bocquené confirmed to me in a personal communication in 1969), slavery persisted in several lamidates of Adamawa into the 1950s. The French colonial administration, not wishing to destabilise the political situation in northern Cameroon,

tacitly (and sometimes even overtly) gave its support to this state of affairs. Both the Protestant and the Catholic missions therefore often found themselves in conflict with the colonial administrators on this issue.

5. Circumcision is commonly practised among most of the peoples of Adamawa and therefore is no bar to Islamic conversion.

6. I use the male pronoun here consciously. The 'passing' of women into the Fulbe category, and their conversion to Islam, is generally accomplished in the context of marriage to a Fulbe or Fulbeising husband, and their prayers are less subject to public scrutiny.

7. See note 6 in Chapter 2 for an explanation of the ethnic label *kambari*. *Kambariire* is the language spoken by *kambari*.

8. As Riesman (1977: 127) explained:

> According to our scientific conception of heredity, only skin color and physical type are almost totally determined by the parents' genes; moral qualities depend on education and on the individual's surroundings during his childhood. We have just seen, however, that the Fulani do not make a distinction between heredity and environment; even if they admit in some contexts the existence of a Fulani role which one plays or not according to the situation, they firmly believe that it is membership in the Fulani 'race' which makes a man capable of this.

9. *Pulaaku* is certainly a pervasive notion in all Fulani groups in Cameroon, the Central African Republic, Nigeria and Niger among whom I have personally worked or who are discussed in the literature. The conversations I have had with anthropologists who have lived among more westerly Fulani groups have also convinced me that the concept is widespread in those groups, although I cannot say that it is universal there. It is also the case that, given grammatical variations between the eastern and western dialects of Fulfulde/Fula, the concept of *pulaaku* is expressed in some western dialects using a different but cognate term: for example, *pulaagu* (Ndongo 1986: 15).

10. See, for example, Eguchi (1974) for a substantial compilation of racial and ethnic epithets, insults, jokes, praise songs, etc., in the Maroua dialect of Fulfulde, which amply illustrates Fulbe feelings of superiority. See also Pfeffer (1939) and Lebeuf and Lacroix (1972).

11. See Adler and Zempléni (1972) and Schilder (1994) for the comparable case of the Mundang people. Schilder writes (1994: 33):

> This time-honoured (Mundang) cosmology, which has many similarities with the religious life of other indigenous ethnic groups in northern Cameroon, such as the Massa, Tupuri, Giziga and Gidar, clearly contradicts the teachings of Islam. In contrast with Islam, the people tend to lend an ethnic significance to these religious beliefs and practices: 'We, the Mundang, we . . .' followed by a reference to one or another local religious custom . . .
>
> The rejection of Islam and the assertion of independent sources of self-esteem in the form of an ethnicised cultural repertoire, leaves us with a picture of a self-conscious and independent group of people, which regards itself as equal, if not superior, to its ethnic neighbours. However, this is only the positive pole of ethnic identity, as Epstein calls it, which depends upon inner concepts of exclusiveness, inner strength and resources. This positive self-image should not blind us to the existing ethnic stratification in the region, which is responsible for a (rather submerged) strand of imposed, negative identity in Mundang ethnicity.

12. In querying informants in these surveys concerning their ethnic affiliation, I used the Fulfulde word *lenyol*, which can refer either to ethnic group or to descent group, depending on the context of the question. In my surveys, my informants responded to this question quite uniformly at the ethnic group level, understanding correctly that I was not asking a more detailed question about, for example, their clan or lineage (cf. Schultz 1979: 243–4).

13. The phrase '*pullo pir*' is quite commonly heard in the Fulfulde spoken in the Mbere Department and is used to describe someone of 'pure' Fulani descent. One is tempted to see this phrase as a borrowing of the French word *pur* (pure), but some of my Fulani informants argued that this was unadulterated Fulfulde, with '*pir*' playing the role of an ideophonic strengthener comparable to the role of words like '*tal*' and '*kurum*' in the phrases '*daneejum tal*' (pure white, whitest of white) and '*baleejum kurum*' (jet black).

14. See Chapter 4, note 6 for a discussion of the term *mbisa*.

15. Three billion CFA francs represented about (US) $10,000,000 at the time of my survey (i.e., prior to the 1993 devaluation of the CFA franc). In 1994, one US dollar equalled about 575 CFA francs.

16. The two Gbaya household heads in my samples were butchers. They were residing in Fulbe residential quarters, rather than in adjacent Gbaya quarters, both to keep close links with the Fulbe cattle merchants with whom they had regular dealings as well as to emphasise their Muslim faith and correct slaughtering practices, which are crucial to maintain their Muslim clientele.

CHAPTER 4

1. See Burnham, Copet-Rougier and Noss (1986) for a discussion of linguistic classifications of Gbaya dialects.

2. Heinrich Barth (1857, II: 613–21; see also Burnham 1981) collected Hausa traders' itineraries, referring to the 1840s period when the Gbaya were first contacted by them, which speak repeatedly of visiting 'Baya'. In the case of the letters of de Brazza and his associates describing their first penetration of the Haute-Sangha region in 1891–2 (Rabut 1989; Burnham in press), the Gbaya were called 'N'dri' or 'N'dere' by the riverine peoples on the lower Sangha, who acted as interpreters and intermediaries between the French and the Gbaya at the start of the de Brazza expedition (and did their best to obstruct French efforts to contact the Gbaya first-hand). Once the French had advanced further upriver and had begun to deal with the Gbaya directly, the French documents begin to speak of the 'Baya'. The reports of Clozel's expedition through the Haute-Sangha region to the Ouham river valley in 1894–5 indicate the widespread usage of this ethnic label among the local populations at this period, and Clozel's brief monograph *Les Bayas: Notes Ethnographiques et Linguistiques* (1896) is our earliest first-hand ethnographic account published on the Gbaya.

3. In fact, although non-Yaayuwee Gbaya are liable to stress the Fulbe influences on Gbaya culture, many of these Yaayuwee traits seem to have been received from the Mbum, who formerly were much more numerous in the Mbere region. See Burnham (1980a: 297) and Hino (1978) for a partial list of Mbum material culture and social organisational vocabulary which is used in the Gbaya Yaayuwee dialect.

4. Coquery-Vidrovitch (1988: 179) argues that the Karnu Rebellion was the largest peasant insurrection in sub-Saharan Africa between the two World Wars. See also Nzabakomada-Yakoma (1986).

5. Philip Noss has recently compared the character of Wanto, the trickster figure

of Gbaya folktales, with that of Karnu, seeing both of them as heroes – if of a different sort. Noss writes (1993: 216, my translation):

> Perhaps Karnu is different [from Wanto] because he loses his life. However, in oral tradition, he does not die. It is only the official history which seeks to bring the story to an end by proclaiming the hero dead. In Gbaya life and thought, he continues to live and to assert his identity in the contemporary Gbaya world, just as Hare, Black Ant, Chameleon, Blue Duiker, and Tortoise continue to live and reaffirm Gbaya values as bequeathed by the ancestors.

6. The etymology of the term *mbisa* (sometimes pronounced *mbusa*), which is used today by the Gbaya to refer to non-Gbaya Muslims in general (including Hausa, Fulbe and Mbum), is possibly linked with the Mbum political formation of that name which was one of the tributary slave-raiding chiefdoms of the Ngaoundere state in the pre-colonial period. (See Blanchard and Noss 1982: 296, 305 and Faraut 1981.) When Gbaya wish to speak of the Fulani specifically, as distinct from other non-Gbaya Muslims, they often use the term *bira*, which is likely to have been borrowed from the Mbum language (Hino 1978: 163).

7. On the basis of my more recent periods of fieldwork among the Gbaya, I have the impression (which I have not sought to quantify) that Gbaya residential mobility has tended to decrease over the past ten to fifteen years, as a result of the stabilising effects of village infrastructural developments such as schools and wells, as well as more permanent methods of house construction. However, the contingent quality of social relations in Gbaya *ndok fuu* units does not appear to have changed.

8. One indication of the low degree of Gbaya involvement in commerce in Meiganga is provided by an analysis of the ethnic affiliations of the 111 named individuals in Meiganga listed as having a telephone in the 1990 national telephone directory. Only seven were Gbaya, thirty were from ethnic groups hailing from southern or western Cameroon, and seventy-four were Fulbe, Hausa or from other Muslim peoples.

9. The most recent census giving information on religion by ethnic group dates to 1961 (Callies 1968: 50). These data indicate that 46.4 per cent of the Gbaya population declared themselves to be Christian, 44.6 per cent Muslim and 9.0 per cent 'animist'. Thirty years later, the proportion of Gbaya Christians in the Mbere Department has grown substantially, although Islam is still very widespread.

10. The historical domination of the Fulbe states of Adamawa against which the Gbaya are reacting in their usage of the term *bara mbisa* is well-described in this text from Garoua (Bassoro and Mohammadou 1980: 86–7, my translation):

> The majority of the slaves at Garoua originated from the lamidates of Ngaoundere and Rei [Bouba], which is the reason why they are referred to in an undifferentiated manner as 'Laka' or 'Gbaya' . . . Among the titled officials of the [Garoua] *laamiido* drawn from conquered peoples, only the Laka and the Gbaya were truly of slave status [*jeyaaɓe* – from the verbal root *jeya* – to possess or own], although they were often freed when they assumed their offices.

It is hardly surprising that Gbaya do not wish to become involved in social contexts in which they are viewed as mere '*possessions*', although it is in this wider Fulbe-dominated world that many economic and political opportunities lie.

11. Norwegian Lutheran missionaries have long worked in close collaboration with the American Lutherans, many of whom themselves are of Scandinavian descent. For more details on the involvement of Norwegian missionaries in Adamaoua, see Christiansen (1956) and Lode (1993).

12. Gbaya Lutherans evidently feel that their denomination is lacking in methods to obtain supernatural influence and efficacity in everyday life, despite their putative belief in the power of prayer. A local Catholic priest once mentioned to me that he was continually surprised to be called upon to say prayers over sick Gbaya Lutherans, which he interpreted as evidence of Gbaya belief in an active, rather than only a symbolic power of the Catholic sacraments. Lutheran pastors also bemoan the fact that Gbaya church members may consult a Muslim *mallum* in times of illness or other difficulty in order to drink Koranic medicines or to obtain amulets.

13. In the few cases known to me in recent years where members of the Gbaya elite have attempted the 'straddling' strategy, using government employment as a springboard to obtain substantial bank loans for personal business investments, these activities have come to grief, leading to substantial losses.

CHAPTER 5

1. Fulbe, in common with Gbaya, particularly delight in telling ethnic jokes that emphasise the purportedly naïve and rustic nature of the Mbororo. A popular one I heard in the Mbere Department concerned an Mbororo who was continually being bothered by mosquitoes. Hearing of a new 'marvel' called a 'mosquito net', he visited the marketplace where he was sold one at an exorbitant price by a clever Hausa trader. Having returned to the bush and as night fell, the Mbororo attached the net to a tree and lay down to sleep beside it. As the mosquitoes began to bite him, he leapt up and cried, 'Kai! You mosquitoes! Here I've bought you this new house and you refuse to use it!'
   For further information on this point, see Dupire (1981: 170–1) for a listing of ethnic stereotypes applied to Fulani peoples, particularly the Mbororo.

2. The works of several authors who have recently written on the Fulani of Cameroon suffer from their failure to distinguish clearly between the sedentary Fulbe and the pastoral nomadic Mbororo. Thus, Gondolo (1986: 301) confuses the Wodaabe, an Mbororo group, with the Wolarbe, the Fulbe clan that conquered Ngaoundere. This leads him to engage in some fruitless speculation regarding the shift of the Fulbe of Ngaoundere from a nomadic to a sedentary lifestyle. In the case of Njiasse Njoya and Zouya Mimbang (1988), who write on Islamic law in Ngaoundere, they erroneously assume that the form of marriage practised by the Mbororo in Adamaoua (as reported by Dupire 1970 and Bocquené 1986) is the same as that practised by the Fulbe at Ngaoundere.

3. See Dupire (1970: photo following p. 618) for a photograph of this ceremony taken among the Jafun of the Meiganga region.

4. Compare Stenning's (1959: 225 *et seq.*) discussion of the tendency of Wodaabe in Bornu to 'become Kanuri' as a result of being named to village headships.

5. According to a survey carried out in 1985–6, 37 per cent of the herders in the Mbere Department had been resident there for fewer than five years, 16 per cent for five to ten years, 32 per cent for ten to twenty-five years and 15 per cent for more than twenty-five years (personal communication: M. Doufissa Albert, head of the Service d'Elevage in the Mbere Department). See Boutrais (1978: 39 *et seq.*) for further discussion of socioeconomic and ethnic differentiation among the pastoral populations of Cameroon.

6. Personal communication: M. Doufissa Albert, head of the Service d'Elevage in the Mbere Department.

7. We can get some impression of the sense of personal identification and pride felt by an Mbororo for his herd in this passage from Ndoudi Oumarou's autobiography (Bocquené 1986: 103, my translation):

> What a feeling of pride for the herdsman who walks alone at the head of his herd! He begins to run. The cattle are on his heels. He almost feels their horns in his back. He controls their speed with his herding staff. And when other Mbororo, who have already set up camp, see him pass by at such a pace, there are praises on everyone's lips, 'Ah! There is someone who knows how to care for his animals! Look how closely they follow him! But isn't that So-and-So, son of So-and-So? Well, it's no surprise; isn't his father reputed for his knowledge of cattle medicines?'

8. The marked contrast between the effectively more indirect mode of colonial rule employed by the French in northern Cameroon with the more direct administration of southern Cameroon, is quite noteworthy. In the north, the French administration relied much more heavily on the 'traditional' chiefs of local ethnically defined social groups. Moreover, ethnically differentiated taxation rates, according to which politically or economically dominant groups like the Fulbe and Mbororo paid higher taxes than *kirdi* groups like the Gbaya, were general throughout the region. (See the *Rapports Annuels du Gouvernement Français à l'Assemblée Générale des Nations Unies sur l'Administration du Cameroun Placé sous la Tutelle de la France*.)

9. As Ndoudi Oumarou remarks on this theme (Bocquené 1986: 378, my translation):

> Yes, wherever we go, we Mbororo, no one gives us any consideration. How can one explain this? We are a people without villages or land; we are illiterate and know little about our religion or the wider world. We are only feared for our magical knowledge . . .
>
> Such is our fate, we people of the bush. Nomads without education, we are only good for being exploited by everyone everywhere. Wherever we are, we are strangers. Wherever a nomad is, he is one too many. He came from someplace else, so let him return there! . . .
>
> I have heard tell that it was the great Shehu Usumanu who organised the Fulani to conquer the pagans and bring them to Islam. He gave them banners for each territory they submitted. It is said that a large group of Fulani refused to join his forces. Those were the Mbororo. They didn't participate in the holy war. They placed their love for their cattle ahead of religion. This is the origin of the irrational disdain that some Fulbe hold for us.

10. See Bocquené (1986: Chap. 13 *et passim*) for Ndoudi Oumarou's vivid account of the magical practices associated with the *soro* contests.

11. Unfortunately, I do not possess a sufficiently large sample of herd data to demonstrate in a statistically conclusive manner this shift in herd structures. My statements are based, rather, on a close familiarity with a small number of herdsmen and on explicit statements by them to this effect. Boutrais (1978: 53–4) also discusses herd structure data from Mbororo and Fulbe groups in Adamawa and although he too notes sex and age structure differences, his data sets are not refined enough to detect the process I am discussing here.

12. As Dupire (1970: 244) has remarked, it is not surprising that the poetry recited

by Fulbe poets in honour of Ardo Idje passes largely in silence over Idje's resistance to the *laamiido* of Ngaoundere (Lacroix 1965, I: 106–13).

13. The precise meaning and etymology of the term *huya'en* (singular, *huyaajo*) have been the subject of some discussion. Taylor's (1932) dictionary defines it as 'the name given to the settled Fulani by the Mbororo; so called from the Mbororo word for *suudu* (house) = *huyaaru*'. Dognin (1981: 140), while not contradicting Taylor, offers some more fanciful suggestions. Mbororo informants in the Mbere Department explained to me that *huya'en* had a pejorative sense, which could be translated approximately as 'scavenger dogs of the towns', playing on an association between *huyaaru* and other words in the *-ndu* noun class (cf. *rawaandu* – dog).

14. Stenning (1959: 145) discusses a similar conflict of values between *deetuki* (cf. *deetawal*) and Islam among the Wodaabe of Bornu.

CHAPTER 6

1. Ndoudi Oumarou's autobiography (Bocquené 1986: Chap. 8) contains an excellent description of an Mbororo life-cycle ceremony and Mbororo ethnic stereotypes of the various guests in attendance.

2. 'Bokassa grass' (*l'herbe de Bokassa*, that is, *Chromolaena odorata*, cf. *Eupatorium odoratum*), an exotic weed which is said to have been introduced to West Africa as part of an agricultural development project, spread rapidly throughout the pastoral zones of Cameroon during the 1970s and 1980s. Noxious dictators seem to have often given their names to noxious weeds – further north in West Africa it is known as 'Acheampong weed' (Sebastian Amanor and Paul Richards, personal communications)!'

CHAPTER 7

1. See Lucas (1994) for a comparable discussion of the role of regional elites associations in northern Nigeria.

2. The political contraditions faced by the *laamiido* of Ngaoundere during this period are graphically portrayed in *The Sultan's Burden* (Whyte 1993), a television documentary made under the ethnographic supervision of Lisbet Holtedahl. Although the autochthonous Mbum people have often been viewed as substantially Fulbeised since the nineteenth-century conquest of Adamawa, the Mbum-Fulbe ethnic cleavage figured prominently in the political unrest in Ngaoundere in 1991 and 1992. The *laamiido*, who is of mixed Fulbe and Mbum parentage, found himself in the middle of this conflict as the Biya regime's insistence that he publicly support the government party helped to create conditions which set both the Mbum and many of his Fulbe supporters against him.

   The situation of the Fulbe *laamiido* of Rei Bouba has been somewhat different during this period. His connivance with the Biya regime has recently given him space to return to his repressive political ways which, to some extent, had been suppressed in the last years of Ahidjo's rule. This has led to bloody clashes between local Mbum villagers, who support opposition political parties, and the retainers of the *laamiido* (Amnesty International 1994a).

3. See, for example, the interview with Oumarou Koué, Governor of Adamaoua Province, published in the *Cameroon Tribune* of 23 April 1992.

4. The term *kirdi*, apparently a word of Bornu or Mandara origin, is a (pejorative) label that is applied collectively to non-Muslim peoples in the far north of Cameroon. In its usage, it bears a strong resemblance to the Fulfulde term *haaɓe*, which is more widely used in Adamaoua Province.

5. At present, the rise of multi-party politics has opened a larger space within

Cameroonian political discourse for arguments concerning political legitimacy. And it remains the case at the time of this writing (May 1994) that at least some of Biya's political opponents have refused to be co-opted. The SDF with its strong base in the anglophone region retains the highest political profile among the opposition, but other parties, or factions of parties, including elements of the UPC and the UNDP, also continue to contest the legitimacy of the Biya regime. At the same time, with the greater (although hardly satisfactory) press freedom now practised in Cameroon, opposition newspapers such as *Le Messager*, *La Nouvelle Expression*, and *Dikalo* add their voices to the protests broadcast daily on the 'sidewalk radio' (*radio trottoir*). See, for example, Amnesty International 1991a and 1991b.

6. As this book was going to press, I received a letter from a member of MOINAM which announced (my translation): 'I must not forget to tell to you that the Gbaya people are, from now on, on their feet – with the appointment of M. Bello Mbele André as Minister of Mines and Energy.'

7. See, for example, *La Nouvelle Expression* No. 134 of 1–7 March 1994, *La Nouvelle Expression* No. 146 of 19–25 April 1994, Amnesty International 1994a, Amnesty International 1994b, and Amnesty International 1994c. A common factor in facilitating much of the current banditry and warfare in northern Cameroon is the easy availability of modern weapons from neighbouring countries, especially from Chad in the aftermath of its various civil wars. For example, from time to time over the past ten years, the roads to Djohong and Ngaouwi in the northeastern section of the Mbere Department have been subject to banditry by groups of '*jargina*' and in 1987, while I was conducting fieldwork in that area, several members of one of these gangs were killed and others captured by local villagers deputised by the Cameroon gendarmerie. The term *jargina* is said to derive from the brand name of a popular blueing agent, which is purportedly used by bandits to render themselves 'invisible'.

8. I am in agreement here with Miller (1994: 306) who writes:

> There is no one response to the conditional factors which define modernity, and I would strongly assert, contrary to most authorities, that the modern condition is just as varied and plural as the non-modern. There is no global homogenisation except in the most superficial sense.

CHAPTER 8

1. Anderson (1991: 6) explains his concept of the nation as an 'imagined community' as follows:

> It is *imagined* because the members of even the smallest nation will never know most of their fellow-members, meet them, or even hear of them, yet in the minds of each lives the image of their communion.

2. A further source of weakness in Bayart's understanding of ethnicity, as in that of Amselle (1990: Chap. III), is his failure to maintain clear and consistent distinctions between ethnicity and culture, as well as between the (physical) persons who possess cultural knowledge, the roles they play as social actors, and the content of cultural knowledge itself. Ethnicity is, I repeat, a cultural phenomenon – a set of inter-subjectively transmitted and acknowledged understandings of cultural difference which are available to actors as resources in their sociopolitical practice.

3. Amselle's (1990: 77) attempt to discount an ethnic reading of the account of

Sonni Ali's desire to exterminate the Fulani in the *Tarikh el-Fettach* (Kati 1964: 83–4) on the grounds that his hostilty was based on religious principles is not convincing. Religion is as much open to use as a basis for ethnic distinction as any other cultural attribute, and we have seen how, in the pre-colonial and colonial periods, the Fulbe of Cameroon 'appropriated Islam for their own benefit' (Lacroix 1966: 402, my translation). Moreover, in conflicts between Muslims, it was normal tactics to damn the opposition for their purportedly un-Islamic conduct – in this case, their practice of enslaving free Muslims.

4. My own reading of the African literature leads me to the view that separatist movements are by no means as rare as Bayart claims, but we lack a convenient means of quantifying such impressions. In any case, as Bayart (1993: 253–5) notes, many 'small men' in Africa have developed a quite refined set of evasive tactics which permit them to 'never pay more than lip-service to their adhesion to the state'. However, regarding such 'strategies of extraversion and escape' (1993: 263), Bayart argues that (1993: 209):

> We should not attempt in an academic and artificial balancing act, to oppose the statist 'totalising' work with the divergent tactics of 'detotalising', even if the latter more than any others do lead directly to the erosion and dilution of the State. In reality, the logic of deconstruction in the statist arena is not so easily separated from the logic of its construction.

Such an argument is probably inevitable, given Bayart's all-encompassing definition of the state.

5. While Bayart's view of the state does not partake of this simple monolithic conception, he does attempt to expand the meaning of 'the state' to encompass the total realm of the political in all its manifestations – as in the following passage (1993: 249):

> In order to understand 'governmentality' in Africa we need to understand the concrete procedures by which social actors simultaneously borrow from a range of discursive genres, intermix them and, as a result, are able to invent original cultures of the State. We can then see that the production of a political space is on the one hand the work of an ensemble of actors, dominant and dominated, and that on the other hand it is in turn subject to a double logic of totalitarianising and detotalitarianising.

It is also apparent that when Bayart (1993: 266) speaks of 'government in the strict sense of the term', he wishes to make it clear that his conception of the state is much broader than this. Of course, such an expansive concept of the state has advantages as a literary device in a book like his *The State in Africa*, which seeks to encompass the broad sweep of modern African political behaviour, but it runs the risk of itself becoming a '*passe-partout*' notion (cf. Bayart 1986: 9), virtually equivalent to the general concept of 'society', which soon overreaches its analytic value.

6. Amselle's attempt (1990: 74) to deconstruct Fulani ethnicity, on the grounds that key elements of the Fulani conception of *pulaaku* are not unique to Fulani peoples, is fundamentally flawed by his failure to distinguish between actor's and analyst's viewpoints.

7. Although most Jafun living in the Mbere Department today are wont to approve of Ardo Idje's abolition of the *soro*, since it is consonant with their more Fulbeised style of life, their relatives living in the Benue valley, who still practise the *soro*, see this as a betrayal of *pulaaku* (see Bocquené 1986: 357–8). Once again, we are reminded of the relativity of such cultural judgements.

8. It is important to recall the basic definitional distinction established by Hobsbawm (1983: 1–2) between 'invented tradition' and 'custom':

> 'Invented tradition' is taken to mean a set of practices governed by overtly or tacitly accepted rules and of a ritual or symbolic nature, which seek to inculcate certain values and norms of behaviour by repetition, which automatically implies continuity with the past. In fact, where possible, they normally attempt to establish continuity with a suitable historic past . . . 'Tradition' in this sense must be distinguished clearly from 'custom' which dominates so-called 'traditional' societies. The object and characteristic of 'traditions', including invented ones, is invariance. The past, real or invented, to which they refer imposes fixed (normally formalised) practices, such as repetition. 'Custom' in traditional societies has the double function of motor and fly-wheel. It does not preclude innovation and change up to a point, though evidently the requirement that it must appear compatible or even identical with precedent imposes substantial limitations on it. What it does is to give any desired change (or resistance to innovation) the sanction of precedent, social continuity, and natural law as expressed in history . . . 'Custom' cannot afford to be invariant, because even in 'traditional' societies life is not so.

While Hobsbawm's use of the term 'custom' in this context could be improved upon with reference to practice theories like that of Bourdieu (1977), the above quotation does go a considerable distance toward capturing the way in which a sense of cultural continuity is maintained through the flow of history.

9. Speaking of the phenomenon of cultural creolisation more generally, there may well be settings in West African society, particularly in more impersonal urban contexts, in which dominant cultural logics have as much to do with events in Paris or London as they do with locally rooted African cultures (Hannerz 1987: 549). But we must specify the historical conditions under which such situations emerge and the contemporary social conditions that perpetuate them. Vague generalisations about the world system and globalisation are not sufficient.

10. For example, Bayart argues against Bourdieu (1993: 248):

> In reality, these 'fields of the politically thinkable' are composite and at least partially reversible. They consist of ensembles, relatively integrated but nevertheless incomplete, disparate genres of discourse which the competing social actors mix enthusiastically.

However, as I have argued above, this style of analysis does not address the question of what makes sense to actors and what doesn't, or what is seen as a moral imperative and what isn't. Of course, new cultural elements are continually being brought into play, but they tend to become creatively integrated in, or encompassed by, conceptual logics in place – culture change is not a free-for-all. These 'discourses' take place in 'language' ('genres' if you will) which is still, in large measure, derived from locally grounded and culturally rooted understandings. Indeed, although the fashionable concept of 'discursive genres', (which Bayart [1993: 243–4] has borrowed from Mikhail Bakhtin) would itself seem to imply rather more in the way of cultural structuring than does his use of the concept of creolisation, Bayart does not pursue the implications of this point.

GLOSSARY

(Abbreviations: A. = Arabic; F. = Fulfulde; Gb. = Gbaya; H. = Hausa; K. = Kanuri; P.E. = Pidgin English)

al hajji (F.)	title given to a man who has made the pilgrimage to Mecca (*hajj*)
alkali (pl. *alkali'en*, F.)	Muslim judge
arɗo (pl. *arɗo'en*, F.)	leader, esp. of an Mbororo migratory group
arɗo bariki (F.)	an Mbororo leader recognised by the government for tax collection purposes
ari (Gb.)	vengeance killing
arnaaɗo (pl. *arnaaɓe*, F.)	chief of subject pagan people (*haaɓe*)
baleeɓe (sing. *baleejo*, F.)	literally 'black people'; often used synonymously with *haaɓe*
baŋtal (F.)	final stage in Mbororo *koobgal* marriage; ceremony held when the wife leaves her parents' home, with the couple's newly weaned child, to join her husband
bara mbisa (Gb.)	a slave of Muslims
barkehi (F.)	species of tree whose leaves are used by Mbororo as a sign of blessing; *Piliostigma reticulatum*
bilkiire (F.)	the language of simpletons; said of the poor Fulfulde spoken by non-native speakers
bira (Gb.)	Fulani peoples
bodeeji (F.)	a breed of large, long-horned red zebu cattle favoured by Jafun Mbororo
bodeejum (F.)	red, descriptive of the ideal skin colour of Fulani peoples
chofol (F.)	grazing tax levied by state on nomadic pastoralists
daneeji (F.)	breed of small white short-horned zebu cattle
dan komisio (F.)	a commission agent
deetawal (F.)	Mbororo marriage by elopement
do'a (F.)	prayers; a Muslim prayer ceremony
dimɗinaaɗo (pl. *rimɗinaaɓe*, F.)	manumitted slave
dimaajo (pl. *rimaiɓe*, F.)	slave born in captivity
dimo (pl. *rimɓe*, F.)	freeman
fukaraaɓe (sing. *pukaraajo*, F.)	pupils, usually of a Koranic school
fulɓe bamle (F.)	Fulani living among non-Fulani pagans
fulfulde (F.)	the language of the Fulani peoples

fulfulde laamnde (F.)	'clear', grammatically correct Fulfulde
fulfulde luumo (F.)	vehicular Fulfulde
garafi (P.E.)	people originating from the Grassfields region of western and northwestern Cameroon, including the Bamileke
gaarewol (F.)	flowing robe worn by Fulani men; cf. *gandura* (H.)
gaynaako (pl. *waynaabe*, F.)	a herdsman, especially a hired herdsman
ginaaji (sing. *ginaawol*, F.)	jinn; spirits
girka (F.)	a ceremony seeking control over spirits (*ginaaji*); spirit possession practitioner; cf. *bori* (H.)
gudaali (sing. *wudaale*, F.)	stocky, short-legged zebu cattle breed favoured by sedentary Fulani in Adamaoua Province, Cameroon
haabe (sing. *kaado*, F.)	servile, non-Fulani peoples; pagans (i.e. non-Muslim)
hadaande (F.)	government prohibition
hakkiilo (F.)	intelligence; foresight; said to be one of the core values of *pulaaku*
huya'en (sing. *huyaajo*, F.)	pejorative term used by the Mbororo to refer to town Fulani
indeeri (F.)	infant naming ceremony
jaoro (pl. *jaoro'en*, F.)	village or quarter chief in settled Fulani village
jargina (F.)	slang term for modern bandits; said to be derived from the brand name of a blueing agent used to render the bandits magically invisible
jeyaado (pl. *jeyaabe*, F.)	slave, literally 'a person who is owned'
jihad (F.)	Islamic holy war
jizya (F.)	tribute paid by conquered pagan peoples (*haabe*) to their Muslim overlord
kam (Gb.)	manioc porridge staple food; food in general
kambari (F.)	non-Fulani Muslim ethnic groups
kambariire (F.)	the imperfect Fulfulde spoken by persons of mixed parentage
keefeero (F.)	unbeliever, cf. *kafir* (A.)
kirdi (?K.)	pejorative label applied collectively to non-Muslim peoples of the far north of Cameroon; cf. *haabe*
kirsol (F.)	cattle killed at Mbororo marriage ceremony
koobgal (F.)	Mbororo infant betrothal marriage
kori'en (sing. *koriijo*, F.)	Mbororo age class for young men, immediately senior to *sukaabe*
laamiido (pl. *laamiibe*, F.)	Fulani superior chief; emir
laawol pulaaku (F.)	the Fulani way; Fulani custom
labbaare (F.)	agricultural settlement of Mbororo slaves; cf. *rumnde*
lekki bushin (F.)	'medicine' offering protection against dangers, especially iron weapons
lekki njamndi (F.)	see *lekki bushin*
lekki yaashin (F.)	'medicine' to enable one to locate lost or stolen property
lekki yusufu (F.)	'medicine' to ensure success in romantic affairs
lenyol (F.)	descent group; clan; ethnic group
lukudi (F.)	magical technique to form alliance with satanic spirits to obtain great wealth

maccuɗo (pl. *maccuɓe*, F.)	slave
madugu (pl. *madugai*, H.)	caravan leader
mai bornu (F.)	title given at Ngaoundere to chief of the Bornuan residential quarter
mallum (pl. *mallum'en*, F.)	a person with Koranic schooling; someone versed in the Koran who provides religious services
mallum'en bitiri (F.)	venal *mallum'en* specialising in writing charms
mbisa (Gb.)	non-Gbaya Muslims
munyal (F.)	patience; self-mastery; said to be one of the core values of *pulaaku*
naŋgardu (F.)	the first stage of Mbororo *koobgal* marriage; infant betrothal ceremony
ndem nam (Gb.)	a village composed of conquered or subordinated peoples of heterogeneous origins
ndok fuu (Gb.)	clan-based residential quarter
ngapaleewol (F.)	see *gaarewol*
parkeejo (F.)	licensed cattle buyer
perol (F.)	flight from an unjust ruler; Mohammed's flight from Mecca
pulaaku (F.)	morally correct and prestigious Fulani style of life; the customs of the Fulani
pullo gawra (F.)	a Fulani person from Garoua; often used with the implication of having assimilated or 'passed' into the Fulani ethnic category
pullo pir (F.)	a true or pure Fulani
rubu (F.)	brideprice
rumnde (pl. *dumɗe*, F.)	slave village
saŋyeere (F.)	fortified military camp where slaves would be sold after battles
sarki bindiga (F.)	leader of the corps of musketeers
sarki hausawa (F.)	title given at Ngaoundere to chief of the Hausa residential quarter
sarki lifida (F.)	leader of the heavy cavalry
semteende (F.)	shame; modesty; reticence; said to be one of the core values of *pulaaku*
siiri (F.)	sorcery
soobaajo (F.)	friend; bond friendship between Mbororo and Gbaya
soro (F.)	competitive stick beating contests between Jafun Mbororo youth
sukaaɓe (sing. *sukaajo* or *suka*, F.)	Fulani youth; the Mbororo age-class which participates in the *soro* competitions
suudu (F.)	house; sub-clan
tabajeeji (F.)	hemp smoked for narcotic effect
tabur (F.)	petty 'table-top' trade
tarbiyya (F.)	colloquial name for Al Hajj Ibrahim Niasse's branch of the Tijaniyya Islamic brotherhood
tarkase (F.)	the small stock of goods of a *tabur* trader; cf. *tarkace* (H.)
teegal (F.)	Islamic marriage ceremony
tokkal (pl. *tokke*, F.)	political following of a Fulani leader
tokkuɓe (sing. *tokkujo*, F.)	members of the political following of a Fulani leader

walaba (F.)	divination
yaafi (F.)	paganism
'yiiwugo islama (F.)	ceremony of Islamic conversion
zu duk (Gb.)	clan; ethnic group

BIBLIOGRAPHY

Abdoullaye, Hamadjoda and Eldridge Mohammadou. 1972. *Les Yillaga de la Bénoué: Ray ou Rey-Bouba*. Yaounde: Ministère de l'Information et de la Culture.

Abraham, R. C. 1962. *Dictionary of the Hausa Language* (2nd edn). London: University of London Press.

Adler, Alfred. 1982. *La Mort est le Masque du Roi: la Royauté Sacrée des Moundang du Tchad*. Paris: Payot.

Adler, Alfred and Andras Zempléni. 1972. *Le Bâton de l'Aveugle: Divination, Maladie et Pouvoir chez les Moundang du Tchad*. Paris: Hermann.

Al-Hajj, Mohammed and Murray Last. 1965. 'Attempts at defining a Muslim in 19th century Hausaland and Bornu'. *Journal of the Historical Society of Nigeria* 3: 231–40.

Almond, Gabriel and James Colemen (eds). 1960. *The Politics of Developing Areas*. Princeton: Princeton University Press.

Amnesty International. 1984. *Summary Trials and Secret Executions in the Republic of Cameroon* (AI Index: AFR 17/08/84). London: Amnesty International.

Amnesty International. 1985. *People Imprisoned after the April 1984 Coup Attempt* (AI Index: AFR 17/06/85). London: Amnesty International.

Amnesty International. 1986. *People Imprisoned after the April 1984 Armed Mutiny* (AI Index: AFR 17/05/86). London: Amnesty International.

Amnesty International. 1987. *Amnesty International's Concerns Arising from the April 1984 Coup Attempt* (AI Index: AFR 17/03/87). London: Amnesty International.

Amnesty International. 1989. *Cameroon: Harsh Prison Conditions for Criminal and Political Prisoners* (AI Index: AFR 17/03/89). London: Amnesty International.

Amnesty International. 1991a. *Cameroon: Human Rights Developments during the First Half of 1991* (AI Index: AFR 17/07/91). London: Amnesty International.

Amnesty International. 1991b. *Cameroon: Torture and Ill-Treatment* (AI Index: AFR 17/09/91). London: Amnesty International.

Amnesty International. 1994a. *Cameroon: 1993: Political Arrests and Torture Continue* (AI Index: AFR 17/02/94). London: Amnesty International.

Amnesty International. 1994b. *Cameroon: Extrajudicial Executions/Torture/Death in Custody* (AI Index: AFR 17/03/94). London: Amnesty International.

Amnesty International. 1994c. *Cameroon: Extrajudicial Executions* (AI Index: AFR 17/06/94). London: Amnesty International.

Amselle, Jean-Loup. 1985. 'Ethnies et espaces: pour une anthropologie topologique'. In J.-L. Amselle and E. M'bokolo (eds) *Au Coeur de l'Ethnie: Ethnies, Tribalisme et Etat en Afrique*. Paris: Editions La Découverte.

Amselle, Jean-Loup, 1990. *Logiques Métisses: Anthropologie de l'Identité en Afrique et Ailleurs*. Paris: Editions Payot.

Amselle, Jean-Loup and Elikia M'bokolo (eds). 1985. *Au Coeur de l'Ethnie: Ethnies, Tribalisme et Etat en Afrique*. Paris: Editions La Découverte.

Anderson, Benedict. 1991. *Imagined Communities* (2nd edn). London: Verso.

Arnott, D. W. 1970. *The Nominal and Verbal Systems of Fula*. Oxford: Oxford University Press.

Asad, Talal. 1992. 'Conscripts of western civilisation'. In C. Gailey (ed.) *Civilization in Crisis: Anthropological Perspectives*, Vol. I of *Dialectical Anthropology: Essays in Honor of Stanley Diamond*. Gainesville: University of Florida Press.

Augé, Marc. 1977. *Pouvoirs de Vie, Pouvoirs de Mort*. Paris: Flammarion.

Austen, Ralph. 1992. 'Tradition, invention and history: the case of the *Ngondo* (Cameroun)'. *Cahiers d'Etudes Africaines* 126, XXXII (2): 285–309.

Azarya, Victor. 1978. *Aristocrats Facing Change*. Chicago: University of Chicago Press.

Balandier, Georges. 1970. *Political Anthropology*. London: Allen Lane.

Bandolo, Henri. 1985. *La Flamme et la Fumée*. Yaounde: SOPECAM.

Barkindo, Bawuro. 1993. 'Growing Islamism in Kano City since 1970: causes, form and implications'. In L. Brenner (ed.) *Muslim Identity and Social Change in sub-Saharan Africa*. London: Hurst.

Barley, Nigel. 1983. *Symbolic Structures: an Exploration of the Culture of the Dowayos*. Cambridge: Cambridge University Press.

Barth, Fredrik. 1969. Introduction. In F. Barth (ed.) *Ethnic Groups and Boundaries: the Social Organization of Cultural Difference*. Oslo: Universitetsforlaget.

Barth, Fredrik. 1984. 'Problems in conceptualising cultural pluralism, with illustrations from Somar, Oman'. In D. Maybury-Lewis (ed.) *The Prospects for Plural Societies* (Proceedings of the American Ethnological Society 1982). Washington, DC: American Ethnological Society.

Barth, Heinrich. 1857. *Travels and Discoveries in North and Central Africa*. 5 Vols. London: Longman, Brown, Green, Longmans and Roberts.

Bassoro, Modibbo A. and Eldridge Mohammadou. 1980. *Garoua: Tradition Historique d'une Cité Peule du Nord-Cumeroun*. Paris: Centre National de la Recherche Scientifique.

Bayart, Jean-François. 1985. *L'Etat au Cameroun* (2nd edn). Paris: Presses de la Fondation Nationale des Sciences Politiques.

Bayart, Jean-François. 1986. 'La société politique camerounaise (1982–86)'. *Politique Africaine* 22: 5–36.

Bayart, Jean-François. 1989. *L'Etat en Afrique: la Politique du Ventre*. Paris: Fayard.

Bayart, Jean-François. 1993. *The State in Africa: the Politics of the Belly*. London: Longman.

Baxter, Paul. 1975. 'Some consequences of sedentarization for social relationship'. In T. Monod (ed.) *Pastoralism in Tropical Africa*. London: Oxford University Press for the International African Institute.

Bickerton, Derek. 1981. *Roots of Language*. Ann Arbor: Karoma.

Blanchard, Yves and Philip Noss. 1982. *Dictionnaire Gbaya-Français: Dialecte Yaayuwee*. Meiganga: Centre de Traduction Gbaya.

Bocquené, Henri. 1981. 'Note sur le pulaaku'. In Anon. (ed.) *Itinérances en Pays Peul et Ailleurs*. (Mémoires de la Société des Africanistes) 2: 229–46.

Bocquené, Henri. 1986. *Moi un Mbororo: Ndoudi Oumarou, Peul Nomade du Cameroun*. Paris: Editions Karthala.

Boeke, J. H. 1942. *The Structure of the Netherlands Indian Economy*. New York: Institute of Pacific Relations.

Bourdieu, Pierre. 1977. *Outline of a Theory of Practice*. Cambridge: Cambridge University Press.

Boutrais, Jean. 1973. *La Colonisation des Plaines par les Montagnards au Nord du Cameroun*. Paris: ORSTOM.

Boutrais, Jean. 1978. *Deux Etudes sur l'Elevage en Zone Tropicale Humide (Cameroun)*. Paris: Editions de l'ORSTOM.

Boutrais, Jean. 1982. 'Consommation et production de blé au Cameroun: une difficile indépendance alimentaire'. *Revue de Géographie du Cameroun*. 3 (1): 67–80.

Boutrais, Jean. 1983. *L'Elevage Soudanien: des Parcours de Savannes aux Ranchs*. Paris: Editions de l'ORSTOM.

Boutrais, Jean. 1986. 'L'expansion des éleveurs peul dans les savanes humides du Cameroun'. In M. Adamu and A. Kirk-Greene (eds) *Pastoralists of the West African Savanna*. Manchester: Manchester University Press for the International African Institute.

Boutrais, Jean. 1988. *Des Peul en Savannes Humides: Développement Pastoral dans l'Ouest Centrafricain*. Paris: Editions de l'ORSTOM.

Boutrais, Jean. 1994. 'Les Foulbé de l'Adamaoua et l'élevage: de l'idéologie pastorale à la pluri-activité'. *Cahiers d'Etudes Africaines* 133–5, XXXIV (1–3): 175–96.

Boutrais, Jean (ed.). 1993. *Peuples et Cultures de l'Adamaoua (Cameroun)*. Paris: ORSTOM.

Boutrais, Jean et al. 1984. *Le Nord du Cameroun: des Hommes, une Région*. Paris: ORSTOM.

Boyle, C. Vicars. 1910. 'Historical notes on the Yola Fulani'. *Journal of the African Society* 10 (37): 73–92.

Brenner, Louis. 1993. 'Introduction: Muslim representations of unity and difference in the African discourse'. In L. Brenner (ed.) *Muslim Identity and Social Change in Sub-Saharan Africa*. London: Hurst.

Brenner, Louis and Murray Last. 1985. 'The role of language in West African Islam'. *Africa* 55 (4): 431–46.

Burnham, Philip. 1972. 'Racial classification and identity in the Meiganga region: North Cameroon'. In P. Baxter and B. Sansom (eds) *Race and Social Difference*. Harmondsworth: Penguin.

Burnham, Philip. 1974. 'Ethnic correlates of differential fertility in northern Cameroon'. In B. Adadevoh (ed.) *Fertility and Infertility in Africa*. Ibadan: Caxton Press.

Burnham, Philip. 1975. '*Regroupement* and mobile societies: two Cameroon cases'. *Journal of African History* 16: 577–94.

Burnham, Philip. 1979. 'Spatial mobility and political centralization in pastoral societies'. In Equipe Ecologie et Anthropologie des Sociétés Pastorales (eds) *Pastoral Production and Society*. Cambridge: Cambridge University Press.

Burnham, Philip. 1980a. *Opportunity and Constraint in a Savanna Society: the Gbaya of Meiganga, Cameroon*. London: Academic Press.

Burnham, Philip. 1980b. 'Raiders and traders in Adamawa'. In J. Watson (ed.) *Asian and African Systems of Slavery*. Oxford: Basil Blackwell.

Burnham, Philip. 1981. 'Notes on Gbaya history'. In C. Tardits (ed.) *Contribution de la Recherche Ethnologique à l'Histoire des Civilisations du Cameroun*. Paris: Centre National de la Recherche Scientifique.

Burnham, Philip. 1982. 'The Gbaya and the Sudan Mission: 1924 to the present'. In P. Noss (ed.) *Grafting Old Rootstock*. Dallas: International Museum of Cultures.

Burnham, Philip. 1987. 'Pastoralism and the comparative method'. In L. Holy (ed.) *Comparative Anthropology*. Oxford: Basil Blackwell.

Burnham, Philip. 1991. 'L'ethnie, la religion et l'état: le rôle des Peuls dans la vie politique et sociale du Nord-Cameroun'. *Journal des Africanistes*. 61 (1): 73–102.

Burnham, Philip. In press. 'Political relations on the eastern marches of Adamawa in the late 19th century: a problem of interpretation'. In I. Fowler and D. Zeitlyn (eds) *Cameroon Crossroads: Anthropological and Historical Encounters in Africa*. Oxford: Berghahn Books.

Burnham, Philip and Thomas Christensen. 1983. 'Karnu's message and the "War of the Hoe Handle": interpreting a Central African religious movement'. *Africa* 53 (4): 3–22.

Burnham, Philip, Elisabeth Copet-Rougier and Philip Noss. 1986. 'Gbaya et Mkako: contribution ethno-linguistique à l'histoire de l'Est-Cameroun'. *Paideuma* 32: 87–128.

Burnham, Philip and Murray Last. 1994. 'From pastoralist to politician: the problem of a Fulbe "aristocracy"'. *Cahiers d'Etudes Africaines* 133–5, XXXIV (1–3): 313–57.

Büttner, Thea. 1967. 'On the social-economic structure of Adamawa in the nineteenth century: slavery or serfdom?'. In W. Markov (ed.) *African Studies*. Leipzig: Karl Marx University Press.

Callies, J. M. 1968. *Enquête Démographique au Cameroun: Résultats Définitifs pour la Région Nord*. Yaoundé: Service de la Statistique du Cameroun.

Chapman, Malcolm, Maryon McDonald and Elizabeth Tonkin. 1989. Introduction. In E. Tonkin, M. McDonald and M. Chapman (eds) *History and Ethnicity* (Association of Social Anthropologists, Monograph 27). London: Routledge.

Charreau, P. 1905. 'Un coin du Congo'. *Mémoires de la Société Nationale de Sciences Naturelles et Mathématiques de Cherbourg* 35.

Chazan, N., R. Mortimer, J. Ravenhill and D. Rothchild. 1992. *Politics and Society in Contemporary Africa* (2nd edn). Boulder: Lynne Rienner Publishers.

Christensen, Thomas. 1990. *An African Tree of Life*. Maryknoll: Orbis Books.

Christiansen, Ruth. 1956. *For the Heart of Africa*. Minneapolis: Augsburg Publishing House.

Clozel, F. 1896. *Les Bayas*. Paris: J. André.

Cohen, Abner. 1969. *Custom and Politics in Urban Africa: a Study of Hausa Migrants in Yoruba Towns*. Manchester: Manchester University Press.

Coleman, James and Carl Rosberg (eds). 1969. *Political Parties and National Integration*. Los Angeles: University of California Press.

Comaroff, John. 1983. 'Of totemism and ethnicity'. *Ethnos* 3 (4): 301–23.

Conte, Edouard. 1983. *Marriage Patterns, Political Change and the Perpetuation of Social Inequality in South Kanem, Chad*. Paris: ORSTOM.

Copet-Rougier, Elisabeth. 1987. 'Du clan à la chefferie dans l'est du Cameroun'. *Africa* 57 (3): 345–63.

Coquery-Vidrovitch, Catherine. 1972. *Le Congo au Temps des Grandes Compagnies Concessionnaires: 1898–30*. Paris: Mouton.

Coquery-Vidrovitch, Catherine. 1988. *Africa: Endurance and Change South of the Sahara*. Berkeley: University of California Press.

David, Nicholas and David Voas. 1981. 'Societal causes of infertility and population decline among settled Fulani of North Cameroon'. *Man* 16 (4): 644–64.

DeLancey, Mark. 1989. *Cameroon: Dependence and Independence*. Boulder: Westview Press.

Despres, Leo. 1984. 'Ethnicity: what data and theory portend for plural societies'. In D. Maybury-Lewis (ed.) *The Prospects for Plural Societies* (Proceedings of the American Ethnological Society 1982). Washington, DC: American Ethnological Society.

Djaboule, Pierre. 1993. '"*Sawtu Linjiila*" (Voix de l'Evangile) et les peuples et cultures de l'Adamaoua'. In J. Boutrais (ed.) *Peuples et Cultures de l'Adamaoua (Cameroun)*. Paris: ORSTOM.

Dognin, René. 1981. 'L'installation des Djafoun dans l'Adamaoua camerounais'. In C. Tardits (ed.) *Contribution de la Recherche Ethnologique à l'Histoire des Civilisations du Cameroun*. Paris: Centre National de la Recherche Scientifique.

Douglas, Mary. 1975. 'Self-evidence'. In M. Douglas (ed.) *Implicit Meanings*. London: Routledge and Kegan Paul.

Dugast, Idelette. 1949. 'Inventaire Ethnique du Sud-Cameroun'. *Mémoires de l'Institut Français d'Afrique Noire* (Centre du Cameroun, Populations Series), 1.

Duffill, Mark. 1985. *The Biography of Madugu Mai Gashin Baki*. Atlanta: Emory University for the African Studies Association.

Dupire, Marguerite. 1962. *Peuls Nomades: Etudes Descriptive des Wodaabe du Sahel Nigérien*. Paris: Institut d'Ethnologie.

Dupire, Marguerite. 1970. *L'Organisation Sociale des Peul*. Paris: Plon.

Dupire, Marguerite. 1981. 'Réflexions sur l'ethnicité peule'. In Anon. (ed.) *Itinérances en Pays Peul et Ailleurs*. (Mémoires de la Société des Africanistes) 2: 165–81.

Dupire, Marguerite. 1994. 'Identité ethnique et processus d'incorporation tribale et étatique'. *Cahiers d'Etudes Africaines* 133–5, XXXIV (1–3): 265–80.

Durkheim, Emile. 1964 [1893]. *The Division of Labor in Society*. New York: Free Press.

Eguchi, Paul. 1974. *Miscellany of Maroua Fulfulde (Northern Cameroun)*. Tokyo: Institute for the Study of Languages and Cultures of Asia and Africa.

Ekeh, Peter. 1990. 'Social anthropology and two contrasting uses of tribalism in Africa'. *Comparative Studies in Society and History* 32: 660–700.

Epstein, A. L. 1978. *Ethos and Identity: Three Studies in Ethnicity*. London: Tavistock Publications.

Fabian, Johannes. 1978. 'Popular culture in Africa: findings and conjectures'. *Africa* 48 (4): 315–34.

Faraut, F. 1981. 'Les Mboum'. In C. Tardits (ed.) *Contribution de la Recherche Ethnologique à l'Histoire des Civilisations du Cameroun*. Paris: Centre National de la Recherche Scientifique.

Flegel, Eduard. 1883. 'Reise nach Adamawa'. *Petermanns Mitteilungen* 29: 241–9.

Flegel, Eduard. 1885. *Lose Blätter aus dem Tagebuch meiner Haussa-Freunde . . . Mai gasin baki*. Hamburg: L. Friedrichsen.

Fox, Robin. 1967. *The Keresan Bridge*. London: Athlone Press.

Froelich, J-C. 1954. 'Le commandement et l'organisation sociale chez les Foulbé de l'Adamaoua'. *Etudes Camerounaises* 45–6.

Froelich, J-C. 1962. *Les Musulmans d'Afrique Noire*. Paris: Editions de l'Orante.

Furnivall, J. S. 1939. *Netherlands India: A Study of Plural Economy*. Cambridge: Cambridge University Press.

Geertz, Clifford. 1963. 'The integrative revolution: primordial sentiments and civil politics in the new states'. In C. Geertz (ed.) *Old Societies and New States*. New York: Free Press.

Geertz, Clifford. 1973. *The Interpretation of Cultures*. New York: Basic Books.

Geertz, Clifford (ed.). 1963. *Old Societies and New States*. New York: Free Press.

Gellner, Ernest. 1964. *Thought and Change*. London: Weidenfeld and Nicholson.

Gellner, Ernest. 1983. *Nations and Nationalism*. Oxford: Basil Blackwell.

Gellner, Ernest. 1992. *Postmodernism, Reason and Religion*. London: Routledge.

Genest, Serge and Renaud Santerre. 1982. 'L'école franco-arabe au Nord-Cameroun'. In R. Santerre and C. Mercier-Tremblay (eds) *La Quête du Savoir: Essais pour une Anthropologie de l'Education Camerounaise*. Montreal: University of Montreal Press.

Geschiere, Peter. 1982. *Village Communities and the State*. London: Kegan Paul.

Geschiere, Peter. 1986. 'Paysans, régime national et recherche hégémonique'. *Politique Africaine*. 22: 73–100.

Geschiere, Peter and Piet Konings (eds). 1993. *Itinéraires d'Accumulation au Cameroun*. Paris: Editions Karthala.

Giddens, Anthony. 1985. *The Nation-State and Violence*. Cambridge: Polity Press.

Gledhill, John. 1994. *Power and Its Disguises: Anthropological Perspectives on Politics*. London: Pluto Press.

Gluckman, Max. 1958. 'Analysis of a social situation in modern Zululand'. *Rhodes-Livingstone Papers* 28.

Gondolo, André. 1986. 'L'évolution du peul urbain: Ngaoundéré'. In M. Adamu and A. Kirk-Greene (eds) *Pastoralists of the West African Savanna*. Manchester: Manchester University Press for the International African Institute.

Gumi, Sheikh Abubakar with Ismaila Tsiga. 1992. *Where I Stand*. Ibadan: Spectrum Books.

Haafkens, J. 1983. *Chants Musulmans en Peul*. Yaounde: Editions CLE.

Hannerz, Ulf. 1987. 'The world in creolisation'. *Africa* 57 (4): 546–59.

Harttmann, Hermann. 1927. 'Ethnographische Studie über die Baja'. *Zeitschrift für Ethnologie* 59: 1–61.

Hino, Shun'ya. 1978. *The Classified Vocabulary of the Mbum Language in Mbang Mboum, with Ethnographical Description*. Tokyo: Institute for the Study of Languages and Cultures of Asia and Africa.

Hobsbawm, Eric. 1983. 'Introduction: inventing traditions'. In E. Hobsbawm and T. Ranger (eds) *The Invention of Tradition*. Cambridge: Cambridge University Press.

Hobsbawm, Eric and Terence Ranger (eds). 1983. *The Invention of Tradition*. Cambridge: Cambridge University Press.

Ibn Khaldun. 1967. *The Muqaddimah: an Introduction to History* (trans. F. Rosenthal and ed. N. Dawood). London: Routledge and Kegan Paul.

Inkeles, Alex. 1966. 'The modernization of man'. In M. Weiner (ed.) *Modernization: the Dynamics of Growth*. New York: Basic Books.

Issa, Adamou and Roger Labatut. 1974. *Sagesse de Peuls Nomades*. Yaounde: Editions CLE.

Jenkins, Richard. 1994. 'Rethinking ethnicity: identity, categorization and power'. *Ethnic and Racial Studies* 17 (2): 197–223.

Kane, Ousmane. 1993. *Les Mouvements Islamiques et le Champ Politique au Nord du Nigeria: Le Cas du Mouvement Izala à Kano*. Doctoral Thesis, Paris: Institut d'Etudes Politiques.

Kapferer, Bruce. 1988. *Legends of People, Myths of State: Violence, Intolerance and Political Culture in Sri Lanka and Australia*. Washington: Smithsonian Institution Press.

Kati, Mahmoud. 1964. *Tarikh El-Fettach* (translation by O. Houdas and M. Delafosse). Paris: Adrien-Maisonneuve.

Kirk-Greene, Anthony. 1986. '*Maudo laawol pulaaku*: survival and symbiosis'. In M. Adamu and A. Kirk-Greene (eds) *Pastoralists of the West African Savanna*. Manchester: Manchester University Press for the International African Institute.

Knorr-Cetina, Karin. 1981. 'The micro-sociological challenge of macro-sociology: towards a reconstruction of social theory and methodology'. In K. Knorr-Cetina and A. Cicourel (eds) *Advances in Social Theory and Methodology: Toward an Integration of Micro- and Macro-Sociologies*. Boston: Routledge and Kegan Paul.

Kuper, Leo and Michael G. Smith (eds). 1969. *Pluralism in Africa*. Los Angeles: University of California Press.

Labatut, Roger. 1973. *Le Parler d'un Groupe de Peuls Nomades: les WoDaaBe Hoore-walde Dageeja Bibbe Bii Siroma (Nord-Cameroun)*. Paris: SELAF.

Lacroix, Pierre. 1952. 'Matériaux pour servir à l'histoire des Peul de l'Adamawa'. *Etudes Camerounaises* 37–8: 3–62.

Lacroix, Pierre. 1959. 'Observation sur la "koiné" peule de Ngaoundéré'. *Travaux de l'Institut de Linguistique* 4: 57–71.

Lacroix, Pierre. 1962. 'Distribution géographique et sociale des parlers peuls du Nord-Cameroun'. *l'Homme* 2 (3).

Lacroix, Pierre. 1965. *Poésie Peul de l'Adamawa*. 2 Vols. Paris: Juillard.

Lacroix, Pierre. 1966. 'L'islam peul de l'Adamaoua'. In I. M. Lewis (ed.) *Islam in Tropical Africa*. London: Oxford University Press for the International African Institute.

Lacroix, Pierre. 1967. 'Quelques aspects de la désintegration d'un système classifica-toire'. In Anon. (ed.) *La Classification Nominale dans les Langues Négro-africaines*. Paris: Centre National de la Recherche Scientifique.

Last, Murray. 1967. *The Sokoto Caliphate*. London: Longman.

Last, Murray. 1987. 'Reform in West Africa: the *jihad* movements of the nineteenth century'. In J. Ajayi and M. Crowder (eds) *History of West Africa* (2nd edn). London: Longman.

Last, Murray. 1988. 'Tradition musulmane et diplomatie'. In D. Bach, J. Egg and J. Philippe (eds) *Nigeria: un Pouvoir en Puissance*. Paris: Editions Karthala.

Last, Murray. 1989. 'The Sokoto caliphate and Borno'. In J. Ajayi (ed.) *General History of Africa* (Vol. VI). Paris: UNESCO.

Lebeuf, J. P. and P. F. Lacroix. 1972. *Devinettes Peules Suivies de Quelques Proverbes et Exemples d'Argots (Nord-Cameroun)*. Paris: Mouton and Co.

LeVine, Victor. 1964. *Cameroons: From Mandate to Independence*. Los Angeles: University of California Press.

Lode, Käre. 1993. 'L'apport culturel de la Mission norvégienne en Adamaoua'. In J. Boutrais (ed.) *Peuples et Cultures de l'Adamaoua (Cameroun)*. Paris: ORSTOM.

Loefler, Capitaine. 1907. 'Les régions comprises entre la Haute-Sangha, le Chari, et le Cameroun'. *Bulletin du Comité de l'Afrique Française, Renseignements Coloniaux* 9: 224–40.

Lovejoy, Paul. 1981. 'Slavery in the Sokoto Caliphate'. In P. Lovejoy (ed.) *The Ideology of Slavery in Africa*. Beverly Hills: Sage Publications.

Lubeck, Paul. 1985. 'Islamic protest under semi-industrial capitalism: Yan Tatsine explained'. *Africa* 55 (4): 369–89.

Lubeck, Paul. 1986. *Islam and Urban Labour in Northern Nigeria: the Making of a Muslim Working Class*. Cambridge: Cambridge University Press.

Lucas, John. 1994. 'The state, civil society and regional elites: a study of three associations in Kano'. *African Affairs* 93: 21–38.

Maquet, Jacques. 1961. *The Premise of Inequality in Ruanda*. London: Oxford University Press for the International African Institute.

Marcus, George. 1986a. 'Taking account of world historical political economy: know-able communities in larger systems'. In G. Marcus and M. Fischer (eds) *Anthropology as Cultural Critique: an Experimental Moment in the Human Sciences*. Chicago: University of Chicago Press.

Marcus, George. 1986b. 'Contemporary problems of ethnography in the modern world system'. In J. Clifford and G. Marcus (eds) *Writing Culture: the Poetics and Politics of Ethnography*. Berkeley: University of California Press.

Martin, Jean-Yves. 1971. 'L'école et les sociétés traditionnelles au Cameroun septen-trionel'. *Cahiers ORSTOM* (série Science Humaines), VIII (3): 295–335.

Martin, Jean-Yves. 1981. 'L'implantation des populations du nord et du centre'. In C. Tardits (ed.) *Contribution de la Recherche Ethnologique à l'Histoire des Civilisations du Cameroun*. Paris: Centre National de la Recherche Scientifique.

Martin, Jean-Yves. 1982. 'Inégalités régionales et inégalités sociales: l'enseignement secondaire au Cameroun septentrional'. In R. Santerre and C. Mercier-Tremblay (eds) *La Quête du Savoir: Essais pour une Anthropologie de l'Education Camerounaise*. Montreal: University of Montreal Press.

Miaffo, Dieudonné and Jean-Pierre Warnier. 1993. 'Accumulation et ethos de la notabilité chez les Bamiléké'. In P. Geschiere and P. Konings (eds) *Itinéraires d'Accumulation au Cameroun*. Paris: Editions Karthala.

Miller, Daniel. 1994. *Modernity, an Ethnographic Approach: Dualism and Mass Consumption in Trinidad*. Oxford: Berg Publishers.

Mizon, L. 1895. 'Itinéraire de la source de la Benoué au confluent de rivières Kadei et Mambéré'. *Bulletin de la Société de Géographie de Paris* (Series 7) 16: 342–69.

Mohammed, Ahmed Rufai. 1993. 'The influence of the Niass Tijaniyya in the Niger-Benue confluence area of Nigeria'. In L. Brenner (ed.) *Muslim Identity and Social Change in Sub-Saharan Africa*. London: Hurst and Co.

Mohammadou, Eldridge. 1969. 'Yeerwa, poème des Peuls Yillaga de l'Adamawa'. *Camlang* 1: 73–111.

Mohammadou, Eldridge. 1978. *Les Royaumes Foulbe du Plateau de l'Adamaoua au XIX Siècle*. Tokyo: Institute for the Study of Languages and Cultures of Asia and Africa.

Mohammadou, Eldridge. 1981. 'L'implantation des Peul dans l'Adamawa: approche chronologique'. In C. Tardits (ed.) *Contribution de la Recherche Ethnologique à l'Histoire des Civilisations du Cameroun*. Paris: Centre National de la Recherche Scientifique.

Mohammadou, Eldridge. 1983. *Peuples et Royaumes du Fombina* (African Languages and Ethnography XVII). Tokyo: Institute for the Study of Languages and Cultures of Asia and Africa.

Mohammadou, Eldridge. 1986. *Traditions d'Origine des Peuples du Centre et de l'Ouest du Cameroun* (African Languages and Ethnography XX). Tokyo: Institute for the Study of Languages and Cultures of Asia and Africa.

Monga, Célestin. 1986. *Cameroun: Quel Avenir?* Paris: Silex Editions.

Monino, Yves (ed.). 1988. *Lexique Comparatif des Langues Oubanguiennes*. Paris: Paul Geuthner.

Mouvement d'Investissement et d'Assistance Mutuelle (MOINAM). 1994. *Documents des Assises: Congrès Général*. Bertoua (photocopy).

Ndongo, Siré Mamadou. 1986. *Le Fantang: Poèmes Mythiques des Bergers Peuls*. Paris: Editions Karthala.

Nelson, Ronald. 1972. 'Bilkiire'. Unpublished paper.

Njeuma, Martin. 1978. *Fulani Hegemony in Yola (Old Adamawa) 1809–1902*. Yaounde: CEPER.

Njiasse Njoya, A. and L. Zouya Mimbang. 1988. 'Contribution à l'étude du droit islamique appliqué au tribunal coutumier de Ngaoundéré: les affaires matrimoniales et successorales chez les Peul'. *Revue Science et Technique* V: 59–76.

Noss, Philip. 1993. 'Les héros et l'héroisme dans la tradition et la vie gbaya'. In J. Boutrais (ed.) *Peuples et Cultures de l'Adamaoua (Cameroun)*. Paris: ORSTOM.

Noss, Philip. n.d. 'Fula – a language of change'. Unpublished paper.

Noye, Dominique. 1971. *Un Cas d'Apprentissage Linguistique: l'Acquisition de la Langue par les Jeunes Peuls du Diamaré (Nord-Cameroun)*. Paris: P. Geuthner.

Noye, Dominique. 1974. *Cours de Foulfouldé*. Paris: Librairie Paul Geuthner.

Nzabakomada-Yakoma, Raphael. 1986. *L'Afrique Centrale Insurgée: la Guerre du Kongo-Wara 1928–1931*. Paris: Editions l'Harmattan.

Paden, John. 1973. *Religion and Political Culture in Kano*. Berkeley: University of California Press.

Passarge, Siegfried. 1895. *Adamaua: Bericht über die Expedition des Deutschen Kamerun-Komitees in den Jahren 1893/1894*. Berlin: Dietrich Reimer.

Peel, John. 1989. 'The cultural work of Yoruba ethnogenesis'. In E. Tonkin, M. McDonald and M. Chapman (eds) *History and Ethnicity* (Association of Social Anthropologists, Monograph 27). London: Routledge.

Pfeffer, Gulla. 1939. 'Prose and poetry of the Fulbe'. *Africa* 12 (3): 285–307.

Podlewski, André-Michel. 1966. 'La dynamique des principales populations du Nord-Cameroun (entre Bénoué et Lac Tchad)'. *Cahiers ORSTOM*, (Sciences Humaines Series), III (4).

Podlewski, André-Michel. 1971. 'La Dynamique des Principales Populations du Nord-Cameroun: 2ᵉ Partie – Piémont et Plateau de l'Adamaoua'. *Cahiers ORSTOM*, (Sciences Humaines Series). VIII, numéro spécial.

Ponel, Edouard. 1896. 'La Haute-Sangha'. *Bulletin de la Société de Géographie de Paris* (Series 7) 17: 188–211.

Rabinow, Paul and William Sullivan. 1979. 'The interpretive turn: emergence of an approach'. In P. Rabinow and W. Sullivan (eds) *Interpretive Social Science: a Reader*. Berkeley: University of California Press.

Rabut, Elisabeth. 1989. *Brazza Commissaire Général: le Congo français 1886–97*. Paris: Ecole des Hautes Etudes en Sciences Sociales.

Ranger, Terence. 1983. 'The invention of tradition in colonial Africa'. In E. Hobsbawm and T. Ranger (eds) *The Invention of Tradition*. Cambridge: Cambridge University Press.

Redfield, Robert, Ralph Linton and Melville Herskovits. 1936. 'A memorandum on the study of acculturation'. *American Anthropologist* 60: 433–41.

République du Cameroun. 1987. *Recensement Général*. Yaounde: Bureau Central du Recensement.

République Unie du Cameroun. 1976. *Recensement Général*. Yaounde: Bureau Central du Recensement.

Riesman, Paul. 1977. *Freedom in Fulani Social Life*. Chicago: University of Chicago Press.

Romaine, Suzanne. 1988. *Pidgin and Creole Languages*. London: Longman.

Ruxton, F. H. 1916. *Maliki Law*. London: Luzac and Co.

Sahlins, Marshall. 1976. *Culture and Practical Reason*. Chicago: Chicago University Press.

Sahlins, Marshall. 1981. *Historical Metaphors and Mythical Realities: Structure in the Early History of the Sandwich Islands Kingdom* (Association for Social Anthropology in Oceania Special Publications No. 1). Ann Arbor: University of Michigan Press.

Santerre, Renaud. 1973. *Pédagogie Musulmane d'Afrique Noire*. Montreal: Montreal University Press.

Santerre, Renaud. 1982. 'Aspects conflictuels de deux systèmes d'enseignement au Nord-Cameroun'. In R. Santerre and C. Mercier-Tremblay (eds) *La Quête du Savoir: Essais pour une Anthropologie de l'Education Camerounaise*. Montreal: University of Montreal Press.

Santerre, Renaud and Céline Mercier-Tremblay (eds). 1982. *La Quête du Savoir: Essais pour une Anthropologie de l'Education Camerounaise*. Montreal: University of Montreal Press.

Schatzberg, Michael. 1988. *The Dialectics of Oppression in Zaire*. Bloomington: Indiana University Press.

Schilder, Kees. 1994. *Quest for Self-Esteem: State, Islam and Mundang Ethnicity in Northern Cameroon*. Leiden: African Studies Centre.

Schultz, Emily. 1979. *Ethnic Identity and Cultural Commitment: a Study of the Process of Fulbeization in Guider, Northern Cameroon* (Doctoral thesis of the University of Indiana). Ann Arbor: University Microfilms.

Schultz, Emily. 1984. 'From Pagan to Pullo: ethnic identity change in northern Cameroon'. *Africa* 54 (1): 46–64.

Shils, Edward. 1957. 'Primordial, personal, sacred and civil ties'. *British Journal of Sociology* 8: 130–45.

Shils, Edward. 1962. *Political Development in the New States*. 's-Gravenhage: Mouton and Co.

Shimada, Yoshihito. 1993. 'Jihad as dialectical movement and formation of Islamic Identity among the Fulbe'. In P. Eguchi and V. Azarya (eds) *Unity and Diversity of a People: the Search for Fulbe Identity*. Senri Ethnological Studies No. 35, Osaka: National Museum of Ethnology.

Smith, Anthony. 1986. *The Ethnic Origins of Nations*. Oxford: Basil Blackwell.

Smith, Michael G. 1969. 'Pluralism in precolonial African societies'. In L. Kuper and M. G. Smith (eds) *Pluralism in Africa*. Los Angeles: University of California Press.

Smith, Michael G. 1974. *Corporations and Society*. London: Duckworth.

Smith, Michael G. 1984. 'The nature and variety of plural unity'. In D. Maybury-Lewis (ed.) *The Prospects for Plural Societies* (Proceedings of the American Ethnological Society 1982). Washington, DC: American Ethnological Society.

Starn, Orin. 1992. '"I dreamed of foxes and hawks": reflections on peasant protest, new social movements and the rondas campesinas of northern Peru'. In A. Escobar and S. Alvarez (eds) *The Making of Social Movements in Latin America*. Boulder: Westview Press.

Stennes, Leslie. 1967. *A Reference Grammar of Adamawa Fulani*. East Lansing: Michigan State University Press.

Stenning, Derrick. 1958. 'Household viability among the pastoral Fulani'. In J. Goody (ed.) *The Developmental Cycle in Domestic Groups*. Cambridge: Cambridge University Press.

Stenning, Derrick. 1959. *Savannah Nomads*. London: Oxford University Press for the International African Institute [reprinted 1994, LIT Verlag].

Stoecker, Helmut (ed.). 1968. *Kamerun unter deutscher Kolonialherrschaft*. Berlin: Deutscher Verlag der Wissenschaften.

Strümpell, Kurt. 1912. 'Die Geschichte Adamauas'. *Mitteilungen der Geographische Gesellschaft in Hamburg* 26: 46–107.

Tardits, Claude (ed.). 1981. *Contribution de la Recherche Ethnologique à l'Histoire des Civilisations du Cameroun* (2 Vols). Paris: Centre National de la Recherche Scientifique.

Taylor, F. W. 1932. *A Fulani-English Dictionary*. Oxford: Oxford University Press.

Tessmann, Günter. 1934. *Die Baja: ein Negerstamm im mittleren Sudan, Teil I, materielle und seelische Kultur*. Stuttgart: Strecker und Schröder.

Tessmann, Günter. 1937. *Die Baja: ein Negerstamm im mittleren Sudan, Teil II, geistige Kultur*. Stuttgart: Strecker und Schröder.

VerEecke, Catherine. 1994. 'The slave experience in Adamawa: past and present perspectives from Yola (Nigeria)'. *Cahiers d'Etudes Africaines* 133–5, XXXIV (1–3): 23–53.

Vincent, Joan. 1974. 'The structuring of ethnicity'. *Human Organization* 33: 375–9.

Von Briesen, Oberleutnant. 1914. 'Beiträge zur Geschichte des Lamidats Ngaundere'. *Mitteilungen aus den Deutschen Schutzgebeiten* 27: 349–59.

Weber, Max. 1947. *The Theory of Social and Economic Organization*. Glencoe: Free Press.

Whyte, Denis. 1993. *The Sultan's Burden*. Directed by Jon Jerstad and Lisbet Holtedahl. A film by Denis Whyte Films and Northern Lights Film for NRK, DRI and BBC.

ARCHIVAL REFERENCES

Meiganga Sub-Prefectural Archives (M)
1. VT/19/15: Notes on origin of Lokoti, 1932.
2. VT/19/49: Rapports de Tourneé, 1933–4.
3. VT/19/32: Agricultural dossiers, 1954–7.
4. VT/19/10: *Elevage* dossiers, 1951–6.
5. VT/19/16: Roads and labour levies, 1943–54.
6. VT/19/12: Schools, 1955–7.
7. VT/19/4 : *Elevage* dossiers, 1949–57.

Archives Nationales, Section Outre-Mer (formerly at Paris, now at Aix-en-Provence) (AN)
1. Gabon-Congo III 13: Rapport de Brazza à M. le Sous-secrétaire d'Etat aux Colonies, Paris-Gaza, 23 April 1892.
2. Gabon-Congo III 14: Rapport de Mission Ponel 1892–3.
3. Gabon-Congo III 18: Rapport de Mission Pedrizet, 1897.
4. Gabon-Congo IV 13: Rapport général sur l'expédition de 1896, A. Goujon à M. de Brazza à Libreville, Nola 23 December 1896.

IRCAM Archives (later transferred to the Institute of Human Sciences, Yaounde and now apparently lost following the demise of this institute) (I)
1. Rapport de Tournée du Chef de Région de l'Adamaoua dans la Subdivision de Meiganga, September 1936.

INDEX